PQ-AGL-061

Movement and Vision
in George Eliot's Novels

Movement and Vision
in George Eliot's Novels

By REVA STUMP

Juanita

Seattle: 1959
University of Washington Press

*This book is published with assistance
from a grant by the Ford Foundation.*

8-23-60

To Rada and Glenvil Stump

Preface

"EVERY limit is a beginning as well as an ending, " says George
Eliot in the Finale to *Middlemarch*. I could wish for no more
fruitful response to this book than that the reader consider its
limit to be a beginning. Although I have made detailed studies
of three of George Eliot's novels I do not in any wise consider
them to be exhaustive studies, nor would I wish them to be exhaustive were it possible to make them so.

Aside from my personal limitations as a reader, I am of
course restricted by the fact that a book of criticism cannot
be as long as, say, *Middlemarch*. At the outset, therefore,
I had to decide whether I would write detailed studies of some
of George Eliot's seven novels or much less detailed analyses
of all seven. When I began writing the section on *Adam Bede*
it became apparent to me that in order to discover what I
wished to know I would have to write an extended analysis of
that novel and presumably of two or three other novels. I
chose *Adam Bede,* then, because it was necessary to begin
at the beginning, *The Mill on the Floss* because I was curious
about what George Eliot would do next, and *Middlemarch* because on the basis of my preliminary reading of all seven
novels I had concurred with the general critical opinion that
it is George Eliot's masterpiece.

After I had made studies of these three novels I then proceeded to make a careful analysis of each of the four remaining novels--*Silas Marner, Romola, Felix Holt,* and *Daniel Deronda*--and to write a general chapter showing how they fit into

the structural and imagistic pattern which I had found in *Adam Bede, The Mill on the Floss,* and *Middlemarch.* At that point I was able to draw some conclusions about George Eliot's novels as a body of work. This chapter, however, was of necessity so short that it proved disproportionate. On the excellent advice of critics who read my manuscript I have dropped it entirely and have tried instead to incorporate some of that material in the notes and within these three individual studies. When I do make references to the other four novels, however, I do it merely for the purpose of comparison and never to prove the point I am making about the book being studied. I find on rereading that some generalizations about George Eliot's work as a whole do remain. Even though I have not been able to demonstrate them here, I am willing to stand on them since they are the result of work I have done on the other novels of George Eliot.

In the course of my work I have had the privilege of accumulating many debts, which I now gratefully acknowledge in so far as acknowledgment is possible. Professors James W. Hall, Robert B. Heilman, and Sophus K. Winther, University of Washington, have read and criticized my manuscript in its original form as a doctoral dissertation. Professor Hall's quiet and sure critical guidance and Professor Heilman's keenly perceptive blue pencil have been invaluable to me. Professor Irving Howe, Brandeis University, first made me aware of George Eliot and suggested that I work with her. Mrs. Katherine Armstrong Stockholder, University of Illinois, has discussed George Eliot with me, and both she and Professor David M. Vieth, University of Kansas, have read and criticized my manuscript. My deepest and least calculable personal debts are to Professor Arnold Stein, University of Washington, and Miss Naomi J. Diamond, Wellesley College. Professor Stein has not read my manuscript; Miss Diamond has not only read it but has also talked, thought, and read George Eliot with me. Miss Diamond's doctoral dissertation on George Eliot, now in the process of completion, will be, among other things, an invaluable companion study to this book.

I wish to express my deep gratitude to the American Association of University Women, under whose auspices as Mar-

garet Snell Fellow during the year July, 1956, to July, 1957,
I was able to do a large part of the work on this book. I am
also indebted to Montana State University for a research grant
to assist in preparation of the manuscript; to Houghton Mifflin
Company for permission to quote from the Warwickshire Edition of George Eliot's works; to the Yale University Press for
permission to quote from Gordon Haight's edition of *George
Eliot's Letters;* to the *English Literary History* for permission to quote from John S. Diekhoff's essay, "The Happy Ending of *Adam Bede";* and to E. P. Dutton for permission to
quote from the Everyman's Library edition of St. Augustine's
Confessions. Obviously, I alone am responsible for weakness
or error in this book.

R. S.

Missoula, Montana
September 22, 1958

Contents

Movement and Vision
in George Eliot's Novels

1. Intention and Procedure

A NOVEL is constructed in time, and the mind of a reader is
guided by the novelist to perform three major actions: it expects the future, it considers the present, and it remembers
the past. "I am about to repeat a Psalm that I know," says
Saint Augustine. "Before I begin, my expectation is extended
over the whole; but when I have begun, how much soever of it
I shall separate off into the past, is extended along my memory; thus the life of this action of mine is divided between my
memory as to what I have repeated, and expectation as to what
I am about to repeat; but 'consideration' is present with me,
that through it what was future, may be conveyed over, so as
to become past."[1] Though in the first reading of a novel the
nature of the expectation is different from that which Saint
Augustine describes as the act of rereading, nevertheless even
the most simple plot is based on such a pattern of action in the
mind. But when one part of a novel passes into the memory in
such a way that its repetition in some variant form is expected
by the reader--though not necessarily on a highly conscious
level--we may say that a rhythm has been established. In each
of the seven novels of George Eliot such a rhythm is established and perpetuated by a complex pattern of vision imagery,
by a group of themes united through the concept of vision, and
by the dramatic action which for the most part derives its tension from the contradictory urges to see and to avoid seeing.
This rhythm, a movement produced by the recurrence of remembered and expected elements connected with vision, is the

structure of all George Eliot's novels. Throughout this study I
shall call it the movement toward and the movement away from
moral vision.

The rhythm works both in terms of the reader who perceives
it as structure and the character with whose vision the novel
is concerned. For the character who moves toward vision is
in the process of learning to expect his future, consider his
present, and remember his past, all in realistic terms and in
relation to a broader referent than self. The character who
moves away from vision has destructive daydreams about his
future, fails to consider his present in terms of the larger pattern of existence, and is frequently cut off from his own and
the larger past. In each case the life pattern of the character
is worked out through the expected recurrence of elements,
a series of progressively clearer or progressively duller visions, depending on the direction of the movement.

It is important to remember that here the term *vision* is
never absolute, always relative. And furthermore it is essential to keep in mind the distinction which George Eliot implies between having a vision and having clear vision. A vision
may be nothing more than a fantastic and vividly imagined daydream, whereas *vision* itself implies some positive degree of
moral perception. Some passages from *Adam Bede* will illustrate the essential distinctions which will need to be made at
the outset. Hetty is daydreaming: "Perhaps some day she
should be a grand lady, and ride in her coach, and dress for
dinner in a brocaded silk. . . . At the thought of all this splen-
dour, Hetty. . . caught the little red-framed glass with the
edge of her scarf, so that it fell with a bang on the floor; but
she was too eagerly occupied with her *vision* to care about
picking it up. . . ."[2] Still within the same general context,
George Eliot says of Hetty: "They are but dim ill-defined *pictures* that her narrow bit of an imagination can make of the future; but of every *picture* she is the central figure in fine
clothes . . ." (p. 219). It is clear that what George Eliot calls
a "vision" in the first passage is the same kind of daydream
that she here calls a "picture." Elsewhere in the same chapter
she says:

It is our habit to say that while the lower nature can never understand the higher, the higher nature commands a complete

view of the lower. But I think the higher nature has to learn
this comprehension, as we learn *the art of vision*, by a good
deal of hard experience, often with bruises and gashes incurred
in taking things up by the wrong end, and fancying our space
wider than it is [p. 229].

Out of context there is some ambiguity in this comparison,
since the act which is being scrutinized--the comprehension
of the lower nature by the higher--is logically a part of the
larger action to which it is being compared: learning the art
of vision. In context, however (Dinah has just failed to understand Hetty's emotional response), the ambiguity is resolved
and the comparison acts as a reminder of the larger issue
which is central throughout all of George Eliot's novels: how
it is that one learns "the art of vision." Clearly, *to have a vision* such as Hetty had is not the same as *to have vision*, that
is, to have deeply felt perception.

The first of these two usages, however, is not restricted
to daydreams but covers the sleeping as well as the waking
dream, the clear insight as well as the illusory, the idle fancy
of Hetty and Rosamond as well as the compelling images which
Dinah and Mordecai consider prophetic. Explaining to Seth her
reason for returning to Snowfield after preaching on the Green,
Dinah says:

> "I'm called there. It was borne in upon my mind while I was
> meditating on Sunday night, as sister Allen, who's in a decline,
> is in need of me. *I saw her as plain as we see that bit of thin
> white cloud*, lifting up her poor thin hand and beckoning me. And
> this morning when I opened the Bible for direction, the first
> words my eyes fell on were, 'And after we had seen the *vision*,
> immediately we endeavoured to go into Macedonia.' If it wasn't
> for that *clear showing* of the Lord's will I should be loth to go
> . . ." [III. 44].

That Dinah sees not herself but someone in need of her help
and sees that absent person as clearly as she sees a "bit of
thin white cloud" indicates the mystical nature and the direc-
tion--perhaps, as we shall later discover, even the deficien-
cy--of her early vision. It will be important to remember that
although in George Eliot's novels some visions or dreams do
help lead the character nearer to a realistic vision of the mor-

al life, others initiate or contribute to the movement away from clear vision.

The central image patterns and themes and much of the dramatic action of George Eliot's novels draw symbolic meaning either tangentially or directly from the most literal implications of the term *vision*. Some of these implications will therefore indicate certain emphases in this study. In its simplest and most literal sense vision is ocular perception, the seeing with the eyes; hence, the emphasis on eyes, on different kinds of sight, and on what is perceived. The pre-essential condition of the act of seeing is that there be light, and consequently the most predominant and most highly complex set of images involves light, or the absence of light, darkness. In order to see consciously and with any degree of clarity one must focus on the object for a length of time to be determined by its complexity. Such a process implies that seeing is an act of will, an implication from which a second important set of images and actions is derived. Those characters who provide the negative movements of George Eliot's novels are often shown to be in a will-less state in which they drift aimlessly or allow themselves to be propelled. The drifting may be mental, as in Hetty's daydreaming, or physical, as in her wandering in the woods. Or the state of will-lessness may even be positive, as when Dinah submits her will to the will of God and waits upon the inner light to give her vision.

On a literal level various conditions help to determine the quality of the vision. Thus a second object may come between the eye and the first object, distorting or concealing it from the line of vision. Or there may be spatial modifications; an object may be so far away from the eye that it is not visible, or too near so that proportion is lost. From these literal extensions are derived images of concealment, distortion, restriction, movement, and space. Central throughout, of course, is the problem of false and deceptive appearances. Light itself is used not only to reveal but to distort and dim. Almost all of the images contain their own antitheses and so interpenetrate that complexity does not yield to analysis until we remember that the complex of imagery pertains to the antithetical movements toward and away from moral vision. As George Eliot conceives it and as the term is used throughout this study, moral vision may be defined as the deeply felt perception of the human condition, a perception so deeply felt that it must profoundly influence what one is in relation to his fellow human beings.

As I have perceived it, the key to the artistic meaning of George Eliot's novels is *vision,* an assumption which because of spatial limitations I shall be able to demonstrate only in *Adam Bede, The Mill on the Floss,* and *Middlemarch.* Since I consider vision the key, I have therefore been concerned with exploring the two antithetical movements toward and away from vision, with discovering what kind of structure they create in each of the three novels examined here, and with finding out how imagery, theme, and dramatic action work together to produce the movements. Because the imagery in these novels is a rich source of meaning which often assists in determining how other elements actually function, I have placed a great deal of emphasis upon it. But I have allowed myself much freedom to maneuver in this analysis, frequently pausing to study nonimagistic elements which seem demandingly relevant. Furthermore I have used the term *imagery* in its widest possible sense to mean figurative language in general and even such rhetorical devices as repetition. This is not, then, a study of imagery but rather a study of structural and thematic movement in which imagery is an essential element.

I have proceeded on the assumption that close analysis of the novels themselves would more readily lead me to discover their artistic meaning than use of pertinent material outside the novels. The most prominent of the critical issues has been dealt with indirectly, but in deference to close analysis it has been necessary to omit extensive reference to critics.

2. *Adam Bede:*
Initial Steps and the Negative Movement

IN *Adam Bede* George Eliot first fully develops the two antithetical movements which provide the structural and thematic basis of all her novels: the movement toward a realistic and relatively comprehensive vision of the moral life and the movement away from such vision toward the darkness of moral insensibility and incapacity. In terms of these two movements, the book falls into three parts: the beginning, in which both movements are simultaneously initiated; the middle, in which the movement toward vision is an undercurrent while the movement away from vision predominates, finally ending in catastrophe; and the end, in which there is only the positive movement, the negative having been dissolved into it. Both of these movements are exceedingly slow. For although vision may seem to come in one sudden brilliant revelation, the process of arriving at that point involves irreparable error, suffering, and grief. A series of incomplete and faltering perceptions gradually leads toward the more comprehensive insight. In the same way, movement away from vision is deceptively gradual, for the disablement of the moral sensibility is not effected by any single action. George Eliot shows how in each case the slow inexorable law of consequences is in operation. It is fitting, then, that both movements should be initiated little by little as the images of the book begin to take shape.

The opening image, a picture of a scene in Jonathan Burge's workshop where we first meet Adam, is clearly literal in meaning:

The afternoon sun was warm on the five workmen there, busy
upon doors and window-frames and wainscoting. A scent of pine-
wood from a tent-like pile of planks outside the open door mingled itself with the scent of the elder-bushes which were spreading their summer snow close to the open window opposite; the
slanting sunbeams shone through the transparent shavings that
flew before the steady plane, and lit up the fine grain of the oak
panelling which stood propped against the wall. On a heap of those
soft shavings a rough grey shepherd dog had made himself a
pleasant bed, and was lying with his nose between his forepaws,
occasionally wrinkling his brows to cast a glance at the tallest
of the five workmen, who was carving a shield in the centre of
a wooden mantelpiece [I. 3].

There are countless scenes of such a literal descriptive nature
in *Adam Bede*. They should never be discounted as relatively
unimportant "background" material. They help create the sense
of life, of calm ordered existence, which is so rich a part of
the cumulative effect, but they usually have a more direct function as well. That the sunlight coming through the open door
and window reveals the grain of the wood is merely pleasant
to consider at this point, and that Adam is carving a shield
seems to be no more than stage business. But soon, when
Adam is described, George Eliot calls attention to the *"keen
glance* of the dark eyes that shone from under strongly marked,
prominent and mobile eyebrows."* In contrast Seth's "eyes are
grey; his eyebrows have less prominence and more repose than
his brother's; and his glance, *instead of being keen,* is confid-
ing and benignant." Although the sunlight clearly reveals even
the minute detail of the wood, Seth does not see what is before
him. He announces the completion of a door he is making, only
to be told by Adam that he has omitted the panels. He simply
has not seen the door! When an argument about religion ensues,
Adam says: "'But t'hear some o' them preachers, you'd think
as a man must be doing nothing all's life *but shutting's eyes and
looking what's a-going on inside him.* . . . But what does the
Bible say? Why, it says as God put his sperrit into the work-
man as built the tabernacle, to make him do all *the carved
work* and things as wanted a nice hand'" (p. 9). And the "nice
hand" implies the keen eye. Though Adam admits that "some's
got one way o' looking at things and some's got another," he

shows little tolerance for the other workmen who stop their work the second that the clock strikes. Thus, although his keen eyesight has been emphasized, the faultiness of his vision has also been noted briefly. He measures the weakness of others against his own strength, and his judgment is sometimes harsh. There can be little doubt that in the first chapter the emphasis is on seeing, on different ways "o' looking at things, " and especially on the way Adam looks at things.

But if there were any doubt about whether the sight image is significant, George Eliot establishes it in the second chapter, where we move from the particular world of Adam's workshop into the larger world of the community whose focal point is the Green. At the present moment the Green is Dinah's workshop, and the attention of the villagers is focused directly on Dinah.

> . . . she stood and turned her grey eyes on the people. There was *no keenness in the eyes;* they seemed rather to be shedding love than making observations; they had the liquid look which tells that the mind is full of what it has to give out rather than impressed by external objects. She stood with her left hand towards the descending sun, and leafy boughs screened her from its rays; but in this sober light the delicate colouring of her face seemed to gather a calm vividness, like flowers at evening [II. 28].

Dinah's eyes, like Seth's, lack the external keenness of Adam's, for she has a different kind of sight.

In such a context as the preaching scene all of the light-sight images are of course ready-made--God is light and only the pure in heart shall see Him--but George Eliot exploits the metaphor artistically. Out of all the potential meaning which the vision image holds, she selects and fixes the particular meaning she wishes to associate with Dinah. Dinah's sermon sets echoing in the reader's ear such phrases as "wilful darkness, " "great darkness, " "poor blind child, " "dark bottomless pit, " and "eternal sun. " The scene foreshadows the emotional atmosphere of some of the events which are to follow. Chad's Bess, upon whom Dinah fixes her eye, prefigures the character of Hetty, and her sense of terror at "some undefined offense" is not unlike what Hetty is to feel. This terror is created in the ignorant and impressionable Bess by Dinah's almost hypnotic emphasis on the visual. Closing her eyes Dinah prays:

"Lord! Thou art with Thy people still: they *see* Thee in the night-
watches. . . . And Thou art near to those who have not known
Thee: *open their eyes* that they may *see* Thee: *see* Thee weeping
over them, and saying, 'Ye will not come unto me that ye might
have life'; *see* Thee hanging on the cross and saying, 'Father,
forgive them, for they know not what they do'; *see* Thee as Thou
wilt come again in Thy glory to judge them at the last. Amen"
[II. 30].

One of the purposes of Dinah's sermon is to compel belief in
the visibility of the literally unseeable: she "had that belief
in *visible* manifestations of Jesus, which is common among
the Methodists, and she communicated it irresistibly to her
hearers: she made them feel that he was among them bodily,
and might at any moment *show* himself to them in some way
that would strike anguish and penitence into their hearts"
(p. 38). Within the art frame the general effectiveness of her
rhetoric is indicated by the fact that the village onlookers are
drawn magnetically into the circle of believers. As Macbeth
through the intensity of his vision compels belief in the image
of the dagger, so Dinah compels belief in what her eyes reveal to her audience that she sees. "'*See!*' she exclaimed,
turning to the left, with her *eyes fixed* on a point above the
heads of the people--'*see* where our blessed Lord stands and
weeps, and stretches out his arms toward you'" (p. 38). After
such preparation as this it is small wonder that Bessy throws
away her earrings and sobs in terror when she becomes the
object of Dinah's full attention. But Dinah is to use her peculiar power to compel belief in the invisible image in a far more
significant context. For although this scene serves many functions, its potentiality is not fully exploited until the famous
prison scene, for which it has been a necessary part of the
preparation.

  With the significance of the sight image fully established in
one context, the two movements are now very subtly suggested
in chapter iv. The opening phrases, although they do not even
make a complete statement, create an image in the reader's
mind: "A green valley with a brook running through it, full
almost to overflowing with the late rains; overhung by low
stooping willows" (p. 52). We soon learn that it is this brook
in which Thias Bede, "the poor wandering father," has been

carried to his death. Adam, angry that his father has not returned home to finish the coffin which has been promised, condemns his father, measuring him (as Adam has previously measured the workmen) in terms of what he, Adam, would have done: "'I'd work my right hand off sooner than deceive people with lies i' that way. It makes me mad to think on't. I shall overrun these doings before long. I've stood enough of 'em'" (p. 55). When Lisbeth persists in talking to Adam, the author observes that "one of the lessons a woman most rarely learns is never to talk to an angry or drunken man," thereby inviting a possible comparison between Adam in his anger and Thias in his drunkenness. Adam's self-righteous anger makes Adam as unaware of his own hardness as Thias' drunkenness has made Thias unaware of his responsibility.

While Adam works on the coffin he has visions of past and future scenes with his father: ". . . his mind seemed as passive as a *spectator* at a diorama: *scenes* of the sad past, and probably sad future, floating before him, and giving place one to the other in swift succession" (pp. 64-65). He observes that his father's situation will become worse since "'there's no *slipping* up hill again, and no standing still when once you've begun to slip down.'" This is the first explicit reference to the will-less state which I have called drifting, for *slipping* also implies involuntary movement. The nature of Thias' death by drowning in the almost overflowing brook further suggests the drifting image, which throughout George Eliot's novels is predominantly associated with the movement away from vision. That his body was found "sticking against the willow" implies that it was carried along by the current until it reached an obstruction. This symbol is subsequently used in *Romola* to define the movement of Tito's life. As Tito drifts downstream toward Baldassarre's avenging hands he is vaguely aware that "the current was having its way with him" and Baldassarre is aware that "something was *being brought* to him" (LXVII. 380). Thias' death at the beginning of *Adam Bede* initiates the theme of drifting and partially defines the nature of the negative movement in George Eliot's novels, but even more important is its immediate function of causing Adam to begin taking account of himself.

Although Adam has a sense of mystery, nevertheless his

keen, literal vision has led him partially to discount the sound
of the willow wand and the image it called up as he worked on
the coffin. He says to himself:

> "It's no use staring about to catch *sight* of a sound. Maybe there's
> a world about us as we can't *see*, but th' ear's quicker than the
> *eye*, and catches a sound from't now and then. Some people
> think they get a *sight* on't too, but they're mostly folks whose
> eyes are not much use to 'em at anything else. For my part, I
> think it's *better to see when your perpendicular's true*, than to
> see a ghost" [p. 69].

But now when he sees his father dead before him, he revaluates
the experience, thus indicating that he is potentially capable of
changing his vision: "This was what the omen meant, then! And
the grey-haired father, of whom he had thought with a sort of
hardness a few hours ago, as certain to live to be a thorn in
his side, [1] was perhaps even then struggling with that watery
death! This was the first thought that flashed through Adam's
conscience . . . " (p. 71). Thias' drifting has taken him to the
point at which his "wide-open glazed eyes" will see no more,
but when "Adam's mind rushed back over the past in a flood
of relenting and pity" the positive and predominant movement
of the book is initiated. Adam's insight has come too little
and too late to modify this situation, but as one of the steps
in the process by which he learns the art of vision, it initiates
the forward movement of the novel.

❖❖❖❖❖

   With the appearance of Arthur and Hetty the countermove-
ment suggested by Thias Bede is now begun. For although Adam in his struggle sometimes contributes to the backward
movement of the book, the drama of Hetty and Arthur is almost
exclusively the vehicle through which that movement is developed.
   Before Arthur's movement is traced, it should be noted that
Arthur has no clear and realistic view of himself and the world
about him but rather that he moves in the illusory world of
fairy tale. His romantic conception of himself is immediately
indicated by what he tells Mr. Irwine: "'. . . I used to think
if ever I was a rich sultan, I would make Adam my grand-

vizier'" (V. 86). And that the dream has really changed not
at all since his childhood is made clear by his plans for his
coming-of-age party:"'The world will not see the grand epoch
of my majority twice. I think I shall have a lofty throne for
you, godmamma . . . that you may sit and look down upon us
like an Olympian goddess' " (p. 89). What could be greater
proof of one's generosity and power than that he be able to en-
throne his godmother ? In all of Arthur's daydreams he is the
generous provider, the noble landlord venerated and loved by
all his people. But he is in the unfortunate position of being
a landlord in dreams only, and actually his actions are rather
aimless, concerned primarily with passing the time pleasantly.
It is such a relatively aimless trip that he makes to the Hall
farm with Mr. Irwine when we first see Hetty. But not really
aimless, for when he enters the Hall farmhouse he looks "eagerly round the kitchen, as if his *eye* were seeking something
it could not find" (VI. 111), and that he has come to see Hetty
becomes increasingly clear.

Later, the tête-à-tête in the dairy accomplished,

> Arthur Donnithorne, riding by Mr. Irwine's side towards the
> valley of the Willow Brook, had . . . certain indistinct anticipa-
> tions, running as an undercurrent in his mind while he was lis-
> tening to Mr. Irwine's account of Dinah;--indistinct, yet strong
> enough to make him feel rather conscious when Mr. Irwine sud-
> denly said, --"What fascinated you so in Mrs. Poyser's dairy,
> Arthur ?" [IX. 143].

Having received a warning from Mr. Irwine about the power
of womanly fascination, Arthur replies: "'Thank you. It may
stand me in good stead some day, though I don't know that I
have any present use for it. Bless me ! how *the brook has over-
flowed*. Suppose we have a canter, now *we're at the bottom of
the hill' "* (p. 145). There can be little doubt that the Willow
Brook in which Thias Bede was drowned has here become a
symbol used to foreshadow the fate of Arthur.

From this point on Arthur fluctuates, making up his mind,
feeling heroic, then drifting into an opposite course of action
and rationalizing in order to secure his own approbation.
"Whether he would have *self-mastery* enough to be always as
harmless and beneficent as his good-nature led him to desire,
was a question that no one had yet decided against him, "

George Eliot says (XII. 177). But it soon becomes clear that
the slight shifting of circumstances from favorable to unfavorable is all that is needed to weaken his will power. Telling himself that he needs a week's fishing trip, he prepares
to go to Eagledale, only to discover that his horse is lame.
Next he plans to "have a gallop on Rattler to Norburne this
morning, and lunch with Gawaine." The aimlessness of such
actions indicates the unsettled state of his mind. "Behind this
explicit resolution there lay an implicit one," George Eliot
explains. Then in an acutely perceptive passage she phrases
his implicit resolution:

> If he lunched with Gawaine and lingered chatting, he should not
> reach the Chase again till nearly five, when Hetty would be safe
> out of his sight in the housekeeper's room; and when she set out
> to go home, it would be his lazy time after dinner, so he should
> keep out of her way altogether. There really would have been
> no harm in being kind to the little thing. . . . But perhaps he
> had better not take any more notice of her; it might put notions
> into her head . . . [p. 181].

That such reasoning as this was implicit is in itself significant,
for to have stated it as the real reason would have been to admit to himself that a problem existed, and at this point Arthur
still tries to delude himself about its existence. Furthermore
it is obvious that Arthur has left himself two loopholes (both
of which he later uses). If he fails to linger chatting, or if he
fails to be lazy in his "lazy time" after dinner, there would
be the possibility of seeing Hetty. Without having acknowledged
this reasoning to himself, he begins the process of assuring
himself that no harm would come of his seeing her anyway.
Thus by a series of rationalizations he moves away from his
resolution, which, after all, he has not made explicit. When
he arrives home again from Gawaine's in a flurry of haste at
three o'clock, George Eliot observes that "it is the favorite
stratagem of our passions to sham a retreat, and to turn sharp
round upon us at the moment we have made up our minds that
the day is our own."

It is this same mistake that Arthur makes consistently: he
overestimates his mastery of himself, thinking that to make
the resolution is all that is necessary. He has no clear insight
about himself and circumstances as they are but rather per-

suades himself that things are as he wants to believe them to be.

> The desire to see Hetty had rushed back like an *ill-stemmed current;* he was amazed himself at the force with which this trivial fancy seemed to *grasp* him. . . . It was because he had made a serious affair of an idle matter, by thinking of it as if it were of any consequence. He would amuse himself by seeing Hetty to-day, and get rid of the whole thing from his mind [pp. 182-83].

Clearly Arthur is caught in the "ill-stemmed current" of a situation he refuses to consider realistically. As this current gathers momentum and his will is more and more submerged in it, his movement ceases to be aimless vacillation and becomes propulsion.

In order to give the reader a sense of the propelling emotional power of the situation which is rapidly seducing Arthur, George Eliot describes in rich, sensuous language the wood where the two lovers are to meet. The whole passage must be examined:

> Arthur's *shadow* flitted rather faster among the sturdy oaks of the Chase than might have been expected from the *shadow* of a tired man on a warm afternoon, and it was still scarcely four o'clock when he stood before the tall narrow gate leading into the *delicious labyrinthine wood* which skirted one side of the Chase, and which was called Fir-tree Grove, not because the firs were many, but because they were few. It was a wood of beeches and limes, with here and there a *light, silver-stemmed* birch--just the sort of wood most *haunted* by the *nymphs*: you *see* their *white sunlit limbs gleaming* athwart the boughs, or *peeping* from behind the *smooth-sweeping* outline of a tall lime; you hear their *soft liquid* laughter--but if you look with a *too curious sacrilegious eye*, they vanish behind the *silvery* beeches, they make you believe that their voice was only a running brooklet, perhaps they *metamorphose* themselves into a *tawny* squirrel that *scampers* away and *mocks* you from the topmost bough. It was not a grove with measured grass or rolled gravel for you to *tread* upon, but with *narrow, hollow-shaped, earthy paths,* edged with faint dashes of delicate *moss--paths* which look as if they were made by the free-will of the trees and underwood, moving *reverently* aside to look at the tall queen of the *white-footed nymphs*.
>
> It was along the broadest of these paths that Arthur Donnithorne passed, under an avenue of limes and beeches. It was a still af-

ternoon--the *golden light* was *lingering languidly* among the upper
boughs, only *glancing* down here and there on the *purple pathway*
and its edge of faintly sprinkled *moss*: an afternoon in which destiny *disguises* her *cold awful face* behind a *hazy radiant veil,* en-
closes us in *warm downy wings,* and poisons us with *violet-
scented breath.* Arthur *strolled along carelessly* . . . his *eyes
would* [author's italics] fix themselves on the distant bend in the
road . . . [pp. 183-84].

It seems an almost dangerously delicate thing that George
Eliot has attempted here: to poise the reader at the door of
enchantment so that he may feel what it is and at the same
time to keep him from becoming enchanted so that he may know
what it is that he feels. It may be for this reason that the passage appears to be somewhat overdone, so that the reader will
pull up short of falling under its spell. In order to make sure
that her reader will maintain this delicate balance between involvement and disinvolvement, George Eliot carefully controls
the illusion she is creating. Almost convinced that he hears
the "liquid laughter" of the nymphs, the reader is reminded
that if he looks with "a too curious sacrilegious eye" "they"
will make him disbelieve. Told further that it is not a civilized grove for human feet to "tread" upon, but a place where
paths are made lightly by movement of trees, the reader is
kept outside the enchantment at the same time that he is per-
suaded to grant it a kind of validity. And when the "hazy radiant veil" has covered all and the "warm downy wings" have
enclosed, the author introduces the shocking contrast of the
"cold awful face" which lies behind the wings and the veil;
she further heightens the effect by indicating that the disguise
has been calculated. At this point it becomes a matter of horror that "Arthur strolled along carelessly," his eyes not sac-
rilegiously curious but impelled to look toward the object of
his desire. It is unfortunate that George Eliot introduced the
somewhat distracting personification of destiny at this point,
for the true horror of the scene does not reside in the im-
pending action of any external force.

The wood is a place of shadows and deceptive lights. What
light does penetrate this enclosed, concealed space does so at
odd angles, "glancing down here and there," but for the most
part "lingering languidly among the *upper* boughs," giving a

warm sense of its presence but creating only illusion. This
is one of countless scenes in *Adam Bede* where light is used
to heighten shadows, point up darkness, and create a haze--
where, in short, it distorts rather than assists vision. That
it is afternoon sunlight will be seen to be significant in terms
of the pattern of light imagery, for, in general, afternoon
light in George Eliot's novels suggests either illusion or reinvestment of meaning after necessary disillusionment.

We can never fully determine how it is that the special effect of the passage is achieved, for we can never fully know
how it is that words interact. But careful scrutiny will reveal
that here the author has worked in a poetic mode--that is, she
has fully exploited the language to achieve an immediate and
whole effect. The words are richly connotative, suggesting for
the most part the qualities of warmth *(warm, sunlit, tawny,
purple, golden, downy)*, quiet *(still, smooth-sweeping, peep-
ing, soft, reverently, languidly, shadow)*, softness *(soft, liquid, earthy, moss, downy, wings)*, smoothness *(silver-
stemmed, gleaming, silvery, moss, smooth-sweeping)*, darkness *(shadow, grove, labyrinthine, wood, underwood, purple,
moss)*, and light *(white, sunlit, gleaming, golden, light, hazy,
radiant)*. There is naturally much overlapping since, except
for light and dark, the qualities are all complementary rather
than contrasting. The contrast between light and dark, however, functions as a necessary part of the deception. All of the
qualities are emphasized not only by connotations but also by
soft liquid consonants, such as the *l* sounds in the phrase "gold-
en light was lingering languidly" and the combination of *l* and
m in "sunlit limbs gleaming" and "silver-stemmed"; long vowel
sounds, in such words as *beech, wood, smooth-sweeping,
tawny, lime, hollow;* and voiceless sounds, *labyrinthine,
earthy, pathway, breath, soft*. The liquid consonants emphasize the smoothness and quietness, and together with the long
vowel sounds they underline the rich mellowness that the warm
afternoon sunlight brings to the scene. The voiceless sounds
add to the sense of softness and quietness; and, particularly by
extending a hushed whisper over everything, they create a
sense of secrecy.

All the qualities mentioned above contribute to the special
effect of the passage: the dangerous enchantment of the "de-

licious labyrinthine wood. " Here *delicious* seems intended to suggest delight and allurement, as its derivation indicates. Considered as a whole and in relation to its larger context, the passage has sexual implications which few twentieth-century readers would miss, and it seems reasonable to assume that George Eliot did not miss them. But even if they are not recognized as such, the value of the scene is not noticeably diminished, for resident in it are the unmistakable elements of seduction. The disappearing and reappearing nymphs with their "sunlit limbs" and "soft liquid laughter, " the earthy moss-edged paths which lead on like a labyrinth, the pliant, bending limes and beeches--all are objectifications of Arthur's own emotional and moral state, the submission of his will and the loss of clear perception which would help him distinguish appearance from reality. It is truly, as the first sentence suggests, "Arthur's shadow" which moves before us, for such a state implies the loss of self. The voluptuous language of the passage creates for the reader the illusion of that seduction.

After the first secret meeting between Arthur and Hetty, Arthur has a momentary insight during which "his feelings were *lit up* for him by a more distinct consciousness. " Now he acknowledges that he is "ready to pitch everything else-- no matter where--for the sake of *surrendering himself* to this *delicious* feeling which had just disclosed itself. It was no use *blinking* the fact now--they would get too fond of each other, if he went on taking notice of her . . ." (XII. 189). Here the use of the words "lit up" and "blinking" throws the emphasis on Arthur's vision. But his recognition of the fact that he has been blinking at rather than seeing the truth of the situation is short-lived. Again resolved not to see Hetty, now he "might give himself up to thinking how immensely agreeable it would be if circumstances were different. . . ." And so he repeats the same pattern of insight, resolution, daydream, rationalization, and finally submission. Then having seen Hetty for the second time in one day, Arthur rushes out of the Grove, which he feels is

> haunted by his evil genius. Those beeches and smooth limes-- there was something enervating in the very sight of them; but the strong knotted old oaks had no *bending languor* in them--the

sight of them would give a man some energy. Arthur *lost him-self* among the *narrow* openings in the fern, *winding about* with-out seeking any issue, till the *twilight deepened almost to night* under the great boughs . . . [XIII. 196].

Although the light and space (here specifically the labyrinth) imagery indicates that Arthur is rapidly becoming so, he is not as yet completely "lost." But the last chapter in Book I, where he plans to dispel the charm by discussing his problem with Mr. Irwine, builds up to the climax. Mr. Irwine warns that keeping unpleasant consequences in mind "gives you a sort of smoked glass through which you may look at the re-splendent fair one and discern her true outline . . ." (XVI. 245). Mr. Irwine is in effect the smoked glass through which Ar-thur could come to discern the true outline of both Hetty and himself; but, unable to accept any such aid to his vision, he fails to confide in Mr. Irwine. This failure, the author sug-gests, is the result of an unacknowledged "backstairs influ-ence" which told him that it would be annoying if he were un-able to carry out his resolutions. That this failure is crucial is indicated by the explicit use of the drifting imagery: "While Arthur was hesitating, the rope to which he might have clung had *drifted* away--he must trust now to his own swimming." That he is no longer able to swim against the current has al-ready been indicated. The drifting which follows is inevitable.

Having established this inevitability, George Eliot shows us mostly an external view of Arthur until the last part of the fight scene in the woods. Here it is "the strange evening *light* which the light clouds had caught up even to the zenith, and were now shedding down between the topmost branches" (XXVII. 11) that reveals part of Arthur's deceit to Adam. And for an instant Arthur stands revealed to himself, *"face to face* with the first great irrevocable evil he had ever committed." The commission of such a wrongdoing is consistently shown to be the result of moral drifting in George Eliot's novels. The rev-elation which is now forced upon Arthur comes too late, for he is already lost, forced by his own action into a position where he must violate his own nature: "The native impulse to give truth in return for truth . . . must be suppressed, and duty was become a question of tactics" (XXVIII. 24). Up to this

point Arthur has been a weak-willed man who misjudged his
self-mastery, but now he suffers a complete loss of moral vision. The deception of Adam, which is clearly wrong, becomes
for Arthur in this blinded state necessarily right. George
Eliot's exploration of this state reveals something about the
nature of vision:

> There is a terrible coercion in our deeds which may first turn
> the honest man into a deceiver, and then reconcile him to the
> change; for this reason--that the second wrong presents itself
> to him in the guise of the only practicable right. The action
> which before commission has been *seen* with that blended com-
> mon sense and fresh untarnished feeling which is the *healthy
> eye of the soul,* is *looked at* afterwards with the *lens* of apolo-
> getic ingenuity, through which all things that men call beautiful
> and ugly are seen to be made up of textures very much alike
> [XXIX. 34-35].

Once the deception has been practiced, that "common-sense"
becomes crafty-sense and the "fresh untarnished feeling" becomes dulled automatic response; the "healthy eye of the soul"
which sees beneath the external appearance becomes a mere
mechanical cameralike "lens" which, incapable of discovering
reality, sees wrong in the "guise" of right. The lens is a device used for *looking,* but the "eye of the soul" (common sense
and fresh feeling) *sees.* This distinction between *looking* and
seeing frequently recurs throughout the pattern of vision imagery. The explicitness of the vision image is significant here,
for this is the nadir of Arthur's negative movement. Heretofore
he has failed to see what he does not wish to see, but now he
converts what he looks at into its opposite. In this blinded state
he "must persuade himself that he had not been very much to
blame; he began even to pity himself for the necessity he was
under of deceiving Adam: it was a course so opposed to the
honesty of his own nature. But then, it was the only right thing
to do" (p. 35). Having thus drifted into a state of moral incapacity, he places the responsibility of decision about the letter
upon Adam: "'I leave it to you to decide whether you will be
doing best to deliver it to Hetty or to return it to me. Ask
yourself once more whether you are not taking a measure which
may pain her more than mere silence'" (XXIX. 39). In this
state, George Eliot leaves Arthur until the time of retribution.

Hetty, who provides the other part of the negative movement away from vision, has a great deal in common with Arthur. Both have a romantic conception of themselves; both have unrealistic visions of themselves as storybook hero and heroine, the noble prince about to inherit the kingdom and the beautiful dairymaid about to be carried away by her princely lover who will surround her with the rich halls, luxurious carriages, and magnificent clothes befitting her beauty. Both are concerned with external appearances, but with one significant difference: Arthur looks not only in the mirror to see the reflection of his handsome face and dashing uniform but also in the faces of his prospective tenants which he hopes will mirror approval of his noble generosity. Everything Hetty looks at mirrors for her only her own physical beauty. The image of himself which Arthur sees reflected in the attitude of the community is, however, less deceptive than the image Hetty sees. For until he becomes involved in deceit, Arthur is more or less the genial, good-natured and well-meaning youth that he appears to be. But from the beginning Hetty's beauty is deceptive.

When we first meet Hetty in the dairy we are told that hers is "a spring-tide beauty; it was the beauty of young frisking things, round-limbed, gambolling, circumventing you by a false air of innocence . . ." (VII. 118). She is frequently compared to a kitten, a lamb, or a child. There is always about her an apple-cheeked innocence, a petal-pink and white purity. But there is something more, a voluptuousness which the author merely suggests when she first presents Hetty:

> The dairy was certainly worth looking at: it was a scene to sicken for with a sort of calenture in hot and dusty streets--such *coolness*, such *purity*, such fresh *fragrance* of new-pressed *cheese*, of firm *butter*, of *wooden vessels* perpetually *bathed* in pure water; such *soft colouring* of *red earthenware* and *creamy surfaces*, *brown wood* and *polished* tin, *grey* limestone and *rich orange-red rust* on the iron weights and hooks and hinges. But one gets only a confused notion of these details when they surround a distractingly pretty girl of seventeen, standing on little pattens and rounding her dimpled arm to lift a pound of butter out of the scale [VII. 116].

Here George Eliot does more than draw a background for the character she is introducing; she creates for the reader a rich

sensuous set of associations which is immediately transferred
to Hetty whose movement of "rounding her dimpled arm to lift
a pound of butter out of the scale" is unmistakably sensuous.
The description of the dairy appeals to the sense of smell,
but especially to that combination of sight and touch suggested
by "wooden vessels perpetually bathed in pure water" and "red
earthenware and creamy surfaces." The sight images here remain somewhat general so that the reader has a sense of rich
color and texture without becoming absorbed in too much detail,
retaining only "a confused notion" which is soon given form by
the presence of Hetty.

Though we have been told that Hetty's beauty is that "of young
frisking things," we see very little of the liveliness the phrase
implies. For the dairy scene with Arthur induces a kind of
sensuous languor in her which is characteristic of that dreamlike state of existence in which she drifts inevitably toward
the darkness of the prison cell. "Hetty came out of the dairy
relieving her tired arms by lifting them up, and clasping her
hands at the back of her head. 'Molly,' she said, rather languidly, 'just run out and get me a bunch of dock leaves; the
butter's ready to pack up now'" (VII.134). We do not see the
initial stages of this dreamlike state, for the author soon tells
us, in a chapter which she entitles "Hetty's World," that

> for the last few weeks a new influence had come over Hetty--
> vague, atmospheric, shaping itself into no self-confessed hopes
> or prospects, but producing a pleasant *narcotic effect,* making
> her tread the ground and go about her work in a sort of *dream,*
> unconscious of weight or effort, and *showing her* all things through
> a *soft, liquid veil,* as if she were living not in this solid world of
> brick and stone, but in a beautiful world, *such as the sun lights
> up for us in the waters*. Hetty had become aware that Mr. Arthur
> Donnithorne would take a good deal of trouble for the chance of
> seeing her. . . . And so poor Hetty had got a face and a presence
> haunting her waking and sleeping *dreams;* bright, soft glances
> had penetrated her, and suffused her life with a strange, happy
> *languor. . . .* For three weeks, at least, her inward life had con-
> sisted of little else than living through in memory the looks and
> words Arthur had directed toward her . . . and now her imagina-
> tion, instead of retracing the past, was busy fashioning what would
> happen tomorrow . . . [IX. 141-43].

Hetty's vision is already dimmed so that she sees (or rather--

note the passivity--is *shown)* "all things through a soft liquid veil, " and the world she lives in is that unreal world of deceptive external appearances "such as the sun lights up for us in the waters. " This is one of many variations on the mirror image which we come to associate with Hetty. We do not see the struggle for self-mastery in Hetty that is so important in the development of Arthur's character; for, as this passage substantially indicates, her will has already become submerged in the dream.

One of the important results of her existence in this dreamworld is her isolation. That she is completely unfeeling about anything which does not relate to her becomes evident by her lack of response to the news that Thias Bede has drowned. "In this state of mind, how could Hetty give any feeling to Adam's troubles, or think much about poor old Thias being drowned? Young souls in such pleasant delirium as hers, are as unsympathetic as butterflies sipping nectar; they are isolated from all appeals by a *barrier of dreams*--by invisible looks and impalpable arms" (IX. 143). But this isolation is to function in two ways. Hetty, who is now isolated to the extent that she not only cannot feel for anyone else but also "hates the leveret that runs across the path . . . hates everything that is not what she longs for" (XIII. 193), later reaches the extreme point of isolation where she can share none of her inner life with anyone else. Arthur's deceit and concealment have isolated him from his best friend Mr. Irwine, the only person who could have helped him. But he is never as completely cut off from human relationship as Hetty, whose pattern of concealment carries her to the point of desperation.

What light there is in Hetty's dreamworld is hazy and deceptive. She feels safe in the deepening twilight of the Grove which she prefers to the "unsheltered road, " and she is also associated with candlelight. (Some of the significance of the candlelight is clarified by Mrs. Poyser, doubtlessly the inventor of daylight saving time, to whom candlelight is for the gentlefolk. "What!" she exclaims to Hetty, "you'd be wanting the clock set by gentle-folk's time, would you? an' sit up burnin' candle, an' lie a-bed wi' the sun a-bakin' you like a cowcumber i' the frame?" [XIV. 207].) In the bedchamber scene (chapter xv) Hetty and Dinah go upstairs in the twilight

to rooms "with *no blinds* to shut out the *light,* which was now
beginning to gather new strength from the *rising of the moon*--
more than enough strength to enable Hetty to move about and
undress with perfect comfort." But Hetty, who is "more bent
on her peculiar form of worship than usual, " opens the locked
drawer which contains her treasures and takes out two wax
candles "secretly bought at Treddleston, " a mirror, and a
large pair of glass earrings. Lighting the candles so that her
vision of herself in the mirror may be improved, Hetty decks
herself in false finery and studies her own image. She, like
Gwendolen Harleth, is a "devout" worshiper performing her
"religious rites" of self-worship before the mirror. The religious imagery which permeates this scene is emphasized by
the use of candles, which naturally suggest church ritual. This
merging of religious and vision imagery occurs frequently in
Adam Bede and throughout the novels. Here, too, the pattern
of concealment which later dominates Hetty's movements is
indicated by the locked bedroom door, the locked treasure
drawer, and secretly purchased candles.

Hetty's action in this scene and the nature of her vision are
pointed up by contrast with Dinah who "delighted in her bedroom window. Being on the second story of that tall house, it
gave her a *wide view* over the fields. " Dinah sits by the window in the moonlight looking out, and when she feels the need
of a "clear showing" she puts her Bible "on the window ledge,
where the light was strongest. " We are told that "there was
light enough for her . . . to discern the text. " Dinah's imagination and sympathy create for her a vision of Hetty's coming trials, "a long toilsome journey" in "hunger and cold and
unsheltered darkness. " When Dinah tells Hetty about the vision, Hetty is momentarily filled with "a vague fear that something evil was sometime to befall her. " But it is only a vague
fear, and Hetty is "soon in the wood again--her waking *dreams*
being merged in a sleeping life scarcely more fragmentary and
confused" (XV. 230).

Nowhere does Hetty struggle to emerge from this dreamworld as Arthur has struggled, for at no time--even after
Arthur's departure--does she have more than a "dim undefined
fear that the future might shape itself in some way quite unlike
her dream" (XXX. 43). And when Adam, in an attempt to help

her face reality, delivers Arthur's letter to her, her vision
is not enlarged. The letter-reading scene, which of course
must be secret, is enacted in Hetty's locked bedchamber by
the dim light of a candle. When Hetty finishes the letter and
looks up, there is "the reflection of a blanched face in the old
dim glass" but she does not see it (XXXI. 61). It is only after
she has finished the second reading that

> she caught sight of her face in the glass; it was reddened now,
> and wet with tears; it was almost like a companion that she might
> complain to--that would pity her. She leaned forward on her el-
> bows, and *looked* into those dark overflooding eyes, and at that
> quivering mouth, and *saw* how the tears came thicker and thicker,
> and how the mouth became convulsed with sobs [p. 62].

Hetty's vision at this crucial moment of revelation extends,
as it always has, no further than her mirror. She neither
looks inside herself, nor outside herself, but only at her own
external appearance, at her own self-pitying face. This is an
extremely passive state in which the action is the observation
of the mechanical response. Hetty merely "sat sobbing till the
candle went out, and then, wearied, aching, stupefied with cry-
ing, threw herself on the bed without undressing, and went to
sleep." The dawn brings her, for the first time, face to face
with the real world--a world divested of romance and filled
with the bare facts of commonplace existence. The setting of
the morning scene is similar to that of several key scenes in
George Eliot's later novels, but Hetty's response is peculiarly
her own:

> There was a *feeble dawn* in the room when Hetty awoke, a little
> after four o'clock, with a sense of dull misery, the cause of which
> broke upon her gradually, as she began to *discern* the objects
> round her in the *dim light.* And then came the frightening thought
> that she had to *conceal* her misery, as well as to bear it, in this
> *dreary daylight* that was coming. She could lie no longer: she got
> up and went towards the table: there lay the letter; she opened
> her treasure-drawer: there lay the earrings and the locket--the
> signs of her short happiness--the signs of the lifelong dreariness
> that was to follow it. Looking at the little trinkets . . .   she
> lived back in the moments when they had been given to her with
> such tender caresses, such strangely pretty words. . . . And
> the Arthur who had spoken to her and looked at her in this way,
> *who was present with her now*--whose arm she felt round her,
> his cheek against hers, his very breath upon her--was the cruel,

cruel Arthur who had written that letter. . . . The half-benumbed mental condition . . . made it necessary for her to look again to see if her wretched thoughts were actually true--if the letter was really so cruel. She had to hold it close to the *window* else she could not have read it by the *faint light*. Yes! it was worse--it was more cruel [XXXI. 62-63].

Thus Hetty evokes the dreamworld, summoning up the past to screen her from the painful present. In this scene light is used not as a symbol of growing spiritual or moral vision but rather to reveal the external reality of objects, the commonplace aspects of everyday life. To Hetty, who is incapable of seeing beyond this external, the commonplace is trivial and depressing. It induces in her a state of oppressive languor unlike that of the earlier sensuous state. As she "began *languidly* to take off the clothes she had worn all the night, that she might wash herself and brush her hair, she had the sickening sense that her life would go on in this way . . ." (p. 64). All things were "flat and dreary to her now: everything would be a weariness: and she would carry about for ever a hopeless thirst and longing." She pauses "in the midst of her *languid* undressing," uncaring even about her own beauty. "Her eyes *wandered* sadly over the dull old chamber, and then *looked out vacantly* towards the growing dawn" (p. 65). In this listless, will-less state, she sees nothing more than that she must run away or do anything that will remove her from the dullness of everyday routine. That Hetty's faulty vision is the cause of her moral drifting which follows is emphasized in the following passage: "Poor Hetty's *vision* of consequences, at no time more than a *narrow* fantastic calculation of her own probable pleasures and pains, was now *quite shut out* by reckless irritation under present suffering, and she was ready for one of those convulsive, *motiveless* actions by which wretched men and women leap from a temporary sorrow into a lifelong misery" (pp. 71-72). That such blind and motiveless action constitutes moral drifting is confirmed by the explicit use of a drifting image; now almost completely adrift, Hetty is compared to "a little vessel without ballast *tossed about* on a stormy sea."

Soon faced with the fact of her pregnancy, Hetty concentrates all of her efforts on concealment and drifts along in the *"blind*

vague hope" that something will happen to change her circumstances. Ironically the people of her community who once made
up that dreary commonplace existence from which she constantly sought escape become "all her world, now her *airy
dream* had vanished" (**XXXV**. 109). When her *"blind* trust in
some unshapen chance" betrays her, she is faced with the
necessity of deciding on a course of action. It is at this point
that the tempo of the negative movement quickens and the images of concealment, darkness, and isolation become more
concentrated. Walking along the road to Treddleston on the
pretext of a shopping trip, Hetty

> hardly knows that the sun is shining. . . . She only wants to be
> out of the *highroad,* that she may walk slowly, and not care how
> her face looks, as she dwells on wretched thoughts; and through
> this gate she can get into a fieldpath behind the wide thick hedge-
> rows. Her great dark *eyes wander blankly* over the fields like the
> *eyes* of one who is desolate, homeless, unloved. . . . At the next
> stile the *pathway* branches off: there are *two roads before her --*
> one along by the hedgerow, which will by and by lead her into the
> road again; the other across the fields, which will take her much
> farther out of the way into the Scantlands, *low shrouded pas-
> tures where she will see nobody.* She chooses this, and begins
> to walk a little faster, as if she had suddenly thought of an ob-
> ject towards which it was worth while to hasten. Soon she is in
> the Scantlands, where the *grassy land slopes gradually down-
> wards,* and she leaves the level ground to follow the slope. Far-
> ther on there is a clump of trees on the low ground, and she is
> making her way toward it. No, it is not a clump of trees, but a
> *dark shrouded* pool, so *full with the wintry rains* that the under
> boughs of the elder-bushes lie low beneath the water. She sits
> down on the grassy bank, against the stooping stem of the great
> oak that hangs over the *dark pool.* She has thought of this pool
> often in the nights of the month that has just gone by, and now
> at last she *comes to see it.* She clasps her hands round her knees
> and leans forward, and *looks* earnestly at it, as if trying to guess
> what sort of bed it would make for her young round limbs [**XXXV**.
> 107-8].

Most of the images of this passage, though firmly grounded
in the literal level of meaning, reach a symbolic level. The
"highroad" is traveled by human beings who, having roots in
one community, move from it by a direct route to another community. In leaving it for "the field-path behind the wide thick

hedgerows" Hetty temporarily cuts herself off from the community. But the choice she makes in taking the path is not final, since the path diverges, making a further choice necessary. Choosing not the road which would eventually take her
back to the "highroad" but that which will take her "much far-
ther out of the way . . . where she will see nobody, " Hetty
rejects the opportunity to reverse her first decision and thus
makes her isolation final. But her movement is not only outward from the human community but also downward toward
despair. She has left the "highroad" for the "low shrouded
pastures" and there the "grassy land, " suggesting the slip-
pery, "slopes gradually downwards. " Then Hetty makes a
further choice when she "leaves the level ground to follow the
slope" which leads down to the "dark shrouded pool, " a choice
which brings her to the point of the final choice involving self-
destruction. A variant of the mirror image, the pool is a symbol which extends beyond the idea of self-worship to suggest
the self-destructiveness of such worship. It is calculated to
recall the story of Narcissus. Filled beyond its normal level
with wintry rains, the pool also brings to the reader's mind
the Willow Brook, which at the time that Thias drowned in it
was "full almost to overflowing with the late rains. " By recalling the fate of one who also drifted too far, it foreshadows
Hetty's fate. Hetty, of course, does not throw herself into the
pool but, thinking with a "sense of lulling warmth" of the possibility that Arthur will take care of her, plans a way by which
she may effect an escape to him. That she does pick up her
basket and go on her way to Treddleston does not in any way
vitiate the symbolic value of the scene. It is a pre-enactment
of the journey in despair which is to follow. On a literal level
it is a necessary preparation for Hetty's succeeding action; the
reader must know something of her state of mind when she begins her journey. With the image of the pool fixed firmly in her
mind, feeling "dimly that she might be travelling all this weary
journey toward the beginning of a new misery" (p. 112), Hetty
begins the long wandering which is to end in exile and death.

  Hetty, whose little world has been limited not only by the
boundaries of Loamshire but also by "her poor narrow thoughts"
(XXXVI. 115), now finds herself moving in a large and alien
world. Although her vision is not greatly enlarged by the suf-

fering she endures during her seven-day journey to Windsor, she does come to see her past life in a new perspective:

> Now for the first time, as she lay down to-night in the strange hard bed, she felt that her home had been a happy one, that her uncle had been very good to her, that her quiet lot at Hayslope among the things and people she knew, with her little pride in her one best gown and bonnet, and nothing to hide from anyone, was what she would like to wake up to as a reality . . . [XXXVI. 118].

She still, however, thinks of that life only in terms of herself; ". . . her own misery filled her heart: there was no room in it for other people's sorrow" (p. 119). But "the new susceptibility" that suffering has awakened in her causes her to take notice of the small dog riding by the driver of a wagon which overtakes her: ". . . she felt as if the helpless timid creature had some *fellowship* with her, and, without being quite aware of the reason, she was less doubtful about speaking to the driver . . ." (p. 121). Though Hetty is still a novice in the school of suffering, this journey has helped prepare her for the hardship which is to come. It has had a goal, has given some hope and direction to sustain her through her first experience in the larger world.

With the extinction of that hope on the day that she discovers Arthur's departure from Windsor comes the loss of direction which completely sets Hetty adrift: ". . . when she lay the next morning looking at the *growing light* which was like a cruel taskmaster returning to urge from her a fresh round of hated hopeless labour, she began to think what course she must take. . . . But which way could she turn?" (XXXVII. 128). She remembers the fields with the high hedges and thinks that "perhaps, when there was nothing else she could do, she could get courage to drown herself in some pond like that in the Scantlands" (p. 131). She considers returning home and also considers seeking out Dinah in order to confess to her. But pride forces her to reject both possibilities. Concealment and the urge to self-destruction become the motivating forces, but the life urge, too, is strong. Now Hetty wanders between life and death, "going on and on *without distinct purpose,* yet strangely, by some *fascination,* taking the way she had come, " moving more slowly than before, "sitting for hours under the hedgerows, *looking* before her with *blank*, beautiful eyes; fancying herself at the edge of a *hidden pool, low down*, like that in the Scantlands . . ." (p. 136). Though Hetty's eyes retain their "dark brightness" they have become "hard" and "fierce," and the image which they see constantly before them is the dark pool in a hidden wood.

So persistent is this miragelike vision that it becomes an obsession[2] with her:

> At last she was among the fields she had been dreaming of, on a long *narrow* pathway leading to a wood. If there should be a pool in that wood! It would be better *hidden* than one in the fields. No, it was not a wood, only a wild brake. . . . She roamed up and down, thinking there was perhaps a pool in every hollow before she came to it, till her limbs were weary, and she sat down to rest. The afternoon was far advanced, and the *leaden sky was darkening, as if the sun were setting behind it.* After a little while Hetty started up again, feeling that *darkness* would soon come on; and *she must put off finding the pool till to-morrow,* and make her way to some shelter for the night. She had quite *lost her way* in the fields, and might as well go in one direction as another, for aught she knew. She walked through field after field, and no village, no house was in sight; but *there* [author's italics], at the corner of this pasture, there was a break in the hedges; the land seemed to *dip down* a little, and two trees leaned toward each other across the opening. Hetty's heart gave a great beat as she thought there must be a pool there. She walked towards it *heavily* over the tufted grass, with pale lips and a sense of trembling; *it was as if the thing were come in spite of herself,* instead of being the object of her search.
> There it was, *black under the darkening sky:* no motion, no sound near. She set down her basket, and then sank down herself on the grass, trembling. *The pool had its wintry depth now* . . . [pp. 138-39].

In this passage and the one following it there occurs the most elemental of all struggles: that between the death urge and the life force. Up to this point the death urge has had the upper hand; for although Hetty drifts about, lost and completely without sense of direction, rationalizing that since darkness will soon come she "must put off finding the pool until tomorrow," she nevertheless does find the pool instead of the shelter she consciously seeks. Or rather it is as if the pool finds her, "were come in spite of herself." No sound or motion has led her to it, only her sight in the semi-darkness and perhaps the feel of the land dipping down. Although it is the kind of pool she has dreamed of, winter-deep and concealed by trees, Hetty does not run toward it but walks "heavily."

Thus it is at this point that the life force asserts itself more strongly and Hetty's drifting becomes positive rather than negative. "But then, there was her basket--she must *hide* that too. . . ." Gathering stones to sink it consumes time and increases her weariness. "There was no need to hurry--there was all the night to drown herself in." Hunger forces her to eat all of her food, and the satisfaction of that need induces a "fixed dreamy attitude" that brings on sleep. Awaking in the "deep night" she feels again the "horror of this cold, and darkness, and solitude--out of all human reach. . . ." Feeling the need of warmth, "She walked backwards and forwards . . . *beginning to discern* something of the objects around her, as her *eyes* became accustomed to the *night:* the *darker* line of the hedge, the rapid motion of some living creature--perhaps a field mouse--rushing across the grass. She no longer felt as if the *darkness* hedged her in . . ." (p. 140). With the aid of her new vision and the comforting sound of sheep in a field, she is able to find a hovel near a sheepfold.

> It was an ill-smelling, close place, but warm, and there was straw on the ground: Hetty sank down on the straw with a sense of escape. Tears came--she had never shed tears before since she left Windsor--tears and sobs of hysterical joy that she had still hold of life, and that she was on the familiar earth, *with the sheep near her*. . . . Soon warmth and weariness lulled her . . . into dozing, *fancying* herself at the brink of the pool again--*fancying* that she had jumped . . . and the poor soul, *driven to and fro* between two equal terrors, found the one relief that was possible to it--the relief of unconsciousness [p. 141].

Divested of both artificial and real finery (the jewelry Arthur had given her), stripped of pride, destitute of everything but life itself, the poor, wandering lamblike Hetty sleeps in the fold. Temporarily she has, like Lear, become "the thing itself." Having suffered the terrors of both life and death, she now stands on the threshold of a new state of existence. If suffering has sufficiently enlarged her vision, she will move back

into the most direct way which leads to the community and
moral responsibility. If that has not yet been accomplished,
she will wander on her isolated way, drifting into the commission of an irrevocably destructive act. This is one of the two
great crises in Hetty's life.

As she awakens, she dreams that her aunt is standing over
her with a candle: "She trembled under her aunt's glance, and
opened her eyes. There was no *candle*, but there was *light*
in the hovel--the *light of early morning* through the open door.
And there was a face looking down on her; but it was an unknown face, belonging to an elderly man in a smock-frock"
(p. 142). What has appeared to be a simple symbol of the
sheepfold, wandering lamb, and shepherd becomes more complex at this point. When the man roughly questions Hetty about
her presence in the hovel she "trembled still worse under this
real fear and shame than she had done in her momentary dream
under her aunt's glance. She felt that she was a beggar already. . . . " Explaining that she was "lost" and "overtaken
by the dark, " Hetty asks for directions to the nearest village.
The man looks at her for several seconds "with a slow bovine
gaze" and then answers:

> "Aw, I can show you the way to Norton, if you like. But what
> do you do *gettin' out o' the highroad*?" he added, with a tone of
> gruff reproof. "Y'ull be gettin' into mischief, if you dooant
> mind. "
> "Yes, " said Hetty, "I won't do it again. I'll keep in the road,
> if you'll be so good as show me how to get to it."
> "Why dooant you keep where there's finger-poasses an' *folks
> to ax the way on*?" the man said, still more gruffly. "Anybody
> '*ud* think you was a *wild woman*, an'look at yer" [XXXVII, 142-
> 43].

Much more is implied in this "gruff reproof" than immediately
appears on the surface. That such a lowly peasant shepherd
should condemn Hetty for her actions, and above all her appearance, is an indication that, as she now is, she would be
unacceptable to any human community. She has taken on the
appearance of a "wild" woman outside the pale of even the
lowest level of society, has become an alien even to an isolated shepherd. The condemnation of one outside and below
her own class is sterner than that within her own class, or

most especially within her own family, would be. By comparison her aunt's glance in the waking dream was not so fearful.
On the symbolic level it might be said that the shepherd's function is to show Hetty, by his rejection of her, the importance
of getting back on the highroad which would lead back to her
proper place in her own community. His condemnation of her
is an indication that her life outside her community will be no
more pleasant than that from which she sought escape. But
Hetty does not make this connection. She is no longer "the
thing itself" but once more a vain woman whose pride is hurt.
Poor as she is, "she thought that she would give him a six-
pence for telling her the way, and then he would not suppose
she was wild." But money cannot always buy approval, and
the peasant refuses the money and remains firm in his opinion
of her. To Hetty "life now, *by the morning light,* with the impression of that man's hard wondering look at her, was as full
of dread as death . . ." (p. 144). The cold, lonely darkness of
night has made her feel the horror of death and the relief at
the presence of living things, but the hard reality of daylight
has caused her to feel a similar horror of life and the pain
of human contact. With her new knowledge, she must again
face what seems this time to be a final decision. If she spends
what remaining money she has on cart or coach fare, she can
reach Dinah quickly--an action which would constitute getting
back on the "highroad" where there are "folks to ax the way
on, " where there would again be the human contact from which
she has isolated herself. The other choice is to live on the
money as long as it lasts, drifting about until something happens to her. And it is this which she must choose, since she
fears the shame of having other people know about her, as
they undoubtedly would if she went to Dinah; ". . . she could
no more rush on that shame than she could rush on death. She
must wander on and on. . . . And yet--such is the strange action of our souls, *drawing us* by a lurking desire towards the
very ends we dread--Hetty, when she set out again from
Norton, asked the straightest road northward towards Stony-
shire, and kept it all that day" (pp. 144-45). Much later, in
the prison scene, she is to tell Dinah: "It was partly thinking
o' you made me come toward Stoniton; and, besides, I was so
frightened at going wandering about till I was a beggar-woman,

and had nothing . . . " (XLV. 236). Poor Hetty--frightened of wandering, of shame, and of death--is no longer capable of affirming any course of action.

3. *Adam Bede:*
The Positive Movement

WHILE THE negative movement away from vision has progressed to a climactic point in *Adam Bede,* slowly at first but progressively faster as the increasing blindness brings on panic and indecision, the positive movement toward vision has been quietly and unobtrusively prepared for. Adam's recognition of his own hardness toward his father has already been cited as the initial step in that movement. But although Adam's self-knowledge (as well as his knowledge of others) is still in an elementary stage, the reader knows more about him. Adam has what Mr. Irwine calls "an excess of pride" (IX. 144), but he also has "a large fund of reverence in his nature" (XVI. 233) and a sense of mystery. To him love is "a mystery we can give no account of" (XI. 174), and feelings are difficult to comprehend: "figures tell us a fine deal, and we couldn't go far without 'em, but they don't tell us about folks's feelings. It's a nicer job to calculate *them"* (XIV. 199-200, author's italics). Unlike Arthur, Adam has an "iron will" which is the source of both his strength and weakness. "I've *seen pretty clear,"* he tells Arthur, "ever since I could cast up a sum, as you can never do what's wrong without breeding sin and trouble more than you can ever *see. . . .* But it isn't my way to be see-saw about anything: I think my fault lies th' other way. When I've said a thing, if it's only to myself, it's hard for me to go back" (XVI. 238-39). As Adam sits meditating during his father's funeral, he comes to an even fuller recognition of his weakness:

36

"It's a sore fault in me as I'm so hot and out o' patience with
people when they do wrong, and my heart gets shut up against
'em, so as I can't bring myself to forgive 'em. I *see clear enough*
there's more pride nor love in my soul. . . . Mayhap the best
thing I ever did in my life was only doing what was easiest for
myself. It's allays been easier for me to work nor to sit still,
but the real tough job for me 'ud be to master my own will and
temper, and go right against my own pride" [XVIII. 290-91].

On the surface, then, it appears that Adam does "see clear
enough" the nature of his past mistakes, but he will have arrived at true vision only when he is able to apply that knowledge to another situation which demands that he submerge his
pride and will in love.

Regardless of fond readers who dote sentimentally on Hetty
or pounce critically upon Dinah, regardless, too, of the well-
known fact that *Adam Bede* grew out of a story about a prison
scene told by the author's aunt, Adam Bede is the center of
the book, as the title indicates that he is intended to be. And
the central, unifying action of the book is Adam's slow and
painful progression to the point at which he has learned "the
art of vision." In an explicit statement the author indicates
how the other major actions in the book are related to this one:

Perhaps here lay the secret of the hardness he [Adam] had ac-
cused himself of: he had *too little fellow-feeling* with the weakness that errs in spite of foreseen consequences. Without this
fellow-feeling, how are we to get enough patience and charity
towards our stumbling, falling companions in the long and change-
ful journey? And there is but one way in which a strong determined soul can learn it--by getting his heart-strings bound round
the weak and erring, so that he must share not only the outward
consequences of their error, but their inward suffering. That is
a long and hard lesson, and Adam had at present only learned
the alphabet of it in his father's sudden death . . . [XIX. 302-3].

Viewed then from this standpoint--the education of Adam's
feelings--it is fortunate that he does bind his heartstrings
round the weak and erring Hetty. Because Hetty does not love
him, however, such a viewpoint is emotionally neither tenable
nor desirable for the reader to hold except in the abstract and
in relation to the whole novel. And so we watch unhappily as Adam dreams of Hetty and the future he hopes to spend with her.

Being a practical man, Adam dreams in practical terms--
of marrying, building more rooms to the old house, and dealing
with the problems his mother would cause--and, being a practical man, he keeps his dream in check:" 'A pretty building I'm
making, without either bricks or timber. I'm up i' the garret
a'ready, and haven't so much as dug the foundation' " (XIX. 302).
It is this sensible but reverent man who puts on his Sunday coat
and calls at the Hall Farm to pay his respects to Hetty. Sent
by the shrewd Mrs. Poyser to the garden on the pretext of
looking after Totty, Adam is soon on his way to see Hetty. It
is

> a true farmhouse garden, with hardy perennial flowers, unpruned
> fruit-trees, and kitchen vegetables growing together in careless,
> half-neglected *abundance*. In that leafy, flowery, bushy time, to
> look for any one in this garden was like playing at "hide-and-
> seek." . . . The garden was so *large*. There was always a *su-
> perfluity* of broad beans--it took nine or ten of Adam's strides
> to get to the end of the uncut grass walk that ran by the side of
> them . . . [XX. 314-15].

In comparison with the first wood scene in which Arthur meets
Hetty, this scene is also richly sensuous, but with a significant
difference: instead of the enervating languor of the secret and
enchanted Grove--an objectification of Arthur's state of being--
there is in the garden an invigorating sense of life and growth.
For it is a vigorous Adam whose state of being is objectified
here. Unlike the narrow, labyrinthine Grove which seemed to
be the haunt of the supernatural nymphs, the Hall Farm garden
is a large, spacious place in which the natural order has been
undisturbed. Flowers, vegetables, and weeds grow together in
happy abundance. Here is God's plenty, a temporary paradise
in which Adam is to have "the first glad moment" of his first
love, "a vision" he is to remember all of his life. Stopping
among the rose trees "all huddled together in bushy masses,
now *flaunting with wide open petals,* --almost all of them of
the streaked pink-and-white kind," Adam chooses *"a compact*
Provence rose that *peeped* out half-smothered by its flaunting
scentless neighbors" and walks on in search of Hetty. He is
not, however, too absorbed in his dream to pluck Totty from
a cherry tree and send her off with a kiss. But Hetty is so
lost in dreams of Arthur that when Adam finds her he mistakes

her startled reaction for love. Thus begins the "sweet delu-
sion" which almost completely blinds Adam to Hetty's true
character. When he presents her with the pure pink budding
rose, which may be taken as a symbol of his ideal concept of
her, she immediately thrusts it in her hair as an ornament.
Adam registers his disapproval:"'Ah,' he said, 'that's like
the ladies in the pictures at the Chase; they've mostly got
flowers or feathers or gold things i' their hair, but somehow
I don't like to see 'em: they allays put me i' mind o' the painted
women outside the shows at Treddles'on fair.'" In contrast he
observes:"'Dinah Morris looks very nice, for all she wears
such a plain cap and gown,'" but he concludes that Hetty has
"'another sort o' face; I'd have you just as you are now without
anything t' interfere with your own looks'" (XX. 322-23). Deceived by Hetty's beauty and her innocent appearance, "the
severe Adam felt no movement of disapprobation" when he
later saw her pouting and quarreling at Totty, but rather "a
sort of amused pity, as if he had seen a kitten setting up its
back, or a little bird with its feathers ruffled" (XXIII. 380).
And when he sees Hetty's locket during the scene at the birthday dance, he invents excuses for her and so goes "to bed com-
forted, having woven for himself an ingenious web of probabil-
ities--the surest *screen* a wise man can place between himself
and the truth" (XXVI. 417). Adam's highly idealized concept of
Hetty is to figure significantly in the crisis he later faces.

But although Adam dreams of his future with Hetty, his daydreams do not, like Hetty's, cut him off in a world apart from
the community. Concerned about his friend Bartle Massey,
who has not been in church as usual on Sunday, Adam stops to
visit Bartle on his way home from the Hall Farm. Entering
the schoolmaster's home while class is in progress, ". . .
even in his present self-absorbed mood, Adam felt a momentary stirring of the old *fellow-feeling,* as he looked at the
rough men painfully holding pen or pencil with their cramped
hands . . ." (XXI. 336). Adam, like these men, has been in-
structed in figuring by Bartle Massey, but Bartle's instruction of Adam is soon to extend far beyond the province of figures. Even now in a conversation with Adam, Bartle defines
Adam's primary weakness:"'. . . you're over-hasty and
proud, and apt to set your teeth against folks that don't square

to your notions' " (XXI. 354). But he also recognizes that for all of Adam's strength, Adam is like everyone else in needing someone to depend on. Thus, as he watches Adam leave, Bartle remarks to himself: "'. . . you wouldn't have been what you are if you hadn't had a bit of old lame Bartle inside you. The strongest calf must have something to suck at' " (p. 356). The importance of this relationship in terms of Adam's vision will be dealt with subsequently.

Although the illusion Adam has about Hetty is not to be easily dispelled, his dreams are soon to be shattered, and his reverent, idealizing nature is to receive an irreparable shock. Part of Adam's pleasure at being chosen as keeper of the woods stems from the high regard he holds for Arthur. Commenting on this attitude, George Eliot says: "A nature like Adam's, with a great need of love and reverence in it, depends for so much of its happiness on what it can believe and feel about others! And he had no ideal world of dead heroes . . ." (XXVII. 9). Thus it is that on that critical evening as Adam enters the gate leading to the Grove he is thinking affectionately of Arthur's good qualities. As he strides along (the verbs used to describe his movement are in contrast to those cited earlier in relation to Arthur: Adam *strides* or *stalks* or *strikes across)*, we see the Grove from a point of view different from that which has previously revealed Arthur's state of mind. The beeches that Arthur thought enervating, Adam finds "grand."

. . . he could not help pausing to look at a curious large beech which he had seen standing before him at a turning in the road, and convince himself that it was not two trees wedded together, but only one. For the rest of his life he remembered that moment when he was calmly examining the beech, as a man remembers his last glimpse of the home where his youth was passed, before the road turned, and he saw it no more. The beech stood at the last turning before the Grove ended in an *archway* of boughs that *let in the eastern light;* and as Adam stepped away from the tree to continue his walk, his eyes fell on two figures about twenty yards before him [XXVII. 9-10].

Adam is "transfixed, " his eyes first showing amazement and then fierceness. Suddenly he understands everything--"the locket, and everything else that had been doubtful to him: *a terrible scorching light showed him* the hidden letters that changed the meaning of the past. " In this stark moment of revelation Adam is torn by passion but does not submit to it. "He stood as if petrified by an unseen force, but the force was his own strong will. " But later, "possessed by rage" and *"blind* with passion, " he provokes Arthur into fighting him. As he waits "in the dim light" for Arthur to rise from his blow, he recognizes "the vanity of his own rage. " Fearing that he has killed Arthur, faced with an "image of death, " Adam is horrified at the possibility that he has again committed the too harsh and too hasty irrevocable act. He confesses to the partially revived Arthur:" '. . . perhaps I judged you too harsh--I'm apt to be harsh; and you may have acted out o' thoughtlessness more than I should ha' believed was possible for a man with a heart and a conscience' " (XXVIII. 24). But when Arthur suggests that Adam is "casting imputations" upon Hetty's character, Adam replies,

> "Nay, sir, things don't lie level between Hetty and you. You're acting *with your eyes open,* whatever you may do; but how do you know what's been in her mind? She's all but a child--as any man with a conscience in him ought to feel bound to take care on. . . . But you seem to make light o' what *she* may feel--you don't think o' that" [p. 27, last italics author's].

Thus, on the basis of reason, Adam passes a second moral judgment on Arthur, holding him completely responsible for the relationship. Ironically, he fails to take account of Arthur's feelings at the same time that he accuses Arthur of not thinking about Hetty's feelings. While he judges Arthur from the absolute standard of "any man with a conscience, " he looks at Hetty from a relative standard and finds her not culpable. " 'I'm not blaming you,' " he tells Hetty when he delivers Arthur's letter, "'for I know it 'ud begin by little and little, till at last you'd not be able to throw it off. It's him I blame . . .' " (XXX. 46). And the author observes that as he walks home his thoughts are engaged "in devising pitying excuses for her folly; in referring all her weakness to the sweet lovingness of her nature; in blaming Arthur, with less and less inclination to admit that *his* conduct might be extenuated too!" (pp. 49-50, author's italics).

Adam has certainly not progressed to the point at which his vision of what constitutes justice is clear, but he has perhaps for the first time in his life made allowance for an action on

the basis of feeling. And furthermore he has himself been in
a position in which it was impossible for him to control his
passion by the exertion of his will. What he has yet to learn
is to recognize the weakness in men and accept it rather than
to evade it and substitute an illusion which will correspond
with his idealized concept of man. Dinah's letter to Seth which
Adam reads at this point in the narrative may be relevant here.
Explaining how the "inward light" works in her, Dinah says:

> " I sit on my chair in the *dark* room and *close my eyes*, and it is
> as if I was *out of the body* and could feel no want for evermore.
> For then, the very hardship, and the sorrow, and the *blindness*,
> and the sin I have *beheld* and been ready to weep over, --yea, all
> the anguish of the children of men, which sometimes wraps me
> round like sudden *darkness*--I can bear with a willing pain, as if
> I was sharing the Redeemer's cross. For I feel it, I feel it--in-
> finite love is suffering too--yea, *in the fulness of knowledge* it
> suffers, it yearns, it mourns; and that is a *blind self-seeking*
> which wants to be freed from the sorrow wherewith the whole
> creation groaneth and travaileth. . . . Sorrow is then a part of
> love, and love does not seek to throw it off " [XXX. 55].

Coming as it does at this stage in his crisis, the letter apparently functions both as a comment on Adam's suffering and as
a means of instructing him in the art of vision. If we may assume such a function, then the letter would seem to be implying that although in his tenderness Adam would weep over the
"hardship and sorrow" of others, he is still unable "in the
fulness of knowledge" to accept the "blindness" and the "sin"
of others. To fail to accept the sorrow is to indulge in "blind
self-seeking"--is in effect to be blind. In time Adam is to
learn to accept the sin of others and the sorrow it causes him.
And it is through this acceptance that he makes his greatest
step toward clear vision. For the time being, however, all
he can do is to make a temporary adjustment.

That adjustment made, he once more feels secure in the
illusion that Hetty loves him. And, ironically, it is even with
"a consciousness of well-being" that Adam begins his "quest"
for Hetty, who has been too long absent from the Hall Farm.
Setting off on foot before sunrise, he is accompanied part of
the way by Seth. "'I wish thee wast going all the way wi' me,'"
he tells Seth, "'and as happy as I am'" (XXXVIII. 147). But not
even a brother could go all of the way with Adam on this jour-

ney from hope to despair. Arriving at Snowfield, Adam discovers that Hetty has disappeared. But "he couldn't bear to blame her: she never meant to cause him this dreadful pain. The blame lay with that man who had selfishly played with her heart--had perhaps even deliberately lured her away" (p. 155). This belief in Hetty's goodness is the one illusion that Adam clings to in the face of the hard reality of his dislocated world.

His work has always been for Adam the foundation of his world, a way of thinking, a whole way of life. As he had said to himself after his father's death:

> "There's nothing but what's bearable as long as a man can work
> . . . the natur o' things doesn't change, though it seems as if
> one's own life was nothing but change. The square o' four is
> sixteen, and you must lengthen your lever in proportion to your
> weight, is as true when a man's miserable as when he's happy;
> and the best o' working is, it gives you a grip o' *things outside
> your own lot"* [XI.164].

But after Adam had seen Arthur and Hetty together he had come to a new realization:"'. . . it 'ud ha' gone near to spoil my work for me, if I'd seen her brought to sorrow and shame . . .'" (XXX. 51). And now, back from his unsuccessful and lonely journey, he sees his world from a different perspective. Sitting in his workshop, he

> stared dully at the wood and the signs of work around him, wondering if he should ever come to feel pleasure in them again.
> . . . Hitherto, since Sunday afternoon, Adam had been constantly
> among strange people and in strange places, having no associations with the details of his daily life; and now that *by the light
> of this new morning* he was come back to his home, and surrounded by the *familiar objects* that seemed for ever *robbed of
> their charm,* the *reality*--the *hard, inevitable reality*--of his
> troubles pressed upon him with a new weight" [XXXVIII. 158].

It is no accident that it is "by the light of this new morning" that he has come to face this reality, for it is a common pattern in George Eliot's novels that such partial recognitions are in some way connected with light, and most often with the early morning light. But this particular kind of scene (another example is Hetty's awaking in the dawn after having read Arthur's letter) is often no more than a recognition that things can never again be as they have been. Divested of their former context of meaning, the commonplace things become oppressive and there is as yet no vision of a new context. For Adam now, nothing remains except duty; but seeing that he is no longer capable of traveling on alone, he does what both Arthur and Hetty have failed to do: he shares the burden with Mr. Irwine. "'It's the right thing,'" he concludes. "'I can't stand alone in this way any longer'" (XXXVIII. 293).

In such a state of acknowledged dependence this strong-willed man approaches the crisis of his life. He is so blinded by grief and passionate anger when Mr. Irwine tells him what has happened to Hetty that he is capable of only one positive action: the acceptance of his two friends, Mr. Irwine and Bartle Massey, whose vision has not been so blurred. And it is through them that he is to arrive at a point where he is capable of clearer vision than he has ever before had. Aside from superficial plot considerations, the real crisis of the book is not Hetty's confession in prison or the last-minute rescue by Arthur. It is, rather, Adam's initiation into a new state of being. The vision imagery, such a subtle part of the texture, here reaches its greatest complexity as it becomes symbolic and merges with a traditional religious symbolism to produce the symbolic moment of the book.

It is a symbolism so firmly grounded in the literal, concrete level of meaning that only a careful examination will reveal the artistry with which it was conceived and executed. Many of the details are in themselves almost too slight to have much symbolic import, but they contribute to the cumulative effect and are largely responsible for the ease with which one level of meaning fades into the other. It is, for example, only natural that one of the physical manifestations of the severe shock Adam suffers should be a vacant stare. But something more than mere description creeps in. He tries unsuccessfully to "fix his eyes steadily" on the letter which informed Mr. Irwine about Hetty, but he can see only an image of the suffering Hetty. He thinks of her "so weak and young":

> The *image* called up by these last words gave a new direction to poor Adam's maddened feelings. He was silent, *looking* at the corner of the room as if he *saw* something there. Then he burst out again, in a tone of appealing anguish, --
> 'I *can't* bear it . . . . O God, it's too hard to lay upon me--it's

too hard to think she's wicked" [**XXXIX.**173-74; last italics and
ellipsis author's].

Once he is in Stoniton he shrinks from seeing Hetty, though
he insists on remaining nearby. "'It's no use, sir,' he said
to the Rector--'it's no use for me to go back. I can't go to
work again while she's here; and *I couldn't bear the sight* o'
the things and folks round home. I'll take a bit of a room, here
where *I can see the prison walls,* and perhaps I shall get, in
time, to bear seeing *her'* "(XL. 178; last italics author's). This
is a time in Adam's life when his outward vision of his work
and of "things and folks round home" has been cut off, and the
room he takes appropriately provides no view beyond the prison
walls. It is for him a time of complete external chaos when
the eye must be turned inward upon the soul. Although his grief
thus isolates him now, his "fellow feeling" has enabled him in
the past to establish meaningful personal relationships. The
"bit of old lame Bartle" is still inside him, and even now it
makes him accessible to that lame old schoolmaster who is
to lead him gently back to the community.

As I have previously suggested, Bartle Massey assumes an
extremely important function during the crisis through which
Adam's vision is enlarged. That function is emphasized by
means of both vision and religious imagery. The latter will
be pointed up presently, but at the moment it is necessary to
determine something about the nature of Bartle's own vision.
One significant detail has constantly recurred whenever Bartle
is on the scene--his spectacles. He sometimes carries them,
sometimes shifts them "to the ridge of his nose, not requiring
them for present purposes" (XXI. 336), sometimes glares
through them ominously. That these spectacles are a symbol
of Bartle's desire to have vision--to have keen insight into
the lives of others so that he may feel with them--is clearly
established in the scene between Bartle and Mr. Irwine by the
action which accompanies the following question: "'Is he [Adam]
very much cut up, poor fellow?' Bartle added, *taking out his
spectacles* and putting them on, *as if they would assist his imagination"* (XL. 187). When Bartle indicates his desire to join
Adam in Stoniton, Mr. Irwine is hesitant: "'I'm afraid you
have too little *fellow feeling* in what you consider his weakness

about Hetty.' " Fellow feeling, always central in vision, is,
however, precisely what Bartle does have; he is most capable
of feeling with Adam because he, too, has presumably had an
experience similar to Adam's. "'Trust to me, sir--trust to
me,' " he tells Mr. Irwine. "'I know what you mean. I've been
a fool myself in my time, but that's between you and me. I
shan't thrust myself on him--only *keep my eye on him*, and
see that he gets some good food, and put in a word here and
there.' " Then, "rising, and taking off his spectacles," Bartle
sets out for Stoniton. This frequent shifting of the spectacles
is symbolic of Bartle's constant struggle to adjust to a given
situation so that he may have the best possible vision. [1] Bartle
is like Adam, "a bit fiery and stiff-backed"; but he has learned
what Adam must learn, to control his "keen, impatient tem-
perament." Bartle Massey is lame--the marks of his past
suffering are upon him--but there is nothing to contradict the
speculation that his lameness may well have been profitably
incurred by his struggling movement toward vision. It is
fitting that such a man should be Adam's teacher in more than
"writing and mapping and mensuration."

The crisis of Adam's life is enacted in two short consecutive
chapters, "The Eve of the Trial" and "The Morning of the
Trial." Except for the two opening paragraphs in the second
of these chapters, the whole action is rendered dramatically
in terms of conversation, action, and stage directions. The
first two paragraphs in "The Eve of the Trial" are unmistakably in the style of stage directions, and the first especially
sets the scene:

> An *upper room* in a *dull* Stoniton street, with two beds in it--one
> laid on the floor. It is ten o'clock on Thursday night, and the
> *dark wall opposite the window shuts out the moonlight* that might
> have struggled with the *light* of the one dip *candle* by which Bartle
> Massey is pretending to read, while he is really *looking* over his
> *spectacles* at Adam Bede, seated near the *dark window* [2] [XLI.
> 190].

But more is accomplished here than stage setting. The spectacles, the candle, and the dark prison wall which obstructs
the vision and darkens the window all are here clearly established as symbols; and the "upper room" introduced in such

a symbolic context might be suspected of the significance the
next chapter confirms.

On the eve of the trial comes Adam's fullest realization of
the pity of it:"'. . . that's the deepest curse of all . . . that's
what makes the blackness of it . . . *it can never be undone.*
My poor Hetty . . . she can never be my sweet Hetty again
. . . the prettiest thing God had made--smiling up at me . . .
I thought she loved me . . . and was good--' " (XLI. 193; author's italics and ellipses). Adam's ideal of goodness and
beauty has been shattered and chaos is come again; he has
been struck at the center of his being, his reverent and idealizing nature. His sense of justice is outraged and his whole
belief held in question:"'. . . if there's a just God, he [Ar-
thur] shall feel what it is t' ha' brought a child like her to sin
and misery.' " Blinded by passion and unable to distinguish between revenge and justice, Adam is reminded by Mr. Irwine:
"'It is not for us men to apportion the shares of moral guilt
and retribution . . . if you were to obey your passion--for
it *is* passion, and you deceive yourself in calling it justice--
it might be with you precisely as it has been with Arthur; nay,
worse; your passion might lead you yourself into a horrible
crime' " (p. 194; author's italics). In an effort to prevent such
"an act of *blind* fury," Mr. Irwine recalls to Adam "a vivid
image" of his fight with Arthur. And Adam is left in medita-
tion.

The next day in the "dull upper room" Adam sits alone in
a state which the author describes in some detail:

> Deep, unspeakable suffering may well be called a *baptism,* a
> *regeneration,* the *initiation into a new state.* The yearning memo-
> ries, the bitter regret, the agonized sympathy, the struggling
> appeals to the Invisible Right--all the intense emotions which
> had filled the days and nights of the past week, and were com-
> pressing themselves again like an eager crowd into the hours of
> this single morning, made Adam *look back* on all the previous
> years as if they had been a *dim sleepy existence,* and he had
> only now *awakened to full consciousness.* It seemed to him as
> if he had always before thought it a light thing that men should
> suffer; as if all that he had himself endured and called sorrow
> before was only a moment's stroke that had never left a bruise.
> Doubtless a great anguish may do the work of years, and we may

come out from that *baptism* of fire with a soul full of new *awe* and *pity*.

"O God," Adam groaned, as he leaned on the table, and looked blankly at the face of the watch, "and men have suffered like this before . . . [author's ellipsis] and poor helpless young things have suffered like her . . . " [XLII. 199].

With the explicit statement of the religious imagery here, the symbolic import of the upper room and the candle of the preceding scene begins to suggest itself. Adam's time of mediation in the upper room has brought him to the point of conversion, "the initiation into a new state," the awakening "to full consciousness." The implications in terms of vision are clear: having undergone the "baptism of fire," he now has "a soul full of new awe and pity" and has therefore become so profoundly aware of the eternally tragic condition of man that he is capable of perceiving the universality of his own and Hetty's suffering. Thus he "looks blankly" at the watch before him, for he has suddenly been shifted to a new plane of reality wherein minutes and hours have no meaning because human existence and human suffering are coeval.

Although Adam's "baptism" by suffering has initiated him into a new state, one more ritual remains to confirm his regeneration. When we remember that the first communion was celebrated in an "upper room," the symbolic significance of this scene is clarified by what follows. Bartle Massey, returning from the trial, removes hat and spectacles and sits in front of Adam.

"And now," he said, *rising* again, "I must see to your having a *bit* of the *loaf*, and some of that *wine* Mr. Irwine sent this morning. He'll be angry with me if you don't have it. Come, now," he went on, bringing forward the bottle and the loaf, and pouring some wine into a *cup*, "I must have a *bit* and a *sup* myself. Drink a drop *with me*, my lad--drink with me" [p. 200].

Thus Bartle Massey invites Adam to partake of the communion which is to serve as the rite of confirmation following his baptism. The details are indeed most subtle. That the wine has been provided by Mr. Irwine, who as rector of the parish is Adam's spiritual guide, symbolically suggests that it is sacramental. But significantly it is proffered by Bartle Massey, who, we remember, has observed that Adam has "a bit of old

lame Bartle" inside him and who has himself undergone his
baptism by fire. Nor is this a mere invitation to Adam to eat
and drink, but rather to "drink a drop *with me, my lad--drink
with me.* " The simple repetition of the phrase suggests the
ritualistic, as does the fact that Bartle has risen and remains
standing. This is a communion in the sense that it is a sharing
of the "cup" of sorrow. The word *cup,* one of whose connotations is that which is to be endured and suffered, is commonly
used to refer to the eucharist. In addition to indicating Bartle's
desire to share,. the statement "I must have a bit and a sup
myself" implies his own very human need for sustenance and
suggests that he hopes by example to instruct Adam in the
ritual wherewith sustenance may be obtained.

But Adam is not yet ready to accept *communion.* Eager for
news of Hetty, he pushes the cup away. Bartle, patiently giving
the news, tells how Martin Poyser appeared in the courtroom:
"'Adam, my boy, the blow falls heavily on him as well as you:
you must help poor Martin; you must show courage. *Drink
some wine now,* and show me you mean *to bear it like a man.* '
Bartle had made the right sort of appeal. Adam, with an air
of quiet obedience, *took up the cup,* and drank a little." Bartle
continues, telling how Mr. Irwine "put himself near" Martin
Poyser and stood by him. "'God bless him, and you too, Mr.
Massey,' said Adam, in a low voice, laying his hand on Bartle's arm." Adam continues his questioning: "is there nobody to
stand by her, and seem to care for her, in the court?" Told
that there is no one but the "sharp ferrety-faced" chaplain,
Adam lapses momentarily into bitterness and then arrives at
his decision:

> "There's one man as ought to be there," said Adam bitterly.
> Presently he drew himself up, and *looked fixedly out of the win-
> dow,* apparently turning over some new idea in his mind.
> "Mr. Massey," he said at last, pushing the hair off his fore-
> head, "I'll go back with you. I'll go into court. It's cowardly
> of me to keep away. *I'll stand by her--I'll own her--for all she's
> been deceitful.* They oughtn't to cast her off--her own flesh and
> blood. We hand folks over to God's mercy and show none our-
> selves. I used to be hard sometimes: I'll never be hard again.
> I'll go, Mr. Massey--I'll go with you."

This is the moment toward which the whole book has been

moving: Adam's fully felt acceptance of weak and erring humanity, his own as well as that of others. Only the ritual remains to be completed. Bartle concludes the communion:

> "Take a *bit,* then, and another *sup,* Adam, *for the love of me. See,* I must stop and eat a *morsel.* Now, you take some."
>
> Nerved by an active resolution, Adam *took a morsel of bread,* and *drank some wine.* He was haggard and unshaven, as he had been yesterday, but *he stood upright again,* and looked more like the Adam Bede of former days [p. 204].

The phrase "for the love of me" echoes the tone if not the exact phrasing of the Christian communion. Once more, and in the manner of the ritual, Bartle instructs by example, taking the bread and wine himself and then presenting it to Adam. This time Adam accepts *both* bread and wine. That it is only a "morsel" of bread and a "sup" of wine which this large strong man partakes of establishes the fact that for both of them the action has only symbolic value. Nowhere else in the book does Adam drink wine, and nowhere else are bread and wine placed in the same context. There can be little doubt that George Eliot intended the symbolism of this scene. It should be noted that Bartle Massey is not a symbol of Christ, but that rather in the role of man and friend of man he assumes a priestlike role. The symbols and the ritual are Christian, but the religion is the religion of humanity. It is "for the love of *me*"--that is, *man*--and not for the love of God that Adam takes communion. And it is for the love of man--that is, for the love of Hetty as human being as well as for Hetty as Hetty--that Adam goes to the court to "stand by" Hetty and "own her." Adam is ready to leave the dark, viewless upper room and go back into the world whose harsh reality he is now strengthened to face.[3]

When Adam leaves off thoughts of revenge under the guise of justice and enters the court of justice to take his place by Hetty's side, "the broad sunlight of the great hall" falls upon his face (XLIII. 205). He has yet to undergo "the supreme moment of his suffering" when he knows that Hetty is guilty of the crime; he has still to suffer the agony of waiting the last night in his dark room and of going to Hetty in the prison cell to tell her good-by. But he has learned how to control the hardness in his nature. When he meets Arthur once more in the Grove, ". . . the figure before him touched him with the

signs of suffering. Adam knew what suffering was--he could
not lay a cruel finger on a bruised man" (XLVIII. 255). It is
true that he is soon tempted to anger, but this time he over-
comes the temptation. "'God forbid I should make things worse
for you,' " he tells Arthur. "'I used to wish I could do it, in
my passion;--but that was when I thought you didn't feel enough.
I'll stay, sir: I'll do the best I can. It's all I've got to think of
now--to do my work well, and make the world a bit better place
for them as can enjoy it'" (p. 264). Once more he asserts the
value of his work:"'I shall learn to like it again some time,
maybe; and it's right whether I like it or not'" (p. 253). And
so it is that Adam begins the reordering of his world.

4. *Adam Bede:*

Merging Movements and the Final Steps

THE POSITIVE movement of *Adam Bede*--that is, the movement toward moral vision--has reached the peak of its momentum with Adam's awaking "to full consciousness" and his
"initiation into a new state." The negative movement away
from vision has been broken off at this point by the occurrence
of the catastrophe toward which it has inevitably been directed.
In its stead begins another positive movement, the penitential
pilgrimage of Arthur and Hetty. Before its beginning, however,
there must come to Arthur and Hetty a partial vision of the
consequences of their actions.

To Arthur this knowledge comes ironically on the eve of his
return to assume his long-dreamed-of role as ideal landlord.
It comes actually at the time of his greatest moral blindness.
For he has quite convinced himself that, aside from the indig-
nity which he himself had suffered during the fight with Adam,
only good would come out of his past actions. As landlord now
he would do more for Adam and Hetty than he would have done
had there been no meetings with Hetty in the Grove. In chapter xliv, which narrates Arthur's return, the description of
the countryside is ironically peaceful and idyllic. Light is used
again as a means of objectifying Arthur's state of mind: "And
here was dear old Hayslope at last, sleeping, on the hill, like
a quiet old place as it was, in the *late afternoon sunlight . . .*"
(p. 220). In this deluded state Arthur prepares to read his
mail which is waiting for him when he arrives: "The level rays
of the low *afternoon sun* entered directly at the *window,* and

as Arthur seated himself in his velvet chair with their pleasant warmth upon him, he was conscious of that quiet well-being which perhaps you and I have felt on a sunny afternoon, when, in our brightest youth and health, life has opened a *new vista* for us . . ." (p. 223). But this is a "late afternoon sunlight" and not the early morning light of reality. The "new vista" which is soon opened for Arthur is the knowledge that, as Adam tells him, "there's a sort o' damage . . . that can't be made up for" (XLVIII. 258).

We see Arthur as he reads Mr. Irwine's letter, and then--aside from his dramatic eleventh-hour appearance--we do not see him again until his second meeting with Adam in the woods. It is dramatically right that there is no single scene in which he, like Adam, is shown in the process of achieving greater vision. The cold hard fact of his own wrongdoing is the catalytic agent which bursts shockingly upon him as he reads the letter: "He started up from his chair and stood for a single minute with a sense of *violent convulsion* in his whole frame, as if the life were going out of him with horrible throbs; but the next minute he had rushed out of the room . . ." (XLIV. 224). This is as much as we are--and as much as we need to be--shown of how it is that Arthur arrives at the insight he later verbalizes to Adam:" 'I never meant to injure her. I deceived you afterwards--and that led on to worse. . . . I was all wrong from the very first, and horrible wrong has come of it. God knows, I'd give my life if I could undo it' " (XLVIII. 262). Arthur Donnithorne and Godfrey Cass are very much alike. Both are well-meaning but weak-willed; both drift into a situation which causes them to rationalize their actions; both finally realize that the consequences of their actions are irrevocable, that it is "too late to mend some things, say what they will" (*Silas Marner*. XX. 255).

For Hetty, whose *"vision* of consequences [has been] at no time more than a narrow fantastic calculation of her own probable pleasures and pains," such knowledge as Arthur arrives at is not possible. But she does come to know that she can no longer follow her pattern of concealment, that her guilt must be admitted not only to others but to herself. Only Dinah is capable of breaking through the dark barrier of concealment and isolation in which Hetty has enclosed herself. When she

comes to Hetty in the dark prison cell there follows the most
concentrated use of light-dark imagery which the book contains
(XLV). The turnkey "struck a *light* as they entered the dark
corridor leading to the condemned cell, and then said in his
most civil tone, 'It'll be pretty nigh *dark* in the cell a'ready;
but I can stop with my *light* a bit, if you like'" (p. 228). Dinah,
however, refuses the offer, depending rather on spiritual
light. What little evening light creeps into the cell gradually
becomes less and less, and Hetty is constantly "sinking helpless in a *dark gulf*." Dinah simply sits silently and waits. "She
did not know how long they sat in that way, but it got *darker*
and *darker,* till there was only a *pale patch of light* on the opposite wall: all the rest was *darkness*. But she felt the Divine
presence more and more . . ." (p. 230). Dinah's power to
compel belief in an invisible presence has already been demonstrated in the preaching scene. Now when she tells Hetty
that "there is some one else in this cell besides me, some
one close to you," Hetty's superstitious fear is aroused.

> Hetty said, in a frightened whisper, "Who?"
> "Some one who has been with you through all your hours of sin
> and trouble--who has known every thought you have had--has
> seen where you went, where you lay down and rose up again, and
> all the deeds you have tried to *hide* in *darkness*. . . . It makes
> no difference--whether we live or die, we are in the *presence*
> of God" [pp. 231-32].

But Hetty, relieved that there is no actual third presence in
the cell, has already stopped listening. Terror-stricken at
the thought of death, she is unable to pray. But she is capable
of one positive action, a partial recognition of her own emotional inadequacy:"'Dinah . . . help me . . . I *can't feel anything* like you . . . my heart is hard'" (author's ellipses).
Dinah's prayer which follows has the same emphasis on the
visual that has been noted in her prayer on the Green. The
climax of the prayer will be sufficient to indicate the nature
of the imagery:

> Yea, Lord, I *see* thee, coming through the *darkness*, coming,
> like the *morning*, with healing on thy wings. The marks of thy
> agony are upon thee--I *see*, I *see* thou art able and willing to
> save--thou wilt not let her perish for ever.
> Come, mighty Saviour! let the dead hear thy voice; *let the*

eyes of the blind be opened: let her *see* that God encompasses
her . . . [p. 235].

At this point Hetty's whole pattern of concealment, which began
with the hiding of the mirror, candle, and earrings and eventually extended to the hiding of the baby under grass and chips,
suddenly breaks down. "'I won't hide it any more,'" she sobs
to Dinah. But her confession is motivated largely by her feeling that she is being watched and by her fear of the image
which she sees always before her *("'I saw nothing but that
place* in the woods where I'd buried the baby'"). She does,
however, feel some genuine sorrow and regret, for, as Dinah
tells Adam the next day, "'Although her poor soul is very *dark,*
and *discerns* little beyond the things of the flesh, she is no
longer hard; she is contrite . . .'" (XLVI. 242-43).

In this state of imperfect contrition, which is as near to vision as Hetty can now come, she begins her long wandering
exile after the "hard-won release from death." She who has
sought always the narrow path, the thick hedgerow, and the
concealed wood is now sent out in the wide and alien world.
Her movement has been constantly away from the fellow feeling of the community, toward isolation. In a lesser way Arthur's actions have also isolated him from his friends and
from the community in which his role as ideal landlord is no
longer possible. Both he and Hetty have sinned against the
community as well as against themselves. Thus their isolated
wandering is a fitting penance they must do before they are
spiritually ready to be returned to the community. From the
first they have both been wanderers in the sense that they have
allowed themselves to drift into a wrong course of action; it
is therefore fitting that they now become wanderers who, like
the Ancient Mariner, must do penance for their sin.

That George Eliot may have intended some suggestion of the
Ancient Mariner here is quite possible. In chapter v, Mrs.
Irwine, like Nello the barber in *Romola,* insists that she can
accurately judge men by their appearance:

"If they make me shudder at the first glance, I say, take them
away. An ugly, piggish, or fishy *eye,* now, makes me feel quite
ill; it's like a bad smell."

"Talking of eyes," said Captain Donnithorne, "that reminds
me that I've got a book I meant to bring you, godmamma. . . .

I know you are fond of queer, wizard-like stories. It's a volume
of poems, 'Lyrical Ballads'; most of them seem to be twaddling
stuff; but the first is in a different style-- 'The Ancient Mariner'
is the title. I can hardly make head or tail of it as a story, but
it's a *strange, striking thing"* [p. 90].

That the story of the Ancient Mariner remains incomprehen-
sible to Arthur is perhaps intended to suggest the immaturity
of his moral perception, but it is significant that the story
fascinates him. In its emphasis on appearance and eyes, this
passage does of course call attention to the main issue of the
book; but it is very possibly intended to be suggestive in relation to Arthur and Hetty. At any rate the comparison is
prompted by other elements in the book. Hetty, it has been
pointed out earlier, "hates the leveret that runs across her
path . . . hates everything that is not what she longs for."
It is because of her lack of feeling and hardness that she, like
the Ancient Mariner, is unable to pray until Dinah has inter-
ceded for her. It is only when she is able to feel something
that she, again like the Ancient Mariner, is granted a reprieve.
The arbitrary nature of this eleventh-hour rescue has brought
much criticism upon the author, but it seems most likely that
she intended it to be interpreted as an act of grace. Hetty's
isolation during her journey in despair is perhaps surpassed
only by the Mariner's isolation. (Even Hester Prynne, an
admirable study of isolation, has little Pearl, and her actions gradually secure a place for her in the community.) Unlike the Mariner, however, Hetty does not see her "own coun-
tree" again. But that the "death of the poor wanderer" occurs
when she is on her way back to Hayslope (see Epilogue) indicates that she has finally expiated her sin. Arthur, who has
consistently manifested more fellow feeling than Hetty has been
capable of, comes back to Hayslope shattered with fever. But
"'the doctors say he'll soon be set right in his own country
air.'" It is a final irony that Arthur, whose dream it was to be
a noble landlord beloved by his community because he took good
care of it, finally returns to be taken care of by the community.

⁂⁂⁂⁂⁂⁂⁂⁂⁂⁂⁂⁂⁂

As the negative movement subsides and the second regenera-

tive movement begins, the positive and predominant movement
slowly but forcefully continues through Adam and Dinah. Both
of these characters have already learned the value of loving,
but they have yet fully to comprehend the value of being loved.
For Dinah especially this is no easy lesson.

Dinah's progression toward a more comprehensive vision
is the most subtle element in the book. That there definitely
is such a progression will be demonstrated; and yet, the constantly reiterated emphasis on Dinah's saintliness (an example
is the already quoted description of her on the Green) often
causes the reader to question whether the author does not intend to imply that Dinah has reached a state of near-perfection
which could not be improved in this life. The reader's disturb-
ance about the character of Dinah seems to me to arise not so
much from the fact that she is so nearly a saint as from the
fact that George Eliot has not yet completely made up her mind
about the desirability of sainthood. By the time of *Middlemarch*
she will have learned what she seems to be in the process of
learning in *Adam Bede*: that self-renunciation is not always
the better part of morality.

Dinah's attitude at the beginning of the book is indicated by
her reason for refusing Seth Bede's proposal of marriage:
"'God has called me to minister to others, not to have any
joys or sorrows of my own . . .'" (III. 46). In order that she
may bring spiritual light to those who are in darkness, Dinah
seems always to move toward the darkness where she may most
readily find such people. Thus she observes a "strange dead-
ness to the Word" in places where people live quietly "among
the green pastures and the still waters, tilling the ground and
tending the cattle," but she finds a rich "harvest of souls up
those *high-walled* streets, where you seem to walk as in a
prison-yard . . . maybe it is because the promise is sweeter
when this life is so *dark* and weary . . ." (VIII. 130). Elsewhere the author emphasizes Dinah's propensity for the dark,
barren, and cramped, and one scene (chapter xi) especially
points up the contrast between her and the Bede brothers'
"way o' looking at things." Practical Adam thinks in terms of
going to work, but he wants space enough to enable him to have
a view sufficiently wide to remind him of his fellow man:
"'. . . I like to go to work by a road that'll take me up a bit of

a hill, and *see the fields for miles round me*, and a bridge,
or a town, or a bit of a steeple here and there. It makes you
feel the world's a *big place*, and there's *other men* working
in it with their heads and hands besides yourself.'" Impractical
Seth wants the present darkness in order that he may have
beautiful dreams of a faraway light. He prefers the hills "'when
the clouds are over your head, and you see the *sun shining
ever so far off*, over the Loamford way, as I've often done o'
late, on the stormy days: it seems to me as if that was heaven
where there's always joy and *sunshine*, though this life's *dark*
and *cloudy.*'" His attitude is similar to Dinah's but with one
significant difference: in looking toward the sunshine of the
rich, fertile Loamford country, Seth turns his back on what
is dark and barren; but Dinah seeks it out:

> "O, I love the Stonyshire side," said Dinah: "I shouldn't like
> to set my face towards the countries where they're rich in corn
> and cattle, and the ground so level and easy to tread; and to turn
> my back on the hills where the poor people have to live such a
> hard life, and the men spend their days *in the mines away from
> the sunlight*. It's very blessed on a *bleak* cold day, when the sky
> is hanging *dark* over the hill, to feel the love of God in one's
> soul, and carry it to the *lonely, bare, stone* houses where there's
> nothing else to give comfort."
> "Eh!" said Lisbeth, "that's very well for ye to talk, as looks
> welly like the snowdrop-flowers as ha' lived for days an' days
> when I'n gethered 'em, wi' nothin' but a drop o' water an' *a peep
> o' daylight;* but the hungry foulks had better leave th' hungry coun-
> try. It makes less mouths for the scant cake" [pp. 170-71].

Lisbeth, however, is not the only one who criticizes Dinah's
way of life. Mrs. Poyser's amazing verbal facility is often
utilized on the subject of her favorite niece. Using the Scrip-
ture to her own advantage, she tells Dinah: "'. . . if you loved
your neighbor no better nor you do yourself, Dinah, it's little
enough you'd do for him'" (XVIII. 274). When Dinah finds much
to her surprise that Mr. Irwine's "countenance is as pleasant
as the *morning sunshine,*" Mrs. Poyser replies:

> 'It's summat-like to see such a man as that i' the desk of a
> Sunday! As I say to Poyser, it's like looking at a full crop o'
> wheat, or a pasture with a fine dairy o' cows in it; it makes you
> think the world's comfortable-like. But as for such creatures

as you Methodisses run after, I'd as soon go to look at a lot o'
bare-ribbed runts on a common. Fine folks they are to tell you
what's right, as look as if they'd never tasted nothing better than
bacon-sword and sour-cake i' their lives" [VIII. 133].

And elsewhere Mrs. Poyser tells Dinah to sit down "'an' look
as if you knowed what it was to make yourself a bit comfortable
i' the world'" (XIV. 208).

That Mr. Irwine has a face like "morning sunshine" is significant in contrast with Dinah, who is repeatedly associated
with moonlight. In contrast also is Mrs. Poyser who is "as
true as the *daylight*" (LIII. 344). On one occasion when Adam
is dreaming of Hetty, Dinah appears. "It was like dreaming
of the *sunshine,* and awaking in the *moonlight*" (XI. 165). In
one moonlight scene Dinah is described as being "almost like
a lovely corpse into which the soul has returned charged with
sublimer secrets and a sublimer love" (XV. 227). This non-
lifelike quality in Dinah is emphasized constantly--in Lisbeth's
comparison of Dinah to the "snowdrop-flowers," in Dinah's
paleness, and in various references to her ghostliness. Dinah
is once said to move "as if she had been a ghost" (XV. 230), and
Hetty's appearance in Dinah's cap makes Mrs. Poyser think
she is seeing a ghost (XX. 329). Thus Dinah's spiritual and
nonworldly quality is emphasized, the moon obviously sym-
bolizing both chastity and spiritual light in darkness. But at
the same time her denial of life is evidenced. Her vision is
not comprehensive enough to include the positive element of
joy. As she sees it, life is dark and barren; and the rich abundance, the God's plenty of Hall Farm, is to Dinah not a mani-
festation of providential generosity but a temptation to the
pleasures of the flesh. She chooses *Snow*field in *Stony*shire
rather than *Hay*slope in *Loam*shire. In her own life she denies
not only the feeling of joy but that of love between man and
woman. When Mr. Irwine questions her about her feelings as
a woman, she says that she has "no room for such feelings"
(VIII. 129). But Adam knows that she is not incapable of love:
"'She's made out o' stuff with a finer grain than most o' the
women; I *can see* that *clear enough*. But if she's better than
they are in other things, I canna think she'll fall short of 'em
in loving'" (XI. 174). Through his suffering Adam learns that
"'it isn't notions sets people doing the right thing--it's feel-

ings'" (XVII. 260). Through Adam, Dinah is to learn the inadequacy of a vision which partially negates feeling. Together,
in Book VI, they continue and conclude the positive movement
of *Adam Bede*.

The Adam we see two years after his great sorrow has
learned to delight in his work almost as before, but he is not
the same man and he has not outlived his sorrow. The author's
comment relevant to Adam's state indicates something more
about the nature of vision:

> It would be a poor result of all our anguish and our wrestling, if
> we won nothing but our old selves at the end of it--if we could
> return to the same *blind* loves, the same self-confident blame,
> the same light thoughts of human suffering, the same frivolous
> gossip over blighted human lives, the same feeble sense of that
> Unknown towards which we have sent forth irrepressible cries
> in our loneliness. Let us rather be thankful that our sorrow lives
> in us as an indestructible force, only changing its form, as forces
> do, and passing from pain into *sympathy--the one poor word which
> includes all our best insight* and our best love. Not that this trans-
> formation of pain into sympathy had completely taken place in
> Adam yet . . . [L. 287-88].

The old Adam had what the new Adam lacks: "a margin of
dreams . . . beyond this daylight reality." Love seems to him
"a limb lopped off," for he "did not know that the power of loving was all the while gaining new force within him . . ."
(p. 289). It is quite natural that Dinah should become his best
friend, "for in the *darkest* moments of memory the thought of
her always came as the first *ray* of returning comfort: the
early days of *gloom* at the Hall Farm had been gradually *turned
into soft moonlight by her presence. . . .*"

But that "moonlight" is very soon to turn into "sunshine," for
Dinah too has changed. There are indications, for example,
that she is growing more like Mrs. Poyser. Her eyes, which
are the same color as her Aunt Poyser's eyes, have lost some
of that "seraphic gentleness of expression" which has been
previously contrasted with the "keenness" of Mrs. Poyser's
eyes. And her cheeks which have almost always been pale are
now frequently blushing. "She looked as if she were only sister
to Dinah" (p. 282). This change in Dinah has been very carefully prepared for, however. As early as chapter xi, when she
first met Adam, "Dinah, for the first time in her life, felt a

painful self-consciousness; there was something in the dark
penetrating glance of this strong man so different from the
mildness and timidity of his brother Seth. A faint blush came,
which deepened as she wondered at it" (pp. 165-66). Since that
time Dinah has been thrown in intimate contact with Adam and
has shared his sorrow, the most binding of all ties. That she
should love him now is quite as natural as that she should feel
it necessary to struggle against her love. When Mrs. Poyser
prevails upon Dinah's sense of duty in order to get her to stay
in Hayslope ("An' who is it, I should like to know, as you're
bound t' help and comfort i' the world more nor your own flesh
and blood") Dinah replies: "your wish for me to stay is not
a call of duty which I refuse to hearken to because it is against
my own desires; it is a temptation that I must resist, lest the
love of the creature should become like a *mist* in my soul
shutting out the heavenly light" (XLIX. 271).

For Adam, however, the "love of the creature" is not a
"mist" shutting out "heavenly light, " but rather it is light it-
self--and sunlight rather than moonlight. When Lisbeth finally
makes Adam aware of the fact that he and Dinah love each
other, he leaves the house and goes into the fields. His realization of that love is rendered solely through the language,
rhythm, and imagery of the scene which immediately follows
the discovery:

> The *sunshine* was on them: that *early autumn sunshine* which
> we should know was not summer's, even if there were not the
> touches of yellow on the lime and chestnut: the *Sunday sunshine*,
> too, which has more than autumnal calmness for the working
> man: the *morning sunshine*, which still leaves the dew-crystals
> on the fine gossamer webs in the shadow of the bushy hedge-
> rows.

> Adam needed the calm influence. . . . Strange, that till that
> moment the possibility of their ever being lovers had never
> crossed his mind, and yet now, all his longing suddenly went
> out toward that possibility; he had no more doubt or hesitation
> as to his own wishes *than the bird that flies towards the open-
> ing through which the daylight gleams and the breath of heaven
> enters.*

> The *autumnal Sunday sunshine* soothed him; but not by pre-
> paring him with resignation to the disappointment if his Mother--
> if he himself--proved to be mistaken about Dinah: it soothed
> him by gentle encouragement of his hopes. *Her love was so like*

that calm sunshine that they seemed to make one presence to
him, and he believed in them both alike. And Dinah was so bound
up with the sad memories of his first passion, that he was not
forsaking them, but rather giving them a new sacredness by loving her. Nay, his love for her had grown out of that past: it was
the *noon of that morning* [LI. 308-9].

It is through the definition and localizing of the sunshine that
the love is defined. At first it is only an abstraction, "the sunshine." But soon it is progressively particularized in terms of
season, day of the week, and time of the day. The autumnal
ripeness, Sunday calmness, and morning beauty of this sunshine are all qualities in Adam's new love. The bird-window
image connects the love with "daylight" and "breath of heaven,"
and the next phrase, "autumnal Sunday sunshine," merges
and echoes the qualities of the sunshine. The now well-defined
sunshine becomes one with Dinah's love and the final step in
the localization and definition of both the sunshine and the love
is contained in the last phrase, "the noon of that morning."
The dawn of that morning, the dreary early morning reality,
had left Adam's life destitute of meaning. By this noontime,
the commonplace things have, like the sunshine, become rein-
vested with meaning. Adam's eyes are once again "eager" and
"intense," looking "as if they saw something very vividly; but
it was not the brook or the willows, not the fields or the sky.
Again and again his *vision* was interrupted by wonder at the
strength of his own feeling . . ." (LI. 310).

Dinah, however, fears the feeling, fears that in loving Adam
she would be rejecting the inner light:"'I should be turning my
back on the *light* that has shone upon me, and *darkness* and
doubt would take hold of me'" (LII. 318). But at this crucial
point Adam brings his hard-earned knowledge to bear:"'I don't
believe your loving me could shut up your heart,' " he tells
Dinah:"'it's only *adding to what you've been before,* not taking
away from it; for it seems to me it's the same with love and
happiness as with sorrow--the more we know of it the better
we can feel what other people's lives are or might be, and so
we shall only be more tender to 'em, and wishful to help 'em.
The more knowledge a man has, the better he'll do's work;
and *feeling's a sort o' knowledge'* "(p. 320). But Dinah remains
silent, her eyes "fixed in contemplation of something visible
only to herself." Finally she answers:"'I must wait for clearer

guidance: I must go from you, and we must submit ourselves
entirely to the Divine Will.' " Adam pleads only briefly, and
then replies:" 'Let us go out into the sunshine, Dinah, and
walk together. I'll speak no word to disturb you.' They went
out and walked towards the fields. . . ." And so, having thus
submitted their own wills to that of God's, they go for an idle
walk in the sunlight. In the sense that it is an aimless action
occasioned by the submission of will, this walk bears some
resemblance to those actions which have been called drifting.
The difference, however, is obvious. Significantly, this action
is a kind of waiting upon God's will which is different even from
that which Dinah has described in several other contexts. In
the letter to Seth (chapter xxx) she speaks of the "blessed time"
when the "outward light" fades. "Then the inward light shines
the brighter, and we have a deeper sense of resting on the Divine strength. I sit on my chair in the *dark* room and *close
my eyes,* and it is as if I was *out of the body* . . ." (p. 55).
Thus she describes a kind of ritualistic invocation which is in
contrast with Adam's simple "let us go out into the sunshine,
Dinah, and walk together." Instead of the dark and enclosed
place is the light, spaciousness of the sunny fields. And instead of the asceticism, the being "out of the body," there is
the rich sensuousness suggested by the following description:
". . . they talked . . . lingering in the *sunshine* to look at the
great *flock* of *geese* grazing, at the new corn-ricks, and at the
surprising *abundance of fruit* on the old pear tree . . ." (LII.
325). The images of sunlight, fertility, and space have been
used here in contrast to those of darkness, sterility, and narrowness with which--in conjunction with the Christian symbol-
ism--Dinah has been primarily associated.

   When Martin Poyser sees Dinah and Adam walking together
across the sunny fields, it suddenly occurs to him that, as he
puts it, " 'it ud' ha' been a pretty thing . . . for 'em t' marry' "
(p. 323)--that is, it would have restored order. There would
seem to be a certain fitness about such a marriage, especially
from Martin Poyser's viewpoint. That one of Poyser's nieces
should in some measure compensate Adam for what the other
niece had cost him is after all a kind of poetic justice. But
it is on just such grounds that George Eliot is criticized for
having brought the marriage about: it smacks of the too tidy,

too "Victorian" ending.[1] Such criticism, it seems to me, fails
to take account of all the facts and misses the central purpose
of *Adam Bede:* to show the process by which the art of vision
is learned. In George Eliot's scheme of things true vision is
moral vision, the deeply felt perception of what it is to be a
human being. It is a perception so deeply felt that it must profoundly influence what one is in relation to all human beings.
And within the art frame of *Adam Bede* the marriage of Adam
and Dinah is the final necessary step in the process of realizing
their potentiality. To quote Adam again, loving is "adding to
what you've been before. . . ." The meaning of the marriage
in terms of Adam's vision is indicated by the author in a passage preceding the meeting on the hill. Adam can feel no "nar-
row-sighted joy" because past wrongs have resulted in good
fortune for him, but, as the author observes,

> it is not ignoble to feel that the fuller life which a sad experience
> has brought us is worth our own personal share of pain; surely it
> is not possible to feel otherwise, any more than it would be pos-
> sible for a man with *cataract* to regret the painful process by
> which his *dim blurred sight* of men as trees walking had been ex-
> changed for clear outline and effulgent day. The *growth of higher
> feeling* within us is like the *growth of faculty,* bringing with it a
> sense of added strength: we can no more wish to return to a nar-
> rower sympathy, than a painter or a musician can wish to return
> to his cruder manner. . . .
>
> Something like *this sense of enlarged being* was in Adam's
> mind this Sunday morning, as he rode along in vivid recollec-
> tion of the past. His feeling towards Dinah, the hope of passing
> his life with her, had been the distant unseen point towards which
> that hard journey from Snowfield eighteen months ago had been
> leading him. Tender and deep as his love for Hetty had been, --
> so deep that the roots of it would never be torn away, --his love
> for Dinah was better and more precious to him; for it was the
> *outgrowth of that fuller life* which had come to him from his ac-
> quaintance with deep sorrow. "It's like as if it was *a new strength*
> to me," he said to himself, "to love her, and know as she loves
> me. *I shall look t' her to help me to see things right.* For she's
> better than I am--there's less o' self in her, and pride" [LIV.
> 348-49].

The growth of higher feeling, here significantly compared to
the growth of sight, gives Adam a "sense of enlarged being"
toward which his whole life has been moving. He has found

a "new strength"; for in this dogmatic man of excessive pride
and stubborn will it is indeed a sign of strength to say: "'I
shall look t' her to help me to see things right.' " "'I've always
been thinking I knew better than them as belonged to me,' "
he continues, "'and that's a poor sort o' life, when you can't
look to them nearest to you t' help you with a bit better thought
than what you've got inside you a'ready.' " Although this new
strength has been growing in Adam since the death of his father, it could hardly have reached such proportion without the
new love. For Adam, the marriage is far more than a device
which will allow him to live happily ever after.

And for Dinah, too, it is a growth and a becoming. In her
own terms it means what she tells Adam when they meet in the
soft afternoon light "almost at the top of the hill": "'I have a
fulness of strength to bear and do our heavenly Father's Will,
that I had lost before' " (p. 352). Her acceptance of Adam as he
stands waiting for her "in the soft October sunshine" under
"the great bracing sky" is an acceptance of all that these light
and space images have come to mean: abundant life and a wider
view of *this* world than her own joyless perspective has af-
forded. It is an acceptance, too, of Mrs. Poyser's belief that
good deeds should begin on and around one's own hearth, and
it is surely an acceptance of Adam's belief that "feeling is a
sort o' knowledge." But it is the significant weakness of the
book that readers are not made to feel unquestionably that
Dinah has ever been lacking in that strength and that her union
with Adam actually adds to her stature. If this had been as un-
falteringly true of Dinah as it is of Adam, the marriage would
never have become the target of criticism.

The wedding of Adam and Dinah, following the harvest sup-
per and in itself a "harvest from that painful seed-time," is
the ceremonial culmination of the autumn harvest of Book VI.
There have been several ceremonies in the book: the funeral,
the games, the birthday dance and feast. And together with
the many descriptive passages--descriptions of the weather
and of the changing seasons and constant references to such
seasonal activities as the plowing, planting, and haying--they
create the great life-rhythm which is substructural. *Adam
Bede,* like the Hall Farm garden, contains God's plenty; and
like that of the garden, its abundance is perhaps sometimes

superfluous. But although it is less organically constructed
than *Silas Marner* or *Middlemarch, Adam Bede* is nevertheless
far more artful in the creation of its order than a first reading
would indicate. Book I begins in the June sunshine, and Book II
"pauses a little" in June; Book III begins in July, and Book IV,
in August, is followed by that dark February of Book V. "The
first autumnal afternoon sunshine of 1801" in the opening of
Book VI is not different from the August sunshine of two years
and two books earlier. But the harvest which follows the introduction of Book IV is a bitter one, the result of the movement
away from vision. The movement toward vision, however, produces the rich harvest of Book VI. And the final affirmation of
the structural order created by the two movements and of the
substructural order created by the life-rhythm is contained in
the June Epilogue.

For the Epilogue is not a conclusion of the life struggle
which *Adam Bede* has examined but rather the conclusion of
one period--metaphorically speaking, one "day"--in the lives
of the characters. The full circle has been drawn, and once
more we are at the beginning. The workshop is closed "and
the *mellow evening light* is falling on the pleasant home with
the buff walls and the soft grey thatch, very much as it did
when we saw Adam bringing in the keys on that June evening
nine years ago." Dinah, "a bit plumper" and "more matronly,"
watches with the children as Adam comes home. Dinah, knowing that the experience of Adam's meeting with Arthur has left
its mark on Adam, and George Eliot, knowing what has made
up the experience of his metaphorical day, both say to him:
"Come in, Adam, and rest; it has been a hard *day* for thee."

5. *The Mill on the Floss:*
The Special Circumstances

IN ONE sense *The Mill on the Floss* is a strange book to follow *Adam Bede*. Ultimately it was the warm, life-giving sunshine which made the final affirmation in George Eliot's first novel, but it is the dark, life-taking (though, paradoxically, life-giving) flood water which makes the only possible affirmation in her second novel. Almost any receptive reader, whether or not he has even so much as visited a chicken yard, comes away from *Adam Bede* with the sense that its characters live in harmony with the land which bred them; the rhythm of their lives, even the lives of the gentry, is in accord with the life rhythm of the land--the plowing, planting, and harvesting. In *The Mill on the Floss* there is no such positive substructure: there is instead the inevitable, fateful movement of the river, the "dark river that flowed and moaned like an unresting sorrow";[1] for the people of St. Ogg's are "a kind of population out of keeping with the earth on which they live . . ." (IV. i. 5). *The Mill on the Floss* is a dark and tragic book; in that sense it is strange that it should have come immediately from the pen which produced *Adam Bede*.

But only in that sense, for George Eliot is still concerned with the nature of moral vision and with those elements in human experience which either enable man to attain vision or prevent him from making progress toward it. Self-renunciation, which was problematical in *Adam Bede*, is here given a more extensive exploration as Maggie searches for "the clue of life" (VI. xiv. 311). In fact it is that search which determines

67

the structure of *The Mill on the Floss*. Much less complex than *Adam Bede*, where the negative movement from vision and the positive movement toward vision produced a structure impossible to define adequately in terms of the narrative, *The Mill on the Floss* has only one primary movement. For it would be inaccurate to describe the negative aspect of this book in the same terms which applied to Hetty and Arthur, as the movement of certain characters away from moral vision. That Hetty and Arthur do actually regress up to the time of the catastrophe which initiates their forward movement has been demonstrated. But the negative element in *The Mill* is far more general and far less calculable: it is a slow process of moral involution, the retrograde development of a whole society. Tom is the character who represents the furthest extension of this movement, although in Tom himself there is no appreciable change from the rigid, severe, narrow person we first see up until the final climactic moment. But although his character does not change until the last moment, that very character indicates a change in the moral status of a retrogressive society. It is this whole society which provides the negative movement away from moral vision.

Instead, then, of the interweaving of the two movements which created a shifting tension and complex structure in *Adam Bede*, there is in *The Mill on the Floss* one fairly direct line of personal positive movement which is held in constant tension by the more ponderous negative movement of a whole society. It is as if Maggie were progressing slowly by running forward on a backward-moving belt. That this particular society is shown in all of its destructiveness is not, however, to be interpreted as an indication that it is society per se that George Eliot is disparaging. Nothing could be further from the meaning of the book. It is rather that at this particular moment during what George Eliot calls the "historical advance of mankind" (IV. i. 6) the characterizing element of a certain kind of society is its retrogressiveness in terms of moral development. Nor does the fact that this society of St. Ogg's is compared unfavorably to a past society--a point which is to be discussed in much detail--imply that George Eliot is advocating the return to a former state of existence. For in spite of the nega-

tive elements in the book, there is still the one primary movement, the forward movement. And what is here called the negative movement of society must therefore be recognized as
relative, meaningful in terms of the particular point in time
which the novel takes as its most immediate province but which
is nevertheless to be ultimately seen in relation to "the onward
tendency of human things" *(ibid.).* However, this larger framework, like the larger framework of *King Lear* or *Othello,* does
not vitiate the tragic elements from which the drama is derived.

One of George Eliot's statements near the end of *The Mill
on the Floss* may be useful in drawing a further comparison
between *Adam Bede* and *The Mill* and thereby clarifying the
emphasis in each novel:

> . . . the man of maxims is the popular representative of the
> minds that are guided in their moral judgement solely by general
> rules, thinking that these will lead them to justice by a ready-
> made patent method, without the trouble of exerting patience,
> discrimination, impartiality--without any care to assure them-
> selves whether they have the *insight* that comes from a hardly-
> earned estimate of temptation, or from a life vivid and intense
> enough to have created a wide fellow feeling with all that is human
> [VII. ii. 350].

Thus the author describes two ways of achieving moral vision,
for although she does not use the term *vision,* that is clearly
what she means by *insight* as it is used in this context. Both
novels illustrate the two ways, but the emphasis is somewhat
different. *Adam Bede* was primarily concerned with showing
how vision may be attained through living "a life vivid and intense enough to have created a wide fellow feeling with all that
is human." But the vision which Maggie achieves is primarily
that which "comes from a hardly earned estimate of temptation." The emphasis in *Adam Bede* is more squarely placed
on the process by which "the art of vision" is learned, on the
method by which one arrives at the deeply felt perception of
what is already clearly established as good in that particular
situation. But the complexity of *The Mill* arises from the ambiguity of the situation; and the central problem is to discover
what is clear vision in such a situation, keeping in mind always

"that the responsibility of tolerance lies with those who have *the wider vision*" (VI. iii. 353). "The man of maxims," that "popular representative of the minds that are guided in their moral judgement solely by general rules," provides no answer more adequate than that what is not white is necessarily black. Ultimately, what *The Mill on the Floss* shows us about the nature of vision is that "the great problem of the shifting relation between passion and duty is clear to no man who is capable of apprehending it" and that "moral judgements must remain false and hollow, unless they are checked and enlightened by a perpetual reference to the special circumstances that mark the individual lot" (VI. ii. 349-50).

In order, then, to reach the core of meaning in *The Mill on the Floss*, the reader must make a careful estimate of those "special circumstances that mark the individual lot" of Maggie, and, therefore, also of those characters who are important in relation to her. Centrally relevant in such an estimate is the nature of the St. Ogg's society.

The famous opening chapter of the book presents an image of what appears to be a naturally harmonious setting. It is one of the three long passages in which the reader is given a general view of the community of St. Ogg's. Examination of these three passages should reveal the larger outline of the "special circumstances" at the same time that it indicates an important pattern of imagery with which George Eliot develops the particulars of the situation.

For the purposes of this study the important thing to note in the opening scene is that the harmony is achieved by a kind of impressionistic fusion:

> A wide plain, where the broadening Floss hurries on between its green banks to the sea, and the loving tide, rushing to meet it, checks its passage with an impetuous embrace. On this mighty tide the black ships--laden with the fresh-scented fir planks, with rounded sacks of oil-bearing seed, or with the dark glitter of coal--are borne along to the town of St. Ogg's, which shows its aged, fluted red roofs and the broad gables of its wharves between the low wooded hill and the river-brink, tingeing the water with a soft purple hue under the transient glance of this February sun. Far away on each hand stretch the rich pastures, and the patches of dark earth, made ready for the seed of broad-leaved green crops, or touched already with the tint of the tender-bladed

autumn-sown corn. There is a remnant still of the last year's
golden clusters of beehive ricks rising at intervals beyond the
hedgerows; and everywhere the hedgerows are studded with trees:
the distant ships seem to be lifting their masts and stretching
their red-brown sails close among the branches of the spreading ash. Just by the red-roofed town the tributary Ripple flows
with a lively current into the Floss [p. 3].

Here George Eliot directs the mind's eye of the reader in such
a way that it performs an action similar to that of observing
a painting. First the eye observes the broad general outline--
"A wide plain, where the broadening Floss hurries on between
its green banks to the sea"--and then it follows the line of the
tide, observing the particularities of the picture, slowly shifting from background to foreground and finally coming to rest
once more on the center of attention, the Floss. Although the
colors are rich and vivid--green, black, red, purple, golden,
red-brown, red--they are merged and muted by the sunlight,
the reflection in the water, and the distance. The town of St.
Ogg's, for example, "shows its aged, fluted *red* roofs and
broad gables of its wharves between the low wooded hill and
the river-brink, *tingeing* the water with a *soft purple hue* under
the transient glance of this February *sun,* " and "the *distant*
ships *seem* to be lifting their masts and stretching their *red-
brown* sails *close among the branches* of the spreading ash. "
The conceptual aspect of the harmony is substantially developed by the fact that everything in the picture is shown to
be functioning in a natural pattern. Thus tributary flows into
river, and river flows into sea, where its passage is checked
"with an impetuous embrace." The sea bears the ships which
are laden with natural products of the land, products which
will build the homes and warm the hearths of St. Ogg's. The
earth has produced rich pastures and tree-studded hedgerows,
is producing the autumn-sown corn, and is made ready for the
seed of springtime. The total effect is harmonious, but it is a
harmony which is achieved by exclusion rather than inclusion,
by distance rather than proximity. No human being is present,
and the details are comparatively general.

In the next paragraph, however, the author moves in closer
to show us Dorlcote mill. Now she observes that "the clouds
are threatening, and it is far on in the afternoon, " a symbolic

suggestion of potential disharmony. But it is only a suggestion, carefully balanced by the sentence which follows it: "Even in this leafless time of departing February it [the mill] is pleasant to look at--perhaps the chill damp season adds a charm to the trimly-kept, comfortable dwelling-house, as old as the elms and chestnuts that shelter it from the northern blast." The next sentence, however, is premonitory, especially so to those readers who recall the Willow Brook and the pool in *Adam Bede:* "The stream is brimful now, and lies high in this little withy plantation, and half drowns the grassy fringe of the croft in front of the house." Careful, however, to assure her readers that it is not water as such that is to be associated with potential disharmony and careful also to preserve the balance which has been established, George Eliot concludes this paragraph:

> As I look at the full stream, the vivid grass, the delicate bright-green powder softening the outline of the great trunks and branches that gleam from under the bare purple boughs, *I am in love with moistness,* and envy the white ducks that are dipping their heads far into the water here among the withes, unmindful of the awkward appearance they make in the drier world above.

Prompted by her observation of the full stream and the lushly growing grass and trees to declare that she is "in love with moistness," the author clearly suggests the traditional symbol: water is fertility, a creative, life-giving force. And the reference to the white ducks is no merely casual detail, for it introduces an important pattern of animal imagery which must later be analyzed in detail.

On this note of harmony, the author moves in still closer to the mill itself. And as she does so, "the rush of the water, and the booming of the mill, bring a dreamy deafness, which seems to heighten the peacefulness of the scene. They are like a great curtain of sound, shutting one out from the world beyond." Thus a further sense of harmony is achieved by further exclusion, but there is in that harmony an almost hypnotic seductiveness which is heightened as we are led to observe the movement of the "unresting wheel sending out its diamond jets of water." And the little girl who stands watching the wheel is "rapt in its movement," completely under its spell and as powerless before it as her dog, which "seems to be leap-

ing and barking in ineffectual remonstrance with the wheel."
From that first general view of the broad Floss and the wide
plain we have been led gradually inward to the center of attention: Maggie, the mill, and the water. And the potentially disturbing elements in the scene have been temporarily suspended
and so muted that an appearance of harmony has been achieved.

In the second of the three long passages which give a general
view of the community, the author examines the town itself.
Now, for the first time, we

> enter the town of St. Ogg's--that venerable town with the red-
> fluted roofs and the broad warehouse gables, where the black
> ships unlade themselves of their burthens from the far north,
> and carry away, in exchange, the precious inland products, the
> well-crushed cheese and the soft fleeces, which my refined read-
> ers have doubtless become acquainted with through the medium
> of the best classic pastorals.
>
> It is one of those old, old towns which impress one as a con-
> tinuation and outgrowth of nature, as much as the nests of the
> bower-birds or the winding galleries of the white ants: a town
> which carries the traces of its long growth and history like a
> millennial tree . . . [I.xii.172].

The details with which the town was described in the opening
paragraph are thus recalled to the reader's mind--"red-fluted
roofs," "broad warehouse gables" and "black ships." But now
we learn what products the black ships carry away from St.
Ogg's, and that the "well-crushed cheese and soft fleeces" are
intended to suggest an idyllically harmonious origin is borne
out by the author's reference to the "best classic pastorals."
It is, we are told, one of those very old towns that "impress
one as a continuation and outgrowth of nature." But this, it
should be remembered, is its appearance, the way it *impresses* one who sees it. And the comparison to the "winding
galleries of white ants" might be somewhat disturbing when
we remember the destructive power of the white ant, or ter-
mite. But it is an old town with a long history, including the
legend of St. Ogg's, and there is about it "no incongruous
new-fashioned smartness, no plate-glass in shop-windows, no
fresh stucco-facing or other fallacious attempt to make fine
old red St. Ogg's wear the air of a town that sprang up yesterday" (p. 175). It is a placid town, secure in the knowledge that

the time was gone for ever when the broad river could bring

up unwelcome ships: Russia was only the place where the linseed
came from--the more the better--making grist for the great
vertical millstones with their scythe-like arms, roaring and
grinding and carefully sweeping as if an informing soul were in
them. The Catholics, bad harvests, and the mysterious fluctua-
tions of trade, were the three evils mankind had to fear: even
the floods had not been great of late. *The mind of St. Ogg's did
not look extensively before or after.* It inherited a long past without thinking of it, and *had no eyes for the spirits that walk the
streets*" [p. 176].

The mind of St. Ogg's, then, has achieved its sense of a calm,
harmonious existence by the same method the author used in
the creation of the first scene: by exclusion. It is a mind limited by its narrow vision, a mind threatened only by minor
annoyances outside itself, a mind which does not "*look* extensively before or after" and has "no *eyes* for the spirits"
of its past. If it is "an outgrowth of nature," it has no knowledge of that nature which gave it birth, remaining placidly
serene in its ignorance.

The third and most significant of the passages under examination occurs at the opening of Book IV just after the fall of the
house of Tulliver. Here the true nature of St. Ogg's is revealed
and the unharmonious elements are no longer excluded. Although the passage is extremely long, it must be quoted almost
in full:

Journeying down the Rhone on a summer's day, you have perhaps felt the sunshine made dreary by those ruined villages which
stud the banks in certain parts of its course, telling how the swift
river once rose, like an angry, destroying god, sweeping down
the feeble generations whose breath is in their nostrils and making their dwellings a desolation. Strange contrast, you may have
thought, between the effect produced on us by these dismal remnants of commonplace houses, which in their best days were but
the sign of a sordid life, belonging in all its details to our own
vulgar era; and the effect produced by those ruins on the castled
Rhine, which have crumbled and mellowed into such harmony
with the green and rocky steeps, that they seem to have a natural fitness, like the mountain pine: nay, even in the day when
they were built they must have had this fitness, as if they had
been raised by an earthborn race, who had inherited from their
mighty parent a sublime instinct of form. And that was a day of
romance! If those robber barons were somewhat grim and drunken

ogres, they had *a certain grandeur of the wild beast* in them--
they were *forest boars with tusks, tearing and rending: not the
ordinary domestic grunter;* they represented the demon forces
forever in collision with beauty, virtue, and the gentle uses of
life. . . . That was a time of colour, when the sunlight fell on
glancing steel and floating banners; a time of adventure and fierce
struggle--nay, of living, religious art and religious enthusiasm;
for were not cathedrals built in those days . . . ? Therefore it
is that these Rhine castles thrill me with a sense of poetry; they
belong to the grand historic life of humanity, and raise up for me
the vision of an epoch. But these dead-tinted, hollowed-eyed,
angular skeletons of villages on the Rhone oppress me with the
feeling that human life--very much of it--is a narrow, ugly,
grovelling existence, which even calamity does not elevate, but
rather tends to exhibit in all its bare vulgarity of conception; and
I have a cruel conviction that the lives these ruins are the traces
of were part of a gross sum of obscure vitality, that will be swept
into the same oblivion with *the generation of ants and beavers*.

Perhaps something akin to this oppressive feeling may have
weighed upon you in watching this old-fashioned family life on
the banks of the Floss, which even sorrow hardly suffices to
lift above the level of the tragi-comic. It is a sordid life, you
say, this of the Tullivers and Dodsons--irradiated by no sublime
principles, no romantic visions, no active self-renouncing faith--
moved by none of those wild, uncontrollable passions which create
the dark shadows of misery and crime--without that primitive
rough simplicity of wants, that hard submissive ill-paid toil,
that childlike spelling-out of what Nature has written, which gives
its poetry to peasant life. Here, one has conventional worldly
notions and habits without instruction and without polish--surely
the most prosaic form of human life: proud respectability in a
gig of unfashionable build: worldliness without side dishes. Observing these people narrowly . . . one sees little trace of
religion, still less of a distinctively Christian creed. Their belief in the Unseen, so far as it manifests itself at all, seems to
be rather of a pagan kind; their moral notions, though held with
a strong tenacity, seem to have no standard beyond hereditary
custom. You could not live among such people; you are stifled
for want of an outlet towards something beautiful, great, or noble; you are irritated with *these dull men and women,* as *a kind
of population out of keeping with the earth on which they live*--
with this rich plain where the great river flows forever onward
and links the small pulse of the old English town with the beatings
of the world's mighty heart. A vigorous superstition, that lashes
its gods or lashes its own back, seems to be more *congruous*

with the mystery of the human lot, than the mental condition of
these *emmet-like* Dodsons and Tullivers [IV. i. 3-5].

Although it has been clearly indicated by the quotation examined immediately before this one that the town of St. Ogg's
looks as if it were "a continuation and outgrowth of nature,"
it is nevertheless clear that in this passage St. Ogg's is to be
identified with those dismal remnants of villages along the
Rhone rather than with "those ruins on the castled Rhine, which
have crumbled and mellowed into such harmony with the green
and rocky steeps, that they seem to have a natural fitness."
It is true that the buildings of St. Ogg's, like those along the
Rhine, must have had this fitness when they were first constructed, as if they too "had been raised by an earth-born
race." But St. Ogg's, we remember, "had inherited a long
past without thinking of it, and had no eyes for the spirits that
walk the streets." And its people have now become like those
"feeble generations whose breath is in their nostrils," far
more comparable to the "ordinary domestic grunter" than to
the "forest boars with tusks" who have "a certain grandeur
of the wild beast."

One of the reasons why I consider this passage so important
is that it clearly establishes the crux of meaning which is resident in the animal imagery. And it is that particular pattern
of imagery which provides several significant clues to the
meaning of *The Mill on the Floss.* [2] For analysis of the animal
imagery points to those elements in the society of St. Ogg's
which are destructive in the sense that they narrowly restrict
the imagination and partially destroy the capacity for adequate
emotional response. Since imagination and feeling are necessary elements in clear vision, the pattern of animal imagery
will therefore be helpful in describing how it is that the whole
society of St. Ogg's provides the negative movement of the
book, the movement away from vision.

The crux of meaning in the animal imagery, then, is contained here, specifically in the image of the "domestic grunter"
and the "forest boars." Now it is not the "romance" or the
"demon force" per se that the author finds commendable in
those robber barons of the castled Rhine when she compares
them to the forest boars. Rather it is that "certain grandeur"
of the untamed spirit which recognizes "beauty, virtue, and

the gentle uses of life" even though that recognition may take the negative form of rebellion. The "ordinary domestic grunter," dulled by habit, tamed and spiritless, is completely unaware of that elemental struggle between the demon forces and those forces which represent beauty and virtue. What George Eliot most deplores is this domestication of the spirit which results in a "narrow, ugly, groveling existence." Lives which have been so dulled are "part of a gross sum of *obscure vitality,* that will be swept into the same oblivion with the *generations of ants and beavers.* " The obscuring of vitality is a violation of man's nature, reducing him to a level of existence which Eliot characterizes as "the generation of ants and beavers."

The occurrence of this image of the ants and beavers should call to the reader's mind an image previously used to describe St. Ogg's. It was a "continuation and outgrowth of nature, as much as the nests of the bowerbirds or the winding galleries of the white ants." The full significance of the bowerbird, a bird of paradise which builds elaborate nests, remains somewhat obscure to me, but the ant and the beaver have in common one very distinct and pertinent characteristic: each belongs to an animal family in which there is some degree of social organization. The ants especially represent a highly organized animal society, and that Eliot intended them to be specifically associated with the Dodsons and Tullivers of St. Ogg's is indicated by the third occurrence of the image, "these emmet-like [that is, ant-like] Dodsons and Tullivers." Now anthood is completely in accord with the nature of an ant, but as the prevailing characteristic of human beings, it constitutes them "a kind of population out of keeping with the earth on which they live." It symbolizes a completely prosaic life, devoid of "that childlike spelling-out of what nature has written" and producing nothing more than "conventional worldly notions and habits without instruction and without polish." Even the wild forest boar is more nearly in accord with the nature of the human being, and "a vigorous superstition, that lashes its gods or lashes its own back, seems to be more congruous with the mystery of the human lot, than the mental condition of these emmet-like Dodsons and Tullivers."

It should be emphasized once more that George Eliot is not

in any way suggesting a return to the state of the noble savage, but rather that she is using the animal images as a means of characterizing and defining temperaments. Nor is she suggesting that the Rhine society (which did exist--her comparisons are never to a Utopia) because it is more appealing to the romantic side of our natures and because it contained a grandeur of impulse and energy is therefore a golden age to which we should return. She is rather using it as a means of defining particular characteristics of the St. Ogg's society: the dullness of mind and spirit, the lack of emotional capacity from which either the dark shadows of misery and crime or the finest cathedrals may derive, the lack of *passionate* adherence to a chosen way of life, the artificial rather than the original.

※ ※ ※ ※ ※ ※ ※

Such, then, is the general condition of those "special circumstances that mark the individual lot" of Maggie. One way in which we can arrive at an understanding of the more particular circumstances is to examine the pattern of animal imagery. All of the characters in the book, with the single exception of Dr. Kenn, are characterized and developed in terms of animal images. The largest group of images in this pattern to be examined is quite naturally that which pertains to Maggie.

The first point which is established about Maggie is that unfortunately she rather than Tom has inherited the Tulliver "acuteness." As Mr. Tulliver puts it:"'That's the worst on't wi' *the crossing o' breeds:* you can never justly calkilate what'll come on't. . . . It's no mischief much while she's a little un, but an over-'cute woman's no better nor a *long-tailed sheep*--she'll fetch none the bigger price for that'" (I. ii. 12). Thus by St. Ogg's standards, Maggie's cleverness is a quality that is as impractical in her as a long tail is on a sheep. It will decrease her market value as a woman. To Mrs. Tulliver, however, Maggie's strangeness is cause for more immediate concern than Mr. Tulliver anticipated:"'. . . wanderin' up an' down by the water, *like a wild thing,* she'll tumble in some day.'" When "this small mistake of nature" enters the room and the reader is given his first close look at her, she is performing a characteristic action, "incessantly tossing her head

to keep the dark heavy locks out of her gleaming black eyes--
an action which gave her very much the air of a *small Shetland
pony"* (I. ii. 14). The image of the pony recurs in several passages dealing with Maggie's childhood. She "stamps" her foot
when she is passionately angry, or she "trots" peacefully along
by Tom's side; and always she is tossing her black "mane"
from her eyes. What Eliot intends the image to suggest is made
explicit when Maggie clings to Tom and begs forgiveness for
having let his lop-eared rabbits die. [3] On this scene the author
comments:

> We learn to restrain ourselves as we get older. We keep apart
> when we have quarrelled, express ourselves in well-bred phrases,
> and in this way preserve a dignified alienation, showing much
> firmness on one side, and swallowing much grief on the other.
> We no longer approximate in our behaviour to *the mere impul-
> siveness of the lower animals,* but conduct ourselves in every
> respect like members of a *highly civilized society.* Maggie and
> Tom were still very much like young animals, and so she could
> rub her cheek against his, and kiss his ear in a random, sobbing
> way; and there were tender fibres in the lad that had been used
> to answer to Maggie's fondling; so that he behaved with a weak-
> ness quite inconsistent with his resolution to punish her as much
> as she deserved: he actually began to kiss her in return, and
> say--
> "Don't cry, then, Magsie--here, eat a bit o' cake."
> Maggie's sobs began to subside, and she put out her mouth
> for the cake and bit a piece; and then Tom bit a piece, just for
> company, and they ate together and rubbed each other's cheeks
> and brows and noses together, while they ate, *with a humiliating
> resemblance to two friendly ponies* [I. v. 53-54].

This behavior which approximates the "mere impulsiveness
of the lower animals" is intended to point up the fact that Maggie and Tom have the capacity for spontaneous emotional response. It is the most (if not the only) genuinely tender moment
Tom is allowed with Maggie until the concluding scene. Such
impulsiveness is, like the "well-bred" restraint of the "highly
civilized society, " capable of producing either morally desirable or undesirable human action, but here it is shown to
be producing natural and harmonious behavior. And although
that behavior is unrestrained, there is about it an element
which gives it form. George Eliot defines this element much
later in Book VI as she recalls the time when the two children

"bit their cake together as a *sacrament* of conciliation" (VI. iv. 192). The Shetland pony is a domesticated animal having perhaps but little or none of that "certain grandeur of the wild beast," but as an image of the natural and spontaneous emotional state it is most effective.

Furthermore the heavy mane and rough shaggy appearance of the pony suggest that Maggie's appearance defies the Dodson standard of neatness. This fact is pointed up by another animal image. The contrast between her careless appearance and her cousin Lucy's "natty completeness" is like that "between a rough, dark, overgrown *puppy* and a white *kitten*. Lucy put up the neatest little rosebud mouth to be kissed: everything about her was neat . . ." (I. vii. 87). On the occasion when Maggie defiantly dips her head in a basin of water to destroy the artificially induced curls, she is compared to an especially shaggy breed of dog: she shook "the water from her black locks as she ran, like a *Skye terrier* escaped from his bath" (I. iv. 36). In addition to the shaggy appearance, something of the intensely loyal and spontaneous emotional response is pointed up by another occurrence of this image. At the mention of Tom's name in a conversation, Maggie "shook her heavy hair and looked up eagerly. . . . Tom's name served as well as the shrillest whistle: in an instant she was on the watch, with gleaming eyes, like a *Skye terrier* suspecting mischief, or at all events determined to fly at anyone who threatened it towards Tom" (I. iii. 18).

Maggie's youthful conception of society is indicated by her speculation about the life of the spiders who inhabit the mill:

> She wondered if they had any relatives outside the mill, for in that case there must be a painful difficulty in their family intercourse--a fat and floury spider, accustomed to take his fly well dusted with meal, must suffer a little at a cousin's table where the fly was *au naturel*, and the lady-spiders must be mutually shocked at each other's appearance [I. iv. 39].

She is aware, then, of the pain of exclusion, that powerful force which society exerts to secure the conformity of its members. But she is aware, too, that there is a world outside the mill society. She knows, for example, that not all animals are domesticated, that there are "elephants and kangaroos, and the civet cat, and the sunfish, and a bird sitting on its tail--

I forget his name. There are countries full of those creatures, *instead of horses and cows,* you know" (I. iv. 40).

But something more decidedly akin to that "certain grandeur of the wild beast" than is suggested by the pony and puppy images is implied in the description of Maggie when she listens to her aunts and uncles join in condemnation of her stricken father. In a state of "trembling indignation," she "suddenly started up and stood in front of them, her eyes flashing like the eyes of a young lioness" (III. iii. 322). The lioness naturally suggests uncontrolled energy which is capable of destruction, but at the same time it also connotes something of the courage and nobility which is commonly attributed to its mate, the king of the lower animals. Both of these qualities are finally applicable to Maggie, whose intense emotional response does bring about both destructive and constructive results. But in this particular context the image seems calculated to accentuate the spirited, untamed quality, the intensity and power of Maggie's emotional response.

At this point the theme of captivity, of restriction or perversion of human nature, appears in the pattern and is more directly stated in a series of images, the first of which precedes the image of the lioness. When Philip first meets Maggie he wonders what it is that makes her "dark eyes remind him of the stories about princesses being turned into animals," and the author concludes: "I think it was that her eyes were full of unsatisfied intelligence, and unsatisfied, beseeching affection" (II. v. 266-67). The idea of a human being who is metamorphosed and held captive in an unnatural state is most effectively presented in a classical image whose relevance should justify its inclusion here, although it is not an animal image. Philip who has long deplored Maggie's immature renunciation of the natural joys of life--"the pity of it, that a mind like hers should be withering in its very youth, like a young forest tree, for *want of the light and space it was formed to flourish in!"* (V. i. 60)--proposes to paint a picture of Maggie as "a tall *Hamadryad,* dark and strong and noble, just issued from one of the fir trees . . ." (V. iii. 88). This image is somewhat paradoxical, for at the same time that it implies an affinity with nature (the hamadryads were, after all, nymphs of the woods), it also implies a kind of unnatural captive existence. The fact

that Philip sees her as "just issued" from her tree is the result of his intense desire that Maggie be released both from
Tom's restrictive influence and from her own asceticism,
which she believes is self-renunciation and Philip tells her
is "a narrow self-delusive fanaticism, which is only a way of
escaping pain by starving into dulness all the highest powers
of your nature" (V. iii. 90). [4] The society of St. Ogg's, however, is hardly one which would encourage or even allow the
development of those highest powers of Maggie's nature. And
although her early asceticism was misguided, it was the only
way she could take to reach a higher value than her society af-
forded. The results, however, were not constructive: ". . .
she often strove after too high a flight, and came down with
her poor little half-fledged *wings* dabbled in the mud" (IV. iii.
36); and furthermore they were, as she herself eventually
comes to realize, actually destructive: "'It is with me as I
used to think it would be with the poor uneasy *white bear* I saw
at the show. I thought he must have got so stupid with the habit
of turning backwards and forwards in that narrow space, that
he would keep doing it if they set him free. One gets a bad
habit of being unhappy'" (VI. ii. 158-59). Thus Maggie identifies
herself with a wild animal whose spirit has been broken or
dulled by enforced (partially self-enforced) confinement. Soon
after the occurrence of this image, however, her dulled sensibilities are reawakened by her love for Stephen; and the remaining animal images suggest an intense emotional state.
When Stephen first pleads for her love, she opens "her eyes
full on his for an instant, like a lovely *wild animal* timid and
struggling under caresses" (VI. xi. 275) and just before she
leaves Stephen she is compared to a frightened bird.

Many of these animal images which apply to Maggie seem
very trivial, even hardly worth noting in themselves. But when
they are seen in relation to the other images in this pattern
they take on greater significance. Maggie has been compared to
"a wild thing," a pony, a puppy, a Skye terrier, a lioness, a
bear, a bird, "a lovely wild animal," all of which in one way or
another suggest a kind of natural, undomesticated state or the
loss of such a state. By contrast, those images which have
reference to the Dodson women are strikingly different in tone.

That tone is characterized in general by an image which de-

scribes the entire Dodson clan as they affect Mr. Tulliver.
After the cessation of a family quarrel which ensued when the
female in-laws tried to dictate Mr. Tulliver's course of action,
"Mr. Tulliver felt very much as if the air had been cleared of
obtrusive flies now the women had left the room" (I. vii. 108).
During that quarrel, Mrs. Glegg's tactics have been far from
admirable, as the author points out: "'Bessy I'm sorry for
you,' said Mrs. Glegg, very much with the feeling of a *cur*
that seizes the opportunity of diverting his bark towards the
man who carries no stick" (p. 106). Mr. Tulliver further describes Mrs. Glegg as forever "gnawing" at people, and Mr.
Glegg's description of his wife is even less complimentary:

> "A woman, with everything provided for her, and allowed to keep
> her own money the same as if it was settled on her, and with a
> new gig stuffed and lined at no end o' expense, and provided for
> when I die beyond anything she could expect . . . to go on i' this
> way, *biting and snapping like a mad dog!* It's beyond everything,
> as God A'mighty should ha' made women *so"* [I. xii. 187; second
> italics and ellipsis are the author's].

With the exception of the reference to the *cur* all of these images indicate the way husbands in this family group look upon
their wives. But even though in everything except housekeep-
ing these women are considered as insignificant as flies, nevertheless they are "obtrusive flies," so obtrusive that in a
very subtle way they actually exert a powerful influence.

Thus Mrs. Tulliver, chosen by her husband "because she
wasn't o'er-'cute . . . 'cause she was a bit weak" (I. iii. 23),
is "a mild woman, but even a *sheep* will face about a little
when she has lambs . . ." (I. vi. 59). Docile as she is, Mrs.
Tulliver does "face about a little" as she tries to keep Mr.
Tulliver from alienating the aunts who will be leaving legacies
to Tom and Maggie. But the effect she achieves is not what she
intends, since she is also a dull-witted woman. Two humorous
and somewhat ironic images are used to characterize Mrs.
Tulliver and to indicate the peculiar influence she exerts. When
she tells Mr. Tulliver that he shouldn't have quarrelled with
Mrs. Glegg (his creditor) because he may have difficulty if
Mrs. Glegg should decide to demand her money, the author
comments:

Mrs. Tulliver had lived thirteen years with her husband, yet she retained in all the freshness of her early married life a facility of saying things which drove him in the opposite direction to the one she desired. Some minds are wonderful for keeping their bloom in this way, as a patriarchial gold-fish apparently retains to the last its youthful illusion that it can swim in a straight line beyond the encircling glass. Mrs. Tulliver was *an amiable fish* of this kind, and, after running her head against the same resisting medium for thirteen years, would go at it again to-day with the same undulled alacrity [I. viii. 110].

The image of Mrs. Tulliver as a goldfish in a bowl is a recurrence of the captive theme in the animal imagery, but there is a significant difference. The lioness makes a stand against her attackers in the hope of protecting her own, and the white bear paces its cage because it knows that it has lost its freedom. But the "amiable fish" continues to run its head against the bowl because it does not even know that the glass exists, thinking each time that it can swim in the direction it wishes and remaining amiable and stupidly unaware when it is unable to do so. The next image indicates the way Mrs. Tulliver reacts when the loss of the mill has forced her into a less amiable state of mind. In the chapter entitled "How a Hen Takes to Stratagem, " Mrs. Tulliver is described as

brooding over a scheme by which she, and no one else, would avert the result most to be dreaded, and prevent Wakem from entertaining the purpose of bidding for the mill. Imagine *a truly respectable and amiable hen,* by some portentous anomaly, taking to reflection and inventing combinations by which she might prevail on Hodge not to wring her neck, or send her and her chicks to market: the result could hardly be other than much cackling and fluttering [III. vii. 369].

It is of course that cackling and fluttering which causes Wakem to purchase the mill, an action which he had not previously considered. In view of this hen image which describes Mrs. Tulliver, Mr. and Mrs. Pullet's name assumes a decided significance. Mrs. Pullet and Mrs. Tulliver are the weakest members of the Dodson clan, having less spirit than the gnawing, biting, snapping Mrs. Glegg.

Lucy, who represents the next generation of Dodson femininity, is characterized by a still different set of animal images. She is "a little white mouse" (I. x. 147), "a white kitten"

(I. vii. 87), "a pretty spaniel" (VI. iii. 178). Her voice is a "pretty treble, like the low conversational notes of little birds" (VI. vii. 217). Something of her passive nature is indicated briefly by the way she "looked on mutely, like a *kitten* pausing from its lapping" during an argument between Tom and Maggie (I. ix. 128). But even more is revealed about Lucy's character by George Eliot's description of the relationship Lucy assumes with animals:

> Sinbad was Lucy's chestnut horse, that she always fed with her own hand when he was turned out in the paddock. She was fond of feeding dependent creatures, .and knew the private tastes of all the animals about the house, delighting in the little rippling sounds of her canaries when their beaks were busy with fresh seed, and in the small nibbling pleasures of certain animals which, lest she should appear too trivial, I will here call "the more familiar rodents" [VI. i. 154].

Suggestive of Chaucer's Prioress, this passage indicates Lucy's romantic, sentimental tendency. One prosperous generation removed from those Dodson women whose primary purpose it was to manage the household with greatest efficiency, Lucy often directs her natural energies and affections toward even more trivial concerns. The role society dictates to her is to be pretty, dainty, and absolutely useless. In her, the feminine qualities have become so refined that many natural qualities of the spirited human being seem entirely lacking at this point in her development. That is not, however, to say that Lucy herself is trivial, for she is obviously well intentioned, and, furthermore, she is eventually to give proof of her ability to step outside the role to which she has been assigned. Like the other Dodson women, Lucy too exerts an influence on those about her. Bringing Maggie into her home among what Philip calls her "whole menagerie of pets" (VI. vii. 218-19), she introduces her to the role of the young lady, for whom there was no "imperative reason for doing one thing more than another" (VI. vi. 202). How Maggie responds under such genuinely tender care as Lucy gives her menagerie must be considered later. But since what has been said about Lucy is of extreme significance in relation to Stephen, it is necessary at this point to explore his character in some detail, even though such exploration seems to involve a partial digression from the pattern of animal imagery.

Although no specific animal image is used to characterize Stephen, the first scene in which he appears shows him to be figuratively as much a part of Lucy's menagerie as her King Charles toy spaniel:

> The neat little lady in mourning, whose light-brown ringlets are falling over the colored embroidery with which her fingers are busy, is of course Lucy Deane; and the fine young man who is leaning down from his chair to snap the scissors in the extremely abbreviated face of the *"King Charles"* lying on the young lady's feet is no other than Mr. Stephen Guest, whose diamond ring, attar of roses, and air of nonchalant leisure, at twelve o'clock in the day, are the graceful and odoriferous result of the largest oil-mill and the most extensive wharf in St. Ogg's. There is an apparent triviality in the action with the scissors, but your discernment perceives at once that there is a design in it which makes it eminently worthy of a large-headed, long-limbed young man; for you see that Lucy wants the scissors, and is compelled, reluctant as she may be, to shake her ringlets back, raise her soft hazel eyes, smile playfully down on the face that is so very nearly on a level with her knee, and, holding out her little shell-pink palm, to say, --
> "My scissors, please, if you can renounce the great pleasure of persecuting *my poor Minny.*"
> The foolish scissors have slipped too far over the knuckles, it seems, and *Hercules* holds out his entrapped fingers hopelessly [VI. i. 143].

That such action as this "Hercules" is engaged in is *not* "eminently worthy" is obviously the point of this passage. And that Stephen sits with the spaniel at Lucy's feet is no more an accident than that the scissors have entrapped his fingers or that the dog with the abbreviated face is a King Charles toy spaniel whom Lucy has named Minny in complete disregard of its supposedly male sex. For the role that society expects of the wealthy Mr. Stephen Guest is that he wear his "diamond ring, attar of roses, and air of *nonchalant* leisure, at twelve o'clock in the day" while he obediently pays court at the feet of a "neat little lady" who sits at her embroidery. But although his role during the courtship demands subjection to what he playfully calls "feminine tyranny, " his glance is "half-ardent, half-

sarcastic, " for (as Philip has disclosed to Lucy) Stephen likes
women "to be rather insipid, " and he knows that "the whole duty of woman" after marriage is expressed in the song "Grace-
ful Consort, " which he asks Lucy to sing: "and from obedience
grows my pride and happiness. " We learn from Lucy that
Philip thinks this whole musical composition "has a sort of
sugared complacency and flattering make-believe in it, " but
Stephen says that it exactly suits his feeling. Thus he is identified with that smug, complacent attitude of mind which, as
has previously been indicated, characterizes the general mind
of St. Ogg's. His sense of harmony is similarly achieved by
exclusion of the unpleasant and undesirable. He is, as he is
expected to be, somewhat different from the ordinary young
man of St. Ogg's, and that difference takes the direction of
foppishness and coxcombry: " 'Guest is a great coxcomb, '
young Torry observed; 'but then he is a privileged person
in St. Ogg's--he carries all before him: if another fellow did
such things [as buying and wearing a scarlet fez of decidedly
feminine appearance which Lucy had embroidered for the society bazaar], everybody would say he made a fool of himself'"
(VI. ix. 249). Because Stephen is a privileged person who is
expected to carry all before him he retains the illusion that
he himself has chosen Lucy, although George Eliot by the tone
of the following passage seems to imply otherwise:

> Perhaps the emphasis of his admiration did not fall precisely on
> this rarest quality [of kindness] in her--perhaps he approved of
> his own choice of her chiefly because she did not strike him as
> a remarkable rarity. A man likes his wife to be pretty; well,
> Lucy was pretty, but not to a maddening extent. A man likes his
> wife to be accomplished, gentle, affectionate, and not stupid;
> and Lucy had all of these qualifications. Stephen was not sur-
> prised to find himself in love with her, and was conscious of ex-
> cellent judgment in preferring her to Miss Leyburn, the daugh-
> ter of the county member, although Lucy was only the daughter
> of his father's subordinate partner; besides, he had had to defy
> and overcome a slight unwillingness and disappointment in his
> father and sisters--a circumstance which gives a young man an
> agreeable consciousness of his own dignity. Stephen was aware
> that he had sense and independence enough to choose the wife who
> was likely to make him happy, unbiased by any indirect consider-
> ations. He meant to choose Lucy: she was a little darling, and ex-

actly the sort of woman he had always most admired [VI. i. 154-
55].

"A man"--that is, any man who plays the role which Stephen
plays in society--likes his wife to be a certain kind of woman--
that is, one who will enable him to fulfill his particular masculine role. And because it is also necessary to his role that
he appear independent, he also likes to oppose "a slight un-
willingness and disappointment in his father and sisters,"
just enough to give him "an agreeable consciousness of his own
dignity" and allow him to retain the illusion that he is "un-
biased by any indirect considerations." At this point in the
narrative, Stephen is himself shown to be what he calls Minny,
"a pampered minion." He is an elegant, foppish favorite in
Lucy's court and in the eyes of society, but he is also a com-
pliant subject of that society. It does not seem unreasonable to
suggest that the role he is expected to play would have eventually unmanned him as surely as Minny has been emasculated.
But Stephen, like Lucy, is also more than the role he plays
and, like her, is capable of moving outside it.

Were this not true, then Maggie's love for Stephen could
not be so convincing without reducing her stature as a character. This interpretation of Stephen, I believe, does much to
explain the sudden fascination Maggie holds for him. From the
first moment Maggie challenges him by refusing to accept the
superficiality of the social situation. She refuses his witty
compliments because (as she had once told Philip) "she didn't
see why women were to be told with a simper that they were
beautiful, any more than old men were to be told that they were
venerable . . ." (VI. ii. 165-66), and because she knows that
he has previously spoken slightingly of her. From the first
Maggie impresses Stephen as "unlike other women" (p. 167).
She is, for example, capable of seeing beneath his satirical
attitude: "'Ah, I see how much penetration you have,' said
Stephen, 'You have discovered already that I am talkative and
impudent. Now superficial people never discern that--owing
to my manner, I suppose'" (p. 169). This sudden understanding which arises between Maggie and Stephen, the mutual
awareness that each has perceived beneath the surface of the
other's personality, creates the sense of a secret relationship

which becomes a strong and compelling force in their love relationship.

There is once again a shift in the tone of animal images when we consider those which refer to Mr. Tulliver. One general image defines a central characteristic of his make-up: speaking of Mr. Tulliver's pride and obstinacy, Eliot observes that "there are *certain animals* to which tenacity of position is a law of life--they can never flourish again, after a single wrench: and there are certain human beings to whom predominance is a law of life--they can only sustain humiliation so long as they can refuse to believe in it, and, in their own conception, predominate still" (III. i. 294). During Mr. Tulliver's illness, when it is no longer possible for him to predominate even in his own conception, he is completely broken in mind and spirit. He receives even Maggie's kiss "as passively as *some quiet animal* might have received it" (III. iv. 334). But slowly his mind struggles back, "like *a living creature* making its way from under a great snowdrift, that slides and slides again, and shuts up the newly-made opening" (III. vii. 365). This is another recurrence of the captive theme; but all of these images are too general to be of much significance except to indicate a contrast to the tone of the previous images. The only important animal image which has reference to Mr. Tulliver repeats the captive theme and recalls something of the spirited quality of the animals used to describe Maggie: Mr. Tulliver is "that pitiable, furious *bull* entangled in the meshes of a net" (p. 379). The significance of this image will be explored in relation to Tom.

When Tom is first introduced in the novel he is described as "one of those lads that grow everywhere in England, and at twelve or thirteen years of age, look as much alike as *goslings*"--that is, the features of his face are indistinguishable from those of any other boy and as such form a strong contrast to "poor Maggie's phiz, which Nature seemed to have moulded and coloured with the most decided intention." But George Eliot goes on to warn us that the appearance of "this pink-and-white bit of masculinity with the indeterminate features" is deceptive: "Under these average boyish physiognomies that she [Nature] seems to turn off by the gross, she conceals some of her most rigid, inflexible purposes, some

of her most unmodifiable characters . . . " (I. v. 44-45). The
image of the gosling should not be pressed too far, but the care
with which Eliot chose all of the animal images seems to justify
the very obvious observation that a gosling is a young goose.
One more fowl image is used to describe Tom, this time
through the eyes of Bob Jakin, whom Tom has tried to punish
for cheating: "'. . . you're a nasty fightin' *turkey cock*, you
are . . .'" (I. vi. 73). But Tom, like Lucy, is most directly
characterized by the relationship he assumes with animals.
Thus Eliot tells us:

> In very tender years, when he still wore a lace border under his
> outdoor cap, he was often observed peeping through the bars of
> a gate and making minatory gestures with his small forefinger
> while he scolded the sheep with an inarticulate burr, intended
> to strike terror into their astonished minds; indicating thus early
> that desire for mastery over *the inferior animals*, wild and do-
> mestic, including cockchafers, neighbour's dogs, *and small
> sisters*, which in all ages has been an attribute of so much prom-
> ise for the fortunes of our race [I. ix. 135].

What kind of promise such a desire for mastery implies for
the fortunes of our race is ultimately shown by the book as
a whole. There is ample evidence that in this respect Tom
changed not at all after the lace border was removed from his
cap. As an older boy he is seen "lowering his piece of string
on the other side [of a poultry-yard fence] as a means of ex-
asperating the turkey cock" (I. x. 152).

One such action of Tom's takes on at least partial symbolic
significance. On an occasion when Tom, Lucy, and Maggie
are playing together, Maggie is so emotionally disturbed by
the uncomfortable tucker her mother makes her wear and by
Tom's inconsiderate treatment when her play houses fall down
(he calls her "a stupid" and says that he wishes Lucy were
his sister) that she accidentally knocks Tom's house down.
She begs for forgiveness, but Tom is so enraged that "he would
have struck her, only he knew it was cowardly to strike a girl,
and Tom Tulliver was quite determined he would never do anything cowardly" (I. ix. 127). And so he

> took no notice of her, but took, instead, two or three hard peas
> out of his pocket, and shot them with his thumbnail against the
> window--vaguely at first, but presently with the distinct aim of

hitting *a superannuated blue bottle* which was exposing its im-
becility in the spring sunshine, clearly against the views of Nature, who had provided Tom and the peas for the speedy destruction of this weak individual [p. 128].

Tom's later rejection of Maggie when she comes to him for
refuge and begs forgiveness is again occasioned by his rigid
conviction that Maggie is a weak individual whose actions have
been clearly against the views of Nature and that his judgment
and punishment of her are clearly in accord with Nature's
views. One more brief reference will illustrate Tom's attitude
toward "the inferior animals": he was "a young gentleman fond
of animals--fond, that is, of throwing stones at them" (p. 130).

The next series of animal images which have reference to
Tom are those which deal with his education under the clergy-
man, Mr. Stelling. Here the focus of the criticism shifts for
the most part to the educational methods which are used. In
fact, the most sympathetic treatment Tom receives in the book
occurs in the passages where he is so obviously the victim in
a situation which is completely out of harmony with his nature.
This state of disharmony is indicated by a recurrence of the
captive image: "At present, in relation to this demand that he
should learn Latin declensions and conjugations, Tom was in
a state of as blank unimaginativeness concerning the cause and
tendency of his sufferings as if he had been *an innocent shrewmouse* imprisoned in the split trunk of an ash tree in order to
cure lameness in cattle" (II. i. 210). This is a variation of the
hamadryad image with which Philip described Maggie's captive
state, but the difference is that whereas the nymph in the tree
suggested a kind of tragic, noble figure, the shrewmouse imprisoned in the tree is merely a pathetic victim who does not
even know why he suffers. The idea expressed by the image is
ironic, since education which is intended to enlighten the individual here actually makes him the object through which a
superstitious charm is supposed to work a cure for ailing
cattle.

The immediate cause of Tom's suffering is, of course, Mr.
Stelling, to whom--as he himself observes--"teaching comes
natural. " But that naturalness George Eliot finds highly questionable, as her choice of images indicates:

Perhaps it was because teaching came naturally to Mr. Stelling, that he set about it with that uniformity of method and independence of circumstances which distinguish the actions of *animals* understood to be under the immediate teaching of Nature. *Mr. Broderip's amiable beaver,* as that charming naturalist tells us, busied himself as earnestly in constructing a dam, in a room up three pairs of stairs in London, as if he had been laying his foundation in a stream or lake in Upper Canada. It was "Binny's" function to build: the absence of water or of possible progeny was an accident for which he was not accountable. With the same unerring instinct Mr. Stelling set to work at his natural method of instilling the Eton Grammar and Euclid into the mind of Tom Tulliver [p. 206].

A second image further emphasizes the limitations of Mr. Stelling's nature:

Besides, how should Mr. Stelling be expected to know that education was a delicate and difficult business? any more than an *animal* endowed with a power of boring a hole through a rock should be expected to have wide views of excavation. Mr. Stelling's faculties had been early trained to boring in a straight line, and he had no faculty to spare [II. iv. 251].

How indeed should he be expected to know what is beyond the understanding of an inferior animal when the limitations of his nature are like those of the animal? Mr. Stelling is certainly one among "the generation of ants and beavers" who have lost sight of the ultimate ends of life and concentrate only on the means. Completely unable to recognize that Tom's mind works in terms of the concrete rather than the abstract, he proceeds in an endeavor as useless and ridiculous as that of Mr. Broderip's beaver. Taking pride in the fact that he is "not the man to enfeeble and emasculate his pupil's mind by simplifying and explaining, or to reduce the tonic effect of etymology by mixing it with smattering, extraneous information, such as is given to girls, " he achieves the opposite of the intended effect. For ". . . under this vigorous treatment Tom became more like a girl than he had ever been in his life before" (II. i. 210-11). [5] Tom's hurt pride gives him "something of the girl's susceptibility" in a situation where he is not the master. That he is a thoroughly conforming member of his society is indicated by George Eliot's analysis of his predicament:

He was of a very firm, not to say obstinate disposition, but there was *no brute-like rebellion or recklessness* in his nature: the human sensibilities predominated, and if it had occurred to him that he could enable himself to show some quickness at his lessons, and so acquire Mr. Stelling's approbation, by standing on one leg for an inconvenient length of time, or rapping his head moderately against the wall, or any voluntary action of that sort, he would certainly have tried it [p. 211].

Obviously it is not only Tom who is being criticized here, but also such "human sensibilities" as are indicated by an inordinate desire for approval and a willingness to conform at any expense, sensibilities which, in some ways at least, occasion too little of the spirited human response.

Thus Tom provides a contrast to his father, whose responses are sometimes too brutelike to be in accord with the best in human nature. Nevertheless Mr. Tulliver's rebellion and recklessness indicate that he is at least one generation closer than Tom to those robber barons of the castled Rhine whose spirited human struggle suggested "a certain grandeur of the wild beast" and aligned them with the "forest boars" rather than "the ordinary domestic grunter." Mr. Tulliver, it has been previously noted, is a "pitiable, furious bull"; but Tom, significantly, is compared to an ox:

The *ox* . . . is not given to use his teeth as an instrument of attack; and Tom was an excellent *bovine* lad, who ran at questionable objects in a truly ingenious bovine manner; but he had blundered on Philip's tenderest point, and had caused him as much pain as if he had studied the means with the nicest precision and the most envenomed spite [II. v. 264].

In context, this image is primarily intended to show Tom's insensitive and even stupid blundering, the tone perhaps unconsciously linking it in the reader's mind with the image of the "truly respectable and amiable hen, by some portentous anomaly, taking to reflection." This linkage is legitimate, since Tom is generally shown to be like his mother and Maggie is consistently more like her father. But at the same time there is also present a suppressed meaning which is significant in the context of the entire pattern of animal imagery: that is, the ox image is suggestive of a dull, stolid, thoroughly domesticated and impotent nature--in short, of the emasculation and perversion of man's essential nature. Actually it is only as a symbolic extension of the society (one generation) that the image works on this level in relation to Tom, for the only real change that takes place in his character occurs at the end of the book. Read on this level, the image supports and underlines the meaning resident in some animal images previously examined and bears a direct relationship to the image which characterizes Philip.

For with one brief exception when he is compared to a mollusc (II. iv. 260), only one image is used to describe Philip. The first occurrence of the image, however, is not explicit. Philip is sitting at the piano in the Stelling drawing room. He is "supremely happy, perched like an amorphous bundle on the high stool, with his head thrown back, his eyes fixed on the opposite cornice, and his lips wide open, sending forth, with all his might, impromptu syllables to a tune of Arne's . . ." (p. 258). The details of this description--the use of the word *perched*, the amorphous shape, the attitude of the head, the absorption in song--all suggest that Philip is birdlike. The next occurrence of the image, somewhat more explicit, is Philip's own description of himself when he tells Maggie: "'. . . I think of too many things--sow all sorts of seeds, and get no great harvest from any one of them. I'm cursed with susceptibility in every direction, and effective faculty in none. . . . I *flutter* all ways, and *fly* in none'" (V. iii. 88-89). This time the bird image is coupled with that of the unproductive seed sowing to emphasize a general state of inefficacy and impotence. Elsewhere Philip's singing is called "warbling." Two more brief recurrences of the image--Stephen speaks of Philip's "ruffled feathers" and later tells Philip: "'. . . I wish you'd conduct yourself a little less like *a sparrow* with a residence on the house-top . . .'" (VI. vii. 223)--emphasize Philip's birdlike qualities and indicate that they are generally apparent. There is undeniably a suggestion of the feminine in the bird image, especially in the particular context of such words as *perched* and *flutter* and in the larger context of the whole pattern where Maggie is the only other character compared to a bird. But here the tone is gentler than it is in the presentation of the ox image. For although Philip has no "effective faculty" and flies in no direction, he does nevertheless "flutter all ways"--that is, he has not been reduced to dull,

bovine stolidity. The most immediate cause of Philip's bird-
likeness--his amorphous shape, his easily ruffled feelings,
his helpless fluttering, his isolated sparrowlike residence on
the housetop--is his humpback. This deformity, which makes
Philip unfit to assume the masculine role in St. Ogg's, determines that he shall be brought up as a girl, thus allowing the
feminine part of his nature to develop more than the masculine:
"Kept aloof from all practical life as Philip had been, and by
nature half-feminine in sensitiveness, he had some of the woman's intolerant repulsion towards worldliness and the deliberate pursuit of sensual enjoyment . . ." (V. iii. 95). Throughout the book there are several indications of Philip's feminine
characteristics, all underlined by the bird image. It seems
reasonable to assume that this feminine quality is one of the
reasons that Maggie is able to confide in Philip as she does
but unable to love him except in a sisterly way.

To some extent most of the animal images examined thus
far have pointed up two contrasting patterns: human response
which is in accord with the full, spontaneous nature of the
human being, whether it be derived from the creative or the
destructive urge; and human response which is destructively
narrow and restricted because it derives from an artificial
impulse produced by an oppressively rigid society. Since all
of the characters discussed are very much the products of
St. Ogg's society, the images have for the most part revealed
some aspect of the second pattern. One figure alone in the
entire book stands out by contrast as being somehow more
independent of that society and therefore decidedly more in
harmony with his own nature and the natural surroundings.
Although he is a minor character relatively unnoticed by the
casual reader, Bob Jakin assumes an extremely significant
role in *The Mill* when we pay close attention to him.

It is necessary to recall once more the key passage in which
Eliot says that the "emmet-like Dodsons and Tullivers" are "a
kind of population out of keeping with the earth on which they
live--with this rich plain, where the great river flows forever
onward. " In the light of this observation, the following image
provides an important clue to Bob's character. When we first
see him, he is walking along by the river, "keeping his blue
eyes fixed on the river, like *an amphibious animal* who *fore-*

saw occasion for darting in" (I. vi. 69). In contrast with the
emmetlike Dodsons and Tullivers, Bob, like an amphibious
animal, is in keeping with both the land and the water. His
amphibious characteristic is emphasized by such details as
the fact that "his trousers were always rolled up at the knee,
for the convenience of wading on the slightest notice" (p. 68)
and that he is not frightened by talk of floods: "'. . . I don't
mind the water, no more nor the land. I'd swim--*I* would'"
(p. 71; author's italics). One of Bob's youthful occupations is
traveling up and down the river on a trading barge, and he later
becomes a packman who travels about the country. When he
marries he moves to "one of those queer old houses, pierced
with surprising passages, by the water-side" (VI. iv. 183), and
when the flood rains finally do come he soothes his womenfolk
by observing that if they had not taken a house by the riverside,
they would have had no boats at all (VII. v. 371). As a boy, Bob
shows his familiarity with the land by his amazing knowledge of
animals: "Bob knew, directly he saw a bird's egg, whether it
was a swallow's, or a tomtit's, or a yellow-hammer's; he
found out all the wasps' nests, and could set all sorts of traps;
he could climb trees like a squirrel, and had quite a magical
power of detecting hedgehogs and stoats . . . " (I. vi. 67). He
shares Tom's enthusiasm for ratcatching, throwing stones at
the sheep, or "killing a cat that was wandering *incognito"* and
his "official if not natural function of frightening the birds"
(p. 67) hardly distinguishes him as a dedicated nature lover.
But the point is that frightening the birds is for Bob a means
of earning a living and that to him trap setting and stone throwing are merely boyish sport, whereas to Tom they are a means
of asserting superiority. Tom never outgrows his desire for
mastery over inferior animals, but in Bob there is a constant
growth. He more than anyone else (with the possible exception
of Dr. Kenn) understands what Maggie means when on the occasion of her father's financial downfall she says: "'. . . everything is going away from us--the end of our lives will have
nothing in it like the beginning!'" Bob stands "looking at her
with the pursuant gaze of *an intelligent dumb animal,* with perceptions more perfect than his comprehension." With the instinct of such an intelligent animal, he, like Maggie, understands how important are the roots in the past life: "I shall

niver grow down'ards again, Mr. Tom, an' you war the little chap as I liked best when *I* war a little chap, for all you leathered me, and wouldn't look at me again" (III. vi. 358-60; author's italics).

Bob also comes to know that there are better ways of making a living than frightening birds, traveling about on a barge, or ratcatching:

> "An' I thought first I'd ha' ferrets an' dogs, an' be a rat-catcher; an' then I thought as I should like a bigger way o' life, as I didn't know so well; for *I'n seen to the bottom o' rat-catching,* an' I thought, an' thought, till at last I settled I'd be a packman, for they're knowin' fellers . . . an' there'd be a use for a feller's tongue, as is no use neither wi' rats nor barges. An' I should go about the country far an' wide, an' come round the women wi' my tongue . . . lors! it 'ud be a lovely life!" [III. vi. 360-61].

It is significant that Bob sees to the bottom of ratcatching and seeks an occupation which will allow him to use all of his faculties. He has a great deal of self-knowledge. Thus he reports to Tom and Maggie what Mr. Torry said about him when he put out a mill fire: "'An' he said first, I was a sperrited chap--but I knowed that afore . . .'" (p. 360). He is, in short, too spirited a chap to find pleasure or profit in ratcatching and so directs his energies toward overcoming a powerful rather than weak adversary. And there is no more powerful adversary in St. Ogg's than the women he "comes round" with his tongue. Unlike Tom, he does not attack the weak because he feels it is his privilege to judge and punish weakness, but rather he attacks the strong who threaten his own freedom. Paradoxically then, it is in this way that he shows himself to be a product of his society, in his spirited rebellion against that society and his assertion of his rights as a human being. When Maggie reprimands him for his skillful but none too honest use of his big thumb as he measures flannel, he explains that his dog Mumps

> "doesn't mind a bit o' cheating, when it's them skinflint women, as haggle an' haggle, an' 'ud like to get their flannel for nothing, an' 'ud niver ask theirselves how I got my dinner out on't. I niver cheat anybody as doesn't want to cheat me, Miss--lors, I'm a honest chap, I am; only I must hev a bit o' sport, *an' now I don't go wi' the ferrets, I'n got no varmint to come over but them haggling women"* [IV. iii. 24-25].

One almost suspects that Bob's big thumb was nature's protective device for one of her own in a society made up of such "varmints" as "them haggling women." Bob's attacks on society are self-protective but not destructive. "'There's no law again' fleabites,'" he tells Tom (III. vi. 363).

In both deeds and words Bob criticizes the society in which he lives. Thus, for example, he tells Maggie about a dog which is "'an uncommon sensible bitch--she means more sense wi' her bark nor half the chaps can put into their talk from breakfast to sundown,'" and of a lowly pot-carrier who criticizes a mongrel for its lack of breeding, Bob says:"'. . . I can't abide to see one *cur* grinnin' at another'" (IV. iii. 23). The crux of his criticism is contained in his insistence that dogs are "better friends nor any Christian" (p. 22). As a further indication of Bob's character and a final comment from Eliot about the nature of the St. Ogg's society compared with the nature of certain animals, Bob presents his dog Mumps to Maggie when she has been rejected and left friendless: "'He's a rare company--Mumps is--he knows iverything, an' makes no bother about it. . . . You'd better let me leave him a bit; he'll get fond on you. Lors, it's a fine thing to hev *a dumb brute* fond on you; it'll stick to you, an' make no jaw'" (VI. i. 336-37).

What has been consistently and repeatedly emphasized by the pattern of animal imagery is a crucial fact in *The Mill on the Floss:* that the role which the society of St. Ogg's forces upon its conforming members is one containing elements which violate their nature as human beings. What has happened generally can be summed up by the following incidental image: "Mr. Moss, who, when he married Miss Tulliver, had been regarded as the *buck* of Basset, now . . . had the depressed, unexpectant air of a *machine-horse*" (I. viii. 120). But more specifically, what the partially suppressed meaning implies is that the men have somehow become submissively less than men and that the women have become both aggressively more and submissively less than women.

Thus when Maggie returns from Mudport, unwed and determined to remain so, she is immediately judged and sentenced by "the world's wife." For "public opinion, in these cases, is always of the feminine gender--not the world, but *the world's wife* . . . " (VII. ii. 338). God might have mercy on her, but ". . . He had not the care of Society on His hands--as the world's wife had" (p. 341). Dr. Kenn, "in attempting to open the ears of women to reason, and their consciences to justice, " finds himself "as powerless as he was aware he would have been if he had attempted to influence the shape of bonnets" (VII. iv. 361). It was not, George Eliot points out, that all of the women of St. Ogg's were devoid of any conscience or tenderness, but rather that

> until every good man is brave, we must expect to find many good women timid: too timid even to believe in the correctness of their own best promptings, when these would place them in a minority. And the men of St. Ogg's were not all brave by any means: some of them were even fond of scandal--and to an extent that might have given their conversation an effeminate character, if it had not been distinguished by masculine jokes, and by an occasional shrug of the shoulders at the mutual hatred of women. It was the general feeling of the masculine mind at St. Ogg's that women were not to be interfered with in their treatment of each other [VII. iv. 363].

And so "the masculine mind of St. Ogg's smiled pleasantly" at Dr. Kenn's attempt to help Maggie, and "the feminine mind, regarded at that period as less powerful, took a more melancholy view of the case" (p. 364).

Dr. Kenn and Bob Jakin are the only whole and brave men in St. Ogg's, for Philip--brave as he is--is ineffectual in the masculine role. By society's standard Dr. Kenn's manners are, as Stephen observes, "'rather cold and severe. There's nothing sugary or maudlin about him'" (VI. ii. 168). In spite of his nonconformity on such matters as sentiment and manners, he is finally forced to submit to the tyrannical influence of the world's wife, for in order to avoid "the appearance of evil--an 'appearance' that is always dependent on the average quality of surrounding minds" (VII. v. 373), he must either advise Maggie to leave St. Ogg's or jeopardize his position among his parishioners. He advises her to leave.

Bob Jakin, finally, remains the most able to fulfill his potentialities as a human being. In his own home, surrounded as he is by mother, wife, and infant daughter, he is clearly the unifying element. Significantly, his is the only child born during the course of the book (with the exception of the Stelling baby which is described as "sickly"), and as son, husband, and father, he fulfills the masculine role. As friend and protector, he fulfills the larger role which transcends that of sex. He is not unlike Ogg, son of Beorl, who (according to the myth of St. Ogg's) said to the pleading, suffering woman, "'I will ferry thee across: it is enough that thy heart needs it.'" Of him alone it can be said, as the Virgin said of Ogg, "'. . . thou didst not question and wrangle with the heart's need, but wast smitten with pity, and didst straightway relieve the same'" (I. xii. 174). When the disgraced and suffering Maggie comes to his home, he takes her in. The simplicity of his action when he brings the child to her room provides one of the rare moments of the book:

> Bob, closing the door behind him, came and stood before her.
> "You see, we've got a little un, Miss, and I wanted you to look at it, and take it in your arms, if you'd be so good. For we made free to name it after you, and it 'ud be better for your takin' a bit o' notice on it" [VII. i. 334].

According to the myth of St. Ogg's the Virgin blessed Ogg, who had listened to the heart's need, saying, "'And from henceforth whoso steps into thy boat shall be in no peril from the storm; and whenever it puts forth to the rescue, it shall save the lives both of men and beasts'" (I. xii. 174). It is Bob Jakin alone who does not wrangle with the heart's need, and it is his boat which miraculously puts forth upon the waters and, paradoxically, saves Maggie in the only way that she can be saved.

⚜ ⚜ ⚜ ⚜ ⚜ ⚜

A second pattern of imagery, much less pervasive and significant than the animal pattern, is important enough to warrant some examination because it emphasizes Maggie's futile search for harmony. This pattern may in general be called the garden or paradisiac imagery, although it ranges through explicit use of the garden of Eden image to general and indirect use of an idyllic or pseudoidyllic setting and concludes in a kind of enchanted pagan paradise. Here also is included a subpattern of diabolical imagery which is significant in relation to the garden imagery of Books I and II.

Analysis of the garden and diabolical imagery of the first
two books helps to throw some light on the almost universally
acknowledged weakness of the book: its conclusion. In the last
chapter of Book II, a chapter entitled "The Golden Gates Are
Passed," George Eliot makes the most specific statement relative to this image pattern. Speaking of the girlish Maggie's
promise to kiss Philip when she next saw him, the author observes: "The promise was void, like so many other sweet,
illusory promises of our childhood; void as promises made
in Eden before the seasons were divided, and when the starry
blossoms grew side by side with the ripening peach--impos-
sible to be fulfilled when *the golden gates* had been passed"
(II. vii. 278-79). At the end of this chapter when Maggie is about
to return to the stricken Tulliver household with Tom (whom
she has come to King's Lorton to bring back), she is touched
by the kindness of Mrs. Stelling, a woman she has never before
liked. The author observes that this was "the first sign within
the poor child of that new sense which is the gift of sorrow--
that susceptibility to the bare offices of humanity which raises
them into a bond of loving fellowship . . ." (p. 287). The description of the scene which immediately follows is, I believe,
intended to evoke something at least akin to (though not of the
same magnitude as) the feeling we have when we read that Adam and Eve, "hand in hand with wand'ring steps and slow, /
Through Eden took their solitary way." Unfair as it is to
George Eliot to juxtapose one of her weakest passages with one
of Milton's best, I nevertheless venture the comparison:

> The two slight youthful figures soon grew indistinct on the dis-
> tant road--were soon lost behind the projecting hedgerow.
> They had gone forth together into their new life of sorrow, and
> they would nevermore see the sunshine undimmed by remembered
> cares. They had entered the thorny wilderness, and the golden
> gates of their childhood had forever closed behind them [p. 287].

That George Eliot finds it necessary at this point to ornament
what would have been far more effective if rendered dramatically is in itself revealing. For had the reader been sufficiently
convinced of the existence of that sorrowless, Edenlike childhood, there would have been no need for such an unfortunate
presentation.

But the reader is not convinced that the gates were really

golden, or that the garden was paradisiacal. At Garum Firs,
for example, "the farmyard life was wonderful . . ." but
"there were white railings and white gates all about, and glit-
tering weathercocks of various design, and garden walks paved
with pebbles in beautiful patterns--nothing was quite common
at Garum Firs . . ." (I. ix. 128-29), or, it may be added, quite
natural. Lacking entirely is the lush, spontaneous profusion
of the Hall Farm garden in which Adam walked with Hetty.
When the children wish to play outdoors, severe restrictions
are placed upon them: ". . . Aunt Pullet gave permission,
only enjoining them not to go off the paved walks in the garden,
and if they wanted to see the poultry fed, to view them from
a distance . . ." (pp. 138-39). It was "so prim a garden"
(I. x. 148), symbolic of the oppressive restriction enforced by
society.

The fields and surrounding countryside where Maggie and
Tom play as children are less restrictive, but there are nevertheless too many disturbing elements present to give them an
Edenlike quality. The most extended passage in which we see
the two children playing happily together is worth examination.
They set off toward "the Round Pool--that wonderful pool,
which the floods had made a long while ago: no one knew how
deep it was; and it was mysterious, too, that it should be almost a perfect round, framed in with willows and tall reeds,
so that the water was only to be seen when you got close to the
brink" (I. v. 55). Now it is obviously true that the origin and
nature of this pool would be a more disturbing element to the
reader than to Tom and Maggie themselves, but the mood it
induces in Maggie as she sits "looking dreamily at the glassy
water" indicates that hers was not a sorrowless existence.
Tom is being unusually kind because Maggie has just caught
a fish.

> There was nothing to mar her delight in the whispers and the
> dreamy silences, when she listened to the light dipping sounds of
> the rising fish, and the gentle rustling, as if the willows and the
> reeds and the water had their happy whisperings also. Maggie
> thought it would make a very nice heaven to sit by the pool in
> that way, and never be scolded [p. 56].

The image of the glassy pool and the dreamy, hypnotic mood

clearly suggest Maggie's desire to escape, possibly even a
death wish. But nevertheless we are told that this

> was one of their happy mornings. They trotted along and sat down
> together, with no thought that life would ever change much for
> them: they would only get bigger and not go to school, and it
> would always be like the holidays; they would always live to-
> gether and be fond of each other. And the mill with its boom-
> ing . . . above all, the great Floss, along which they wandered
> with a sense of travel, to see the rushing spring-tide, the awful
> Eagre, come up like a hungry monster, or to see the Great Ash
> which had once wailed and groaned like a man--these things would
> always be the same to them. Tom thought people were at a dis-
> advantage who lived on any other spot of the globe; and Maggie,
> when she read about Christiana passing "the river over which
> there is no bridge," always saw the Floss between the green
> pastures by the Great Ash [pp. 56-57].

This land of childhood is a place where the "hungry monster"
does not devour and the anthropomorphic ash is merely an object of interest. That the Floss is associated in Maggie's mind
with the river of death is a fact that has more significance for
the reader than for Maggie at this time of her life. However,
since this association is made in a context which also includes
the pool image, its relevance to Maggie's state of mind should
not be completely disregarded.

The first two parts of the book, which take us up to the time
when "the golden gates" close forever behind Maggie and Tom,
actually place more emphasis on the diabolic than the paradisiac. Mr. Tulliver, to whom life is indeed a "puzzling" matter,
believed "that rats, weevils, and lawyers were created by Old
Harry. Unhappily he had no one to tell him that this was ramp-
ant Manichaeism, else he might have seen his error" (I. iii. 16).
His constant references to "Old Harry" have no doubt made
an impression on Maggie's highly imaginative mind. So indeed
have the books at her disposal, as her excited description of
a picture indicates:

> "Oh, I'll tell you what that means. It's a dreadful picture,
> isn't it? But I can't help looking at it. That old woman in the
> water's a witch--they've put her in to find out whether she's a
> witch or no, and if she swims she's a witch, and if she's drowned
> --and killed, you know--she's innocent, and not a witch, but

only a poor silly old woman. But what good would it do her then, you know, when she was drowned? Only, I suppose, she'd go to heaven, and God would make it up to her. And this dreadful blacksmith, with his arms akimbo, laughing--oh, isn't he ugly? --I'll tell you what he is. He's the Devil *really*" (here Maggie's voice became louder and more emphatic), "and not a right black-smith; for the Devil takes the shape of wicked men, and walks about and sets people doing wicked things, and he's oftener in the shape of a bad man than any other, because, you know, if people saw he was the Devil, and he roared at 'em, they'd run away, and he couldn't make 'em do what he pleased" [I. iii. 20-21, author's italics].

The story of the woman who must be drowned before her in-nocence can be proved is (like Maggie's identification of the Floss with "the river over which there is no bridge") most significant to the reader when he sees it in relation to the whole book. It indicates something of the care with which George Eliot has prepared for Maggie's drowning; and although the reader may not remember it specifically, it does, how-ever, add to the cumulative effect. But within its particular context its function is to indicate the fascination such things hold for Maggie. She "can't help looking at" the picture any more than she can keep away from the water. Even more fas-cinating to Maggie is the devil about whom she seems well in-formed, having read *Pilgrim's Progress* and Defoe's *The His-tory of the Devil*. Maggie's youthful impression of Bob Jakin is that he may perhaps be "slightly diabolical, judging from his intimacy with snakes and bats . . ." (I. vi. 67). And when she runs away to the gypsy camp in search of more harmonious surroundings than her home affords, she fears that the devil is nearby: ". . . now she was in this strange lane, she hardly dared look on one side of her, lest she should see the *diabolical blacksmith* in his leathern apron grinning at her with arms akimbo" (I. xi. 159).

Closely related to Maggie's talk of the devil and witches is her superstitious use of the fetish which she keeps hidden in her favorite retreat, the attic. Here "she fretted out all her ill humours, and talked aloud to the worm-eaten floors and the worm-eaten shelves, and the dark rafters festooned with cobwebs; and here she kept *a Fetish* which she punished for all her misfortunes. This was the trunk of a large wooden doll

. . . now entirely defaced by a long career of vicarious suffering. Three nails driven into the head commemorated as many crises in Maggie's nine years of earthly struggle . . ." (I. iv. 37). Maggie's punishment of her fetish should, I believe, come quite naturally to the reader's mind when, much later, he comes upon a previously discussed statement: "A vigorous superstition, that lashes its gods or lashes its own back, seems to be more congruous with the mystery of the human lot, than the mental condition of these emmet-like Dodsons and Tullivers."

The point, then, to be made about the garden imagery of Book I--or the lack of it--and the subpattern of diabolical imagery is this: it *is* far more congruous with the human condition that the childhood of Maggie and Tom be presented as it is, full of restrictions, frustrations, and pain, as well as happiness and joy, than that we be convinced of the unadulterated Edenlike quality of their childhood. For if we were convinced of that, we should find the remainder of the book completely unconvincing. Much of the power of *The Mill* (some critics would say all of it) derives from a presentation which does not exclude "these bitter sorrows of childhood! when sorrow is all new and strange, when hope has not yet got wings to fly beyond the days and weeks, and the space from summer to summer seems measureless" (I. v. 50). This is the reason that I consider the concluding sentence of the flood scene sentimental: ". . . brother and sister had gone down in an embrace never to be parted: living through again in one supreme moment the days when they had clasped their little hands in love, and roamed the daisied fields together." The reader has been too poignantly made aware of the sorrow and pain of childhood to believe that these daisied fields were worth returning to. Had they constituted a paradise for Maggie, she would hardly have found it necessary to leave the farmyard at Garum Firs in search of "her unknown kindred, the gypsies," an action which "seemed to her the only way of escaping opprobrium and being entirely *in harmony* with circumstances . . ." (I. xi. 159, 155).[6]

After the period of childhood is over, Maggie discovers a partial harmony in the idyllic setting of the Red Deeps. Although there is no direct image which identifies it with the earlier garden imagery, the description suggests something of the garden quality: ". . . she could sit on a grassy hollow under the shadow of a branching ash, stooping aslant from the steep above her, and listen to the hum of insects, like tiniest bells on the garment of Silence, or see the sunlight piercing the distant boughs, as if to chase and drive home the truant[7] heavenly blue of the wild hyacinths" (V.i.45-46). Once more the author shows us a harmony which has been achieved through exclusion. The Red Deeps is a place of concealment--a hollow shadowed by the ash tree--and to conceal her actions (it is here that she secretly meets Philip) is not in accord with Maggie's nature.

More specific garden imagery recurs significantly in Book VI, which is entitled "The Great Temptation." In chapter i, "A Duet in Paradise," Lucy and Stephen sing "The Creation," and Stephen says of Philip, who does not like this composition, that "he is *the fallen Adam* with a soured temper." Of Lucy and himself he says: "we are *Adam and Eve unfallen, in Paradise"* (p. 150). But there is a decided note of falseness about this paradise. George Eliot leads the reader to suspect that if Stephen is the unfallen Adam it is because he is too unenergetic and uncaring to have become involved in life's struggles. She notes his air of "supercilious indifference" when he comments that he only knows "half of the names and faces in the neighbourhood in that detached, disjointed way" (p. 146). Speaking casually of an important business action of Tom's which had saved the firm of Guest and Deane a great deal of money, Stephen is unable to recall the details because, as he says, he "was rather drowsy at the time" (p. 149). Lucy playfully tells him:"'. . . I shall not respect an Adam who drags the *tempo,* as you will'" (p. 150), but remarks, "'You do the 'heavy beasts' to perfection'" (p. 151). This air of heavy languor, lack of desire, and will-lessness can hardly be said to describe the ideal state of unfallen man. It defines a state of slavery rather than of Christian liberty, for Stephen--as previously discussed--is enslaved by the role which he is expected to play. He and Lucy temporarily assume the role of the unfallen Adam and Eve, but they are only play acting.

Such is the state of affairs when, after a long period of renunciation and self-imposed exile, Maggie appears as a visitor in her cousin's home. And with her entrance a new element appears in the paradisiacal imagery. Although the Christian overtones of the temptation are retained, what George Eliot now presents is a kind of pagan paradise. There is now a fairy-tale quality, a state of languorous enchantment induced by Lucy's fairy wand: "'I am having a great holiday, am I not?' said Maggie. 'Lucy is like a *fairy godmother:* she has turned me from a *drudge* into a *princess* in no time. I do nothing but indulge myself all day long, and she always finds out what I want before I know it myself'" (VI. vii. 218). Prior to this observation Lucy has said of Maggie: ". . . I want her to have *delicious do-nothing days,* filled with boating, and chatting, and riding, and driving: that is the holiday she needs" (VI. ii. 170-71). Turned "from a drudge into a princess," Maggie, as we shall soon see, is once more metamorphosed and held in a kind of captive state which is unnatural for her. Lucy's romantic nature has been previously noted in connection with the tender care she gives her horse, significantly named Sinbad, and the other members of "her menagerie." Unlike Tom, who does not like "poetry and fairy-tales" (VI. vii. 217), she sees everything in terms of fairy tale and tries to make events fit the pattern. Speaking to Maggie of Maggie's relationship with Philip she says:

> "I can't help being hopeful about it. There is something romantic in it--out of the common way--just what everything that happens to you ought to be. And Philip will adore you like a husband *in a fairy-tale.* Oh, I shall puzzle my small brain to contrive some small plot that will bring everybody into the right mind, so that you may marry Philip. . . . Wouldn't that be a pretty ending to all my poor, poor Maggie's troubles?" [VI. iii. 181].

Lucy's "aerial" quality is constantly emphasized by reference to the slightness of her figure, which is "quite subordinate to her faultless drapery of silk and crape" (VI. ii. 157). Also emphasized is her desire to arrange people and to issue gracious commands: "'. . . come and sit down here,' she went on [speaking to Philip], placing a chair that would suit him best, 'and you shall find yourself treated mercifully'" (VI. vii. 217-18).

The connection between these observations and what has already been stated about Lucy's tender care of her "menagerie" should be obvious. It indicates the way in which one pattern of imagery supports and complements another. This fairyland which is to a certain extent both created and governed by Lucy is, then, a kind of pagan paradise in which once more the appearance of harmony is momentarily secured by the exclusion of discordant elements. It is filled with music, with "sunshine falling on the rich clumps of spring flowers, " with "sweet fresh garden scent" and birds "flitting and alighting, gurgling and singing" (VI. ii. 160). And in it Maggie, hungry for life after long years of dull privation, feels "the half-remote presence of a world of love and beauty and delight, made up of vague, mingled images from all the poetry and romance she had ever read, or had ever woven in her dreamy reveries" (VI. iii. 177). It is a "brighter aerial world" which fills her with sensuous pleasure and a feeling of luxurious ease:"'Life seems to go on without effort, when I am filled with music,'" Maggie tells Lucy (pp. 177, 178).

But "this new sense of leisure and unchecked enjoyment amidst the soft-breathing airs and garden-scents of advancing spring" has an "intoxicating" effect on Maggie (VI. vi. 202). So too does the gentle and inviting voice of Stephen:"'Won't you come out a little way into the garden?'" (p. 212). As this "dim, dreamy state" of intoxication deepens, Maggie comes to sense the unreality of the world in which she now moves. The following passage is an objectification of her state of mind when she walks in the conservatory with Stephen:"'How *strange* and *unreal* the trees and flowers look with the lights among them!' said Maggie in a low voice. 'They look as if they belonged to *an enchanted land,* and would never fade away:--I could fancy they were all made of jewels'" (VI. x. 263). Thus she indicates both her desire to crystallize the beauty of the moment and her awareness that it is an "unreal" and "enchanted land" in which she finds herself. The enchantment, however, is not to remain undisturbed for long, and, soon, as the title of the chapter indicates, "The Spell Seems Broken. " For as Maggie sits alone in the garden Philip enters. Now for the first time made fully aware that her love for Stephen must be disavowed, Maggie "felt as if the enchanted cup had been dashed to the ground" (VI. x. 268). But the spell merely *seemed* to be broken and the "quiescent time" which Maggie spends at the Moss

farm is short. ". . . over the old garden-wall the straggling
rosebushes were beginning to toss their summer weight" and
there is an air of peaceful reality about the scene at the Moss
farm when Stephen arrives to declare his love for Maggie
(VI. xi. 269). Once more the temporary harmony of Maggie's
life is shattered. And two chapters later, she is once more
"being led down the garden among the roses, *being helped*
with firm tender care into the boat . . . all by this stronger
presence that seemed to bear her along *without any act of her
own will* . . ." (VI. xiii. 299).

Some general conclusions may be made about George Eliot's
use of the garden or paradisiac imagery as it ranges from the
Biblical with explicit references to the garden of Eden to the
less direct and non-Biblical. Although the appearance of harmony may have been temporarily established in an idyllic setting, that harmony is always threatened, either by something
within it or by elements which it has excluded. Sooner or later
the real world outside encroaches, urging Maggie further in
her search for the "clue of life. " However, in the enchanted
world where she meets Stephen--and it is a world which seems
to promise a greater happiness than Maggie has ever before
known--she is held fixed in a state of will-lessness which
causes her to drift into the crucial situation of the book. The
luxurious sense of ease, the "delicious do-nothing days, " the
abundance of music and soft garden scents--all a part of the
idyllic setting--create in her a state of languor and passivity
which makes her receptive to Stephen's first admiring glances.
It is at this point in the book that the drifting imagery gradually
begins to appear in much the same way that George Eliot used
it in *Adam Bede* to indicate what happened to Arthur and Hetty.
The enchanted paradise, then, helps to establish a new pattern
of imagery. This pattern, since it helps to define movement,
will be dealt with in the following chapter.

6. *The Mill on the Floss:*
The Antithetical Movements

EVEN IN many of its earliest occurrences, the drifting imagery in *The Mill on the Floss* is derived from a more concrete source than in *Adam Bede.* There is of course the overflowing Willow Brook in *Adam Bede,* but it does not figure so prominently as the Floss, whose presence makes itself felt throughout the whole of *The Mill.* The point is not that there is either more or less or better drifting imagery in one book or the other, but rather that its more literal source in *The Mill* makes it more readily perceivable here and consequently much less in need of detailed analysis.

The actual and obviously symbolic act of drifting down the river is prepared for by Maggie's state of being which has been previously discussed, but it is also anticipated by use of metaphor. For example, Maggie, listening to Stephen singing, is "borne along by a wave too strong for her" (VI. vii. 228). During one of her desperate moments Maggie sees Dr. Kenn's face looking at her, "that plain middle-aged face, with a grave, penetrating kindness in it, seeming to tell of a human being who had reached a firm, safe strand, but was looking with helpful pity towards the strugglers still *tossed by the waves* . . ." (VI. ix. 254). Maggie feels as if she is "sliding downwards in a nightmare" (VI. xi. 273) and that she must "beat and struggle against this *current,* soft and yet strong as the summer stream" (p. 275). Philip has a dream in which "he fancied Maggie was *slipping* down a glistening, green, slimy channel of a *waterfall* . . ." (VI. viii. 242). Images such as this indicate Maggie's sometimes passive, sometimes tortured state of mind, her transient awareness of what is happening to her, and a similar awareness on the part of Dr. Kenn and Philip. They help to prepare the reader either consciously or subconsciously for the flood scene, and they lead quite naturally into the scene of Maggie's boat trip down the river with Stephen.

The boat trip itself (VI. viii) serves several functions. The quiet passive serenity induced by the smooth gliding of the boat and their nearness to each other, the "enchanted haze" in which Stephen and Maggie's love envelops them, provides a sharp contrast to the tortured struggle which is to follow. To the reader, who is outside the enchanted haze, this tranquil part of the trip gives a poignant sense of the transitory beauty of their relationship. But it also symbolizes their subconscious desire to escape coming to terms with their responsibility to ties which bind them morally, and furthermore to escape by drifting rather than by making a definite choice which would constitute an acknowledgment of their moral responsibility.

Stephen, however, is aware on a literal level that they are drifting, more so than Maggie who is "only dimly conscious." But to Stephen who has been rowing "idly, half automatically" it seems that all things conspire to help them along. The boat moves so rapidly, "helped by the backward-flowing tide," that finally Stephen "ceased to row, laid down the oars, folded his arms, and looked down on the water as if watching the pace at which the boat glided without his help. This sudden change roused Maggie." When the hard fact of what has happened does break through her dreamy state, she, unlike Stephen, recognizes its fuller significance and becomes alarmed. Stephen attempts to soothe her by his interpretation of the situation:

> *"See,* Maggie, how everything has come without our seeking--
> in spite of all our efforts. We never thought of being alone to-
> gether again: *it has all been done by others. See how the tide is
> carrying us out*--away from all those unnatural bonds that we
> have been trying to make faster round us--and trying in vain.
> . . . It is the only right thing, dearest: it is the only way of es-
> caping from this wretched entanglement. Everything has con-
> curred to point it out to us. We have contrived nothing, we have
> thought of nothing ourselves" [VI. xiii. 301].

In a man of less intelligence and learning such reading of
events as omens and signs would be pure superstition. In
Stephen, however, it can hardly be anything but rationalization.
It is true that Stephen and Maggie had no control over the
events--Philip's illness and Lucy's calculated absence--which
placed them alone together, but it is equally true that they did
not choose to cancel the boat trip and separate. For at the
moment they entered the boat they were incapable of such
choice: Maggie had submitted to a "stronger presence that
seemed to bear her along without any act of her own will," and
Stephen had voiced their common thought: "we shall not be long
together." Furthermore, what now seems to Stephen a benevo-
lent and designing tide is the same tide that had been carefully
considered before the trip. The "unnatural bonds" which Stephen here uses to his own advantage in his persuasion of Maggie are quite distinctly not the same as the bonds which the St.
Ogg's society has too narrowly imposed on its members. For
these bonds he speaks of are the moral ties derived from a
profound sense of human responsibility within a society.

It is Maggie's most earnest desire to believe Stephen's
rationale, but her own moral nature indignantly asserts itself:

> Maggie listened--passing from her startled wonderment to the
> yearning after that belief *that the tide was doing it* all--that she
> might *glide* along with the swift, silent stream, and not struggle
> any more. But across that stealing influence came the terrible
> shadow of past thoughts; and the sudden horror lest now, at last,
> the moment of *final intoxication* was close upon her, called up
> feelings of angry resistance towards Stephen.
> "Let me go!" she said, in an agitated tone, flashing an indig-
> nant look at him, and trying to get her hands free. "You have
> wanted *to deprive me of any choice*. You knew we were come
> too far--you have dared to take advantage of my thoughtlessness.
> It is unmanly to bring me into such a position" [pp. 301-2].

Stephen's response--"I didn't notice that we had passed Luck-
reth till we had got to the next village; and then it came into
my mind that we would go on"--indicates that he has been as
incapable of choice as Maggie, that he too has been drifting
in the symbolic sense. The unfairness of Maggie's response
in blaming Stephen for taking advantage of what even then she
recognizes as her own "thoughtlessness" soon becomes known

to her. And her feeling for him during his time of self-re-
proach and suffering immediately causes her to fall temporarily into an even more dangerous state: "This yielding to the idea
of Stephen's suffering was more fatal than the other yielding,
because it was less distinguishable from that sense of others'
claims which was the moral basis for her resistance" (p. 303).
Now with a partial awareness that she is drifting both in a
literal and metaphorical sense, Maggie does or says nothing
that will change the course of the boat: "They *glided* along in
this way, both resting in that silence as in a haven. . . ."
And Maggie is "hardly conscious of having said or done anything decisive. All *yielding* is attended with a less vivid consciousness than resistance; it is the *partial sleep of thought;*
it is the *submergence of our own personality by another.* Every
influence tended to *lull* her into *acquiescence* . . ." (p. 304).
No statement could be more explicit than this in defining the
nature of moral drifting as the term is used throughout this
entire study. Such a moment of complete will-lessness in
George Eliot's characters is usually the moment at which
vision is most clouded by illusion. It is a time of moral crisis
after which the character may seek to dispel the illusion and
thereby arrive at clearer vision, or may, like Arthur in *Adam
Bede,* see the first wrong in the guise of the only possible
right, and thereby move further away from clear vision.

In a passage indicating the effects which such moral drifting
produces, George Eliot shows the nature of Maggie's vision
at this critical moment. Maggie dreams of a life

in which affection would no longer be self-sacrifice. Stephen's
passionate words made the *vision* of such a life more fully present to her than it had ever been before; and the *vision* for the
time excluded all realities--all except the returning *sun-gleams*
which broke out on the waters as the *evening approached,* and
mingled with the *visionary sunlight* of promised happiness--all
except the hand that pressed hers. . . .

. . . It was still early, when the fatigues of the day brought
on a drowsy longing for perfect rest, and she laid down her head,
looking at the faint dying flush in the west, where the one *golden
lamp* was getting *brighter* and *brighter.* . . . Behind all the delicious *visions* of these last hours, which had flowed over her
like a *soft stream,* and made her *entirely passive,* there was
the *dim consciousness* that the condition was a transient one, and

that the morrow must bring back the old life of struggle--that
there were thoughts which would presently avenge themselves
for this oblivion. But now *nothing was distinct* to her: she was
being lulled to sleep with that soft *stream* still flowing over her,
with those *delicious visions* melting and fading like the wondrous
aerial land of the west . . . [pp. 307-8].

Here is a merging of several elements which were present
in *Adam Bede* and which, up to this point, have not been so
obviously present in *The Mill*. The pattern is clearly repeti-
tive. It is evening, and the sunlight, as it mingles with "the
visionary sunlight of promised happiness" conceals and distorts reality. Nothing is "distinct, " not even "those delicious
visions"; for they are constantly "melting and fading, " flowing
over Maggie "like a soft stream. " This is a completely passive
time, but the passivity is that which is occasioned by illusion
rather than that which is the natural aftermath of a hard battle
fought and won. Maggie's vision at this point is of the same
order as Hetty's when she fancies herself a lady in fine cloth-
ing. Hetty's daydream indicates her vanity, whereas Maggie's
indicates her desire for a love that is not self-sacrificing,
but both are clearly daydreams which exclude a realistic view
of things. It has been previously pointed out that in George
Eliot's novels such times of greatest moral incapacity and loss
of vision occur in the late afternoon or evening and that they
are followed by the cold hard dawn of reality. Therefore to the
careful reader of *Adam Bede* it should be no surprise that this
scene ends a chapter entitled "Borne Along by the Tide" and
that the next chapter is entitled "Waking. "[1] Here, then, the
pattern of drifting imagery ends, for although Maggie must
still undergo temptation and is still to be swept along by a
greater tide, she no longer drifts in the moral sense.

In the preceding analysis of *Adam Bede* the drifting imagery
pointed up what has been called the negative movement of the
book, the movement away from vision. In *The Mill*, however,
that negative movement away from vision is a far subtler thing
which must be seen in the larger outlines of the book. I have
said that in this book that movement is a slow process of moral
involution, the retrograde development of a whole society.
One key metaphor, however, connects it with the image pattern
just discussed. It should be recalled once more that the people

of St. Ogg's are compared with the inhabitants along the Rhone, "that swift river [which] once rose, like an angry destroying god, *sweeping down* the feeble generations whose breath is in their nostrils . . ." (see my analysis pp. 74-79 above). These people, George Eliot says, are "part of a gross sum of obscure vitality, that will be *swept* into the same oblivion with the generation of ants and beavers." In other words, these "emmet-like Dodsons and Tullivers" who are drifting (the term here is my own) away from those human concerns which give life its fullest significance would eventually after several generations be caught in a swift tide that would destroy them as full human beings, unless, of course, they should become aware of their condition and make a radical change in it. Tom's drowning may be said to foreshadow the eventuality of that symbolic drowning. On this level of interpretation, Maggie's drowning may be considered symbolic of the waste involved, of the total destruction to which this way of life is leading.

The reason that I consider Tom to be the farthest extension of the movement away from vision is that in his rejection of Maggie he moves outside the morality of the St. Ogg's society in a direction which takes him away from its most positive elements. It is true that "the religion of the Dodsons consisted in revering whatever was customary and respectable. . . . The Dodsons were a very proud race, and their pride lay in the utter frustration of all desire to tax them with a breach of traditional duty or propriety" (IV.i.7). But it is also true that "the right thing must always be done toward kindred" (p. 8). Mrs. Glegg, the hardest and most severe of all the Dodson women, illustrates what "the right thing" is by her attitude toward Maggie. Learning of Maggie's return and Tom's rejection of her, Mrs. Glegg

> burst forth in severe reproof of Tom for admitting the worst of his sister until he was compelled. If you were not to stand by your 'kin' as long as there was a shred of honour attributable to them, pray what were you to stand by? . . . The circumstances were unprecedented in Mrs. Glegg's experience--nothing of that kind had ever happened among the Dodsons before; but it was a case in which her hereditary rectitude and personal strength of character found a common channel with her fundamental ideas of clanship, as they did in her lifelong regard to equity in money matters [VI.iii.351-52].

Other characters in the novel indicate the significance of
kinship as a part of the morality of the society. For the weak,
dull-witted Mrs. Tulliver "the only thing clear . . . was the
mother's instinct, that she would go with her unhappy child. "
Frightened as she is, she responds immediately to Maggie's
need: "My child! I'll go with you. You've got a mother" (VII.i.
331). But kinship is important not only to the Dodsons. Mr.
Tulliver, in spite of financial pressures and his disapproval
of his brother-in-law, takes care of his sister. And Wakem,
when he understands Philip's feeling for Maggie, sacrifices
his personal pride in order to give his son a chance for happiness. Furthermore, although it is never stated explicitly in
the novel, Wakem's peculiar interest in young Jetsome, whom
he places in charge of the mill, leads us to believe that he is
taking care of his illegitimate son. If this assumption is true
it provides some reasonable basis for interesting speculation
about the symbolic meaning of the flood.

After Mr. Tulliver loses the mill he considers what it will
mean to him if he refuses to stay on as manager under Wakem.
Discussing it with Luke, he comments: "There's a story as
when the mill changes hands, the river's angry--I've heard
my father say it many a time" (III.ix.397). Somewhat earlier
Mrs. Tulliver has told Wakem: ". . . they *do* say it's always
unlucky when Dorlcote Mill changes hands, and the water might
run away . . . " (III.vii.376, author's italics). In the light of
this superstition, it may be worth noting that the river becomes
angry not when young Jetsome is managing it for Wakem, but
rather when Tom takes it over, for in one sense it has undergone a more radical change of hands under Tom's management.
At the beginning of the last book George Eliot tells us that Tom,
in becoming master of Dorlcote Mill, "had *half*-fulfilled his
father's dying wish. " But she leaves it to the reader to recall that the other half of Mr. Tulliver's wish was that Tom
take care of Maggie: ". . . you must be good to her, my lad.
I was good to *my* sister" (V.vii.137, author's italics). In
turning Maggie away from her old home at the mill, Tom
violates his father's dying wish. And what in terms of the
whole novel is even more important, he violates the moral
code of his society by putting personal pride before clanship.
That his need to reinstate the family name becomes a thing

of personal pride is a logical extension of one element in the code, but it contradicts a more important element. Mrs. Glegg reaffirms the positive value of that code by her acceptance of Maggie, but in Tom she "found a stronger nature than her own--a nature in which family feeling had lost the character of clanship by taking on a doubly deep dye of personal pride" (VII. iii. 353). Thus when Tom takes over, the mill has changed from the hands of one who adhered to the best in St. Ogg's code to one who has established a narrower code. Whether or not it is a part of the author's conscious design, it seems to be of symbolic import that the river becomes angry at this particular time.

That Tom is lacking in clear vision has been substantially indicated throughout the novel. One important difference between Tom and Maggie is pointed up very early by their childish chatter:

> "Oh how brave you are, Tom! I think you're like Samson. If there came a lion roaring at me, I think you'd fight him--wouldn't you Tom?"
> "How can a lion come roaring at you, you silly thing? There's no lions, only in the shows."
> "No; but if we were in the lion countries--I mean in Africa, where it's very hot--the lions eat people there. I can show it to you in the book where I read it" [I. v. 47].[9]

Maggie's active imagination feeds on whatever it can find, but Tom's literal mind dismisses the subject in disdain. "But the lion *isn't* coming. What's the use of talking?" (author's italics). Tom, as the author pointedly indicates elsewhere, has "very *clear prosaic eyes,* not apt to be *dimmed by mists of feeling or imagination*" (IV. ii. 12). That he is capable of seeing only what is immediately and concretely before him does prevent him from making some of the errors which Maggie makes, and his knowledge that he is always right gives him a kind of strength. However, this strength in which Tom takes great pride is the same kind which Adam recognized as a grave fault in himself. It causes Maggie to have "an awe of him, against which she struggled as something unfair to *her consciousness of wider thoughts and deeper motives;* but it was of no use to struggle. A character at unity with itself--that performs what it intends, subdues every counteracting impulse, and has *no visions* beyond the distinctly possible--is strong by its very negations" (V.ii.63). To a certain extent Tom is typical of the St. Ogg's society in that he achieves his inner "unity" by negating or excluding that which is beyond his perception. What is excluded, however, is an essential element in clear vision: he lacks the capacity to sympathize with and forgive the shortcomings of others and he fails to recognize that lack as a shortcoming in himself. Thus in one of her most vehement outbursts against him, Maggie says:

> You have always enjoyed punishing me--you have always been hard and cruel to me: even when I was a little girl, and always loved you better than anyone else in the world, you would let me go crying to bed without forgiving me. You have no pity: you have no sense of your own imperfection and your own sins. It is a sin to be hard; it is not fitting for a mortal--for a Christian. You are nothing but a Pharisee. You thank God for nothing but your own virtues--you think they are great enough to win you everything else. You have not even *a vision* of feelings by the side of which your shining virtues are *mere darkness!* [V.v. 119-20].

Tom has not even *a* vision, that is, one view, of those higher feelings which must be present if one is to have vision. Thus he is completely unequipped to deal fairly with Maggie when she, to all appearances, brings disgrace upon the family: ". . . he judged by what he had been able to see; and the judgement was painful enough to himself. He thought he had the demonstration of the facts observed through years by his own *eyes which gave no warning of their imperfection*, that Maggie's nature was utterly untrustworthy . . ." (VII.iii.352-53). Mrs. Glegg, the matriarch of the Dodson clan who has had a similar set of facts and whose early disapproval of Maggie has been established in much detail, is able to reserve judgment. Tom cannot. He has less sympathy and pity for others than for himself, less feeling of kinship than of personal pride. It is in this sense that he, as a member of the younger generation of Dodsons and Tullivers, represents the farthest extension of the negative movement of the St. Ogg's society, the movement away from moral vision.

❋ ❋ ❋ ❋ ❋ ❋

The positive movement of the book is of course represented by Maggie but also to a certain extent by Philip. His letter to Maggie is all that need be considered here. Speaking of the suffering he had undergone the night before Maggie and Stephen's boat trip when he had become convinced of Maggie's love for Stephen, he asks: ". . . I had never been resigned even to the mediocrity of my powers: how could I be resigned to the loss of the one thing which had ever come to me on earth, with the promise of such deep joy . . . the promise of another self . . . ?" Paradoxically, however, it is loss of Maggie and the recognition that she is capable of placing concern for others above concern for herself that gives Philip that other and new self. It is a self now capable of accepting its limitations with true resignation. It is, he writes Maggie, a "new life" into which he has entered:

> . . . in knowing you, in loving you, I have had, and still have, what reconciles me to life. You have been to my affections what light, what colour is to my eyes--what music is to the inward ear; you have raised a *dim unrest* into a *vivid consciousness*. The new life I have found in caring for your joy and sorrow more than for what is directly my own has transformed the spirit of rebellious murmuring into that willing endurance which is the *birth of strong sympathy*. I think nothing but such complete and intense love could have initiated me into that *enlarged* life. . . . I even think sometimes that this gift of transferred life which has come to me in loving you, may be a *new power* to me [VII. iii. 358-59].

There is no author's comment accompanying this letter, nor does Philip himself say that he has arrived at clearer vision. Yet the "birth of strong sympathy, " the coming of "vivid consciousness, " the initiation into an "enlarged life, " all clearly indicate moral growth. And the "new power" which Philip feels may be present in him is the result of enlarged vision.

Something of the nature of Maggie's way of looking at things has already been briefly indicated. Unlike Tom, whose eyes are "not apt to be dimmed by mists of feeling or imagination, " Maggie as a little girl is often occupied with "refashioning

her little world into just what she should like it to be" (I. vi. 68),
and at that time "her thoughts generally were the oddest mixture of *clear-eyed acumen* and *blind dreams*" (I. xi. 167). The
mists of feeling and imagination often keep her from seeing
clearly, as on the occasion of the hair cutting, but they also
help her to see the larger implications of her actions:

> She *could see clearly* enough, now the thing was done, that it
> was very foolish, and that she should have to hear and think
> more about her hair than ever; for Maggie rushed to her deeds
> with passionate impulse, and then *saw* not only the consequences,
> but what would have happened if they had not been done, with all
> the detail and exaggerated circumstance of *an active imagina-
> tion* [I. vii. 93].

The very act of cutting her hair, although its symbolical implications go much further to indicate her rebellion against
Dodson womanhood, is clearly intended to symbolize her desire to see better. It should be recalled that her characteristic,
childish action--one which heightens her resemblance to a
Shetland pony--is tossing her heavy hair out of her "gleaming
black eyes. " The following description of her during an intensely thoughtful moment crystallizes the image: "Maggie
drew a long breath and pushed her heavy hair back, as if to
see a sudden *vision* more clearly" (IV. iii. 33). Granted that
any presentation of a central character will usually include
a careful description of the eyes, nevertheless there is so
much emphasis on Maggie's eyes that we must concede its
symbolic value. Even Wakem, for example, remarks that
Maggie has "deuced fine eyes" (VI. viii. 243), and Bob Jakin
tells his mother that Maggie has "such uncommon eyes, they
looked somehow as they made him feel nohow" (III. vi. 362).
Philip wishes that he had "a sister with dark eyes" like Maggie's. "They're not like any other eyes, " he tells her. "They
seem trying to speak--trying to speak kindly. I don't like other
people to look at me much, but I like you to look at me, Maggie" (II. vi. 276). Thus he implies that Maggie's eyes are capable of penetrating his misshapen exterior in order to see the
real human being.

It was sometimes Maggie's custom as a child to avoid the
harsh cruelties of life by escaping into a dream world which
her active imagination created for her. Throughout the first

three books of the novel there is considerable emphasis on
Maggie's imaginative faculty and the daydreams which she
fashions, but the vision imagery here is less concrete than
in *Adam Bede.* After the hard experiences occasioned by her
father's bankruptcy, however, Maggie feels the need to search
for some more positive way of living in the world. Chapter iii
of Book IV marks the beginning of her mature search for a
clearer vision of the moral life. The few school books which
have been left her have now become "mere bran."

> Sometimes Maggie thought she could have been contented with
> absorbing fancies; if she could have had all Scott's novels and
> all Byron's poems!--then, perhaps, she might have found hap-
> piness enough to *dull her sensibility* to her actual daily life. And
> yet--they were hardly what she wanted. She could make dream-
> worlds of her own--but no *dreamworld* would satisfy her now.
> She wanted some explanation of this hard, *real* life . . . [IV.iii.
> 26-27].

One afternoon she sits in the sunlight, her dark eyes wandering
from her book; ". . . but they did not seem to be enjoying the
sunshine which pierced the screen of jasmine . . . and threw
leafy shadows on her pale round cheek; they seemed rather to
be searching for something that was not disclosed by the sunshine" (p. 19). It is at this moment that Bob Jakin brings her
a box of books to replace the lost library which his intuition
tells him has had great meaning for Maggie, another example
of his ability to listen to the heart's need. Among them is a
well worn volume by Thomas à Kempis, whose voice questions
Maggie: "why dost thou here *gaze* about, since this is not the
place of thy rest? In heaven ought to be thy dwelling, and all
earthly things are *to be looked* on as they forward thy journey
thither." At this point Maggie thrusts back her hair "as if to
see a sudden vision more clearly." The secret of life, she
believes, is revealed to her:

> . . . here was insight, and strength, and conquest, to be won
> by means entirely within her own soul. . . . It *flashed* through
> her like the suddenly apprehended solution of a problem, that all
> the miseries of her young life had come from fixing her heart
> on her own pleasure, as if that were the central necessity of the
> universe; and for the first time she saw the possibility of shifting
> the position from which she looked at the gratification of her own

desires--of taking her stand out of herself, and *looking at her own life* as an insignificant part of a divinely-guided whole. . . . With all the hurry of an *imagination* that could never rest in the present, she sat in the *deepening twilight* forming plans of self-humiliation and entire devotedness; and in the ardor of first discovery, renunciation seemed to her the entrance into that satisfaction which she had so long been craving in vain [IV.iii.33-35].

But this, it should be noted, is a vision which comes to Maggie as she sits in the afternoon sunlight, and the "deepening twilight" soon falls upon it. Not much attention is given to these details, but they are thoroughly consistent with the pattern George Eliot has established. Maggie has not yet understood the deepest meaning of renunciation. That meaning is to be revealed to her on the morning of her symbolic "waking" after she and Stephen have allowed themselves to be borne along by the tide.

It is at this point in the narrative, the chapter entitled "Waking, " that Maggie's movement toward moral vision gathers momentum. This is not to say that she has previously made no moral progress but rather that having undergone severe temptation she is now ready to gain "the insight that comes from a hardly-earned estimate of temptation. " The symbolic implications of the waking scene will be familiar to the reader of *Adam Bede,* for the pattern is the same. It is the morning after Maggie had gone to sleep lulled by illusory visions; it is, in fact, daybreak. The waking is marked by stages which may be said to symbolize Maggie's life. From deep sleep she moves into a state of vivid dreaming, then to a "false waking" and finally to full consciousness, "to the real waking" under "the awful starlit sky" of dawn. "There was a moment of utter bewilderment before her mind could get disentangled from the confused web of dreams; but soon the whole terrible truth urged itself upon her" (VI.xiv.309-10). She now realizes that the life she dreamed of with Stephen "could have no sacredness" because it would violate the principle of life for which she has been searching and which is now revealed to her. The truth she discovers is that renunciation is really the "clue of life" which she has sought but which she has rejected because she did not know its deepest meaning. For renunciation, she learns, is not an escape into a peaceful state where desire does not enter because the sensibilities have been dulled; rather it is a profound acceptance of pain and sorrow. That she has failed to understand this clue before she has committed "the irrevocable wrong" of bringing sorrow to those who trust her will, she believes, render it ineffectual as a guide for her future life:

> . . . she must forever *sink* and *wander vaguely,* driven by uncertain impulse; for she had let go the clue of life--that clue which once in the far-off years her young need had *clutched* so strongly. She had renounced all delights then, before she knew them, before they had come within her reach. Philip had been right when he told her that she knew nothing of renunciation: she had thought it was quiet ecstasy; she *saw it face to face* now--that sad patient loving strength which holds the clue of life--and *saw* that the thorns were forever pressing on its brow. The yesterday, which could never be revoked--if she could have changed it now for any length of inward silent endurance, she would have bowed beneath that cross with a sense of rest.
>
> *Daybreak came* and the reddening eastern light, while her past life was grasping her in this way, with *that tightening clutch* which comes in the last moments of possible rescue [pp. 310-11].

This, I believe, can legitimately be called an intense moment of vision. There is even a definite indication that the revelation of truth is accompanied by a visual image of the crucified Christ. The experience itself is intentionally suggestive of the moment of drowning. Maggie realizes that she has let go of what she once clutched blindly and that consequently she must forever drift, "forever sink and wander vaguely." And yet there is "that tightening clutch" of her past life which attempts to rescue her. It does not, as the reader knows, prevent her eventual drowning, but it does rescue her in a larger sense.

When Stephen awakens, he tells Maggie that they have both been "rescued from a mistake" (p. 318), that whatever had bound them to Lucy and Philip was unnatural, that "the right course is no longer what it was before" because, as he argues, "you *are* mine now--the world believes it--duty must spring out of that now . . ." (p. 321, author's italics). But that duty must derive from what the world believes, from what society demands in opposition to the demands of the individual conscience, is wholly unacceptable to Maggie. So too is the idea

that their feeling for each other should be placed above other
considerations: ". . . I *see,* if we judged in that way, there
would be a warrant for all treachery and cruelty--we should
justify breaking the most sacred ties that can ever be formed
on earth. If the past is not to bind us, where can duty lie?"
(pp. 316-17). What does tempt her and threaten to blind her
vision is the idea of Stephen's suffering: "A great terror was
upon her, as if she were ever and anon *seeing where she stood
by great flashes of lightning,* and then again stretched forth
her hands in the *darkness"* (pp. 319-20). She knows that once
she lets go of her belief she "should have no *light* through the
darkness of life." Although Stephen tells her, "You_*see* nothing as it really is, " she insists on the validity of her vision:
"Yes, I do. . . . oh, *some* good will come by clinging to the
right" (p. 322, author's italics). Thus the "tightening clutch"
of the past strengthens her moral vision.

Something of the good which came out of Maggie's clinging
to the right has been indicated by Philip's letter. Something
more is indicated by Lucy's visit to Maggie in the little room
at Bob Jaken's, where she has taken refuge. Brooding on the
image of Lucy's face, Maggie "sat *without candle* in the *twilight,* with the *window wide open* towards the river. . . . Seated on a chair against the window, with her arm on the window-
sill, she was *looking blankly* at the flowing river, swift with
the backward-rushing tide--*struggling to see* still the sweet
face in its unreproaching sadness . . ." (VII. iv. 367). The
details of this scene are suggestive of those which describe
Dinah when she sits by the window in her bedchamber thinking
of the suffering of others. Maggie, like Dinah, is without a
candle because she is concentrating on seeing an image of
something which is not visible to her outward eye. When Lucy
suddenly appears before Maggie it is as if she has known how
Maggie has been thinking of her and has come to comfort Maggie. Lucy's recognition of what has actually happened and her
acceptance of the situation for what it is indicates that she has
moved outside her story book world to face a harsh reality:
"I know you never meant to make me unhappy. . . . It is a
trouble that has come on us all:--you have more to bear than
I have--and you gave him up, when . . . you did what it must
have been very hard to do" (VII. iv. 369, author's ellipses).

When Maggie, "with an effort like the convulsed clutch of a drowning man," begs Lucy to forgive Stephen, Lucy says "in a low voice that had the solemnity of confession in it, 'you are better than I am. I can't . . .'" (author's ellipsis). In this way Lucy shows that she is now capable of genuine emotion and that she has gained a new knowledge of herself.

In the final chapter of the book Maggie undergoes "The Last Conflict," and once she has resolved it she arrives at her moment of clearest vision. Then occurs "The Final Rescue." That George Eliot so entitled the last book is extremely significant. Scandalous gossip about Dr. Kenn's relationship with Maggie has forced him to advise her to leave St. Ogg's, and she now realizes that "she must be a lonely wanderer" the rest of her life. Her mind can create 'no image of rest . . . except of that far, far off rest, from which there would be no more waking for her into this struggling earthly life" (VII. v. 372). The only "rescue" possible for her is death.

But if death is to bring to Maggie anything more positive than escape from an unbearable life, there must take place within her something which will reconcile her to life, even such a life as is left for her. She must once more grasp the clue of life, must arrive at not only a full understanding of its meaning but also a complete acceptance of it. In short, she herself must become capable of renunciation. It is after she has visited Dr. Kenn for the last time and returned hopeless, weary, and joyless to her room that the rains come. Three days it rains and three days Maggie sits "in her lonely room, with a window darkened by the clouds and the driving rain, thinking of that future, and wrestling for patience . . ." (VII. v. 374). This dark period in her life is comparable to that in Adam's life when he sits in the dark, viewless upper room and wrestles with himself. Here too, as in the upper room scene where Adam takes communion and undergoes the baptism of suffering, the overtones of Christian symbolism merge with the vision imagery. Maggie has undergone temptation; she has been judged and surely in a sense crucified by "the world's wife" and by her own kin. Now "she must begin a new life. . . ." It is by accepting this new life and renouncing the old that she undergoes spiritual rebirth. The three days are, I believe, intended to suggest--merely to suggest and certainly not in any

exact way--the three days between crucifixion and resurrec-
tion. This interpretation gains support by the previously cited
reference to the cross and the image of Christ and by a later
reference soon to be quoted.

On the third day of her travail Maggie receives a letter
from Stephen begging her to call him back, to call them both
back to life. Thus the final temptation, which George Eliot
clarifies by use of light imagery: "At the entrance of the *chill
dark cavern,* we turn with unworn courage from the *warm light;*
but how, when we have trodden far in the *damp darkness,* and
have begun to be faint and weary--how, if there is a sudden
opening above us, and we are invited back again to the life-
nourishing day?" (p. 375). Although Maggie has had "the vision
of a lonely future" which is here identified with the chill dark
cavern, it is actually the doubt she feels about the "justice of
her own resolve" that causes her to weaken temporarily. But
she recognizes her own weakness and determines to wait and
pray, for she knows that "the *light* that had forsaken her would
come again." The light which she waits for (and the image is
repeated) comes to her as she sits late into the night by the dark
window. The "long past" comes back to her and she hears once
more the words of Thomas à Kempis: "I have received the
Cross, I have received it from Thy hand; I will bear it. . . ."
Maggie's response is only a partial acceptance since it is
negated by a despairing protest: "I will bear it, and bear it
till death. . . . But how long it will be before death comes!
I am so young, so healthy. How shall I have patience and
strength? Am I to struggle and fall and repent again?--has
life other trials as hard for me still?" (p. 377, author's ellipsis). This is the moment of her most intense suffering and
conflict, the moment of greatest spiritual and moral growth,
the moment before she arrives at her clearest vision. "Surely," the author questions, "there was something being taught
her by this experience of great need; and she must be learning a secret of human tenderness and long-suffering, that the
less erring could hardly know?" The question is rhetorical;
it is immediately followed by Maggie's full acceptance, by
her act of complete renunciation: "Oh, God, if my life is to
be long, let me live to bless and comfort--" Further verbali-

zation is unnecessary; Maggie's cry is interrupted by the sudden appearance of the flood.[3] She has grasped the clue of life; she has taken up the cross. That she has arrived at vision is indicated by the flood scene which follows.

The flood scene contains the most highly concentrated use of symbolism in the book. Here the important elements of the novel merge in such a complex way that they cannot logically be separated for discussion. It is necessary to pay particular attention to the use of light imagery and to explore the symbolic meaning of the river in order to discover how it is that the flood scene is a symbolic enactment of Maggie's life, of her movement from darkness to light, from blindness to vision.

In the beginning of this study it was stated that the river is paradoxically both life-giving and life-taking; but some exploration is needed. The difficulty which arises is that this symbol has a multiplex function and that it does involve the primary paradox: the Floss is both the river of death and the river of life. The youthful Maggie, who "when she read about Christiana passing 'the river over which there is no bridge,' always saw the Floss between the green pastures by the Great Ash" (I. v. 57), makes an association which seems calculated to help establish one facet of the symbol. The reference is clearly to the river of death in *The Pilgrim's Progress* which the pilgrims must cross on foot before they can enter the celestial city. Obviously, in Christian terms this river is not merely death but life through death. In George Eliot's terms, however, the paradox of the Floss is more complex: Maggie's belief in death as a means of entering life is unquestionable, but the author makes no such assertion of orthodoxy. She does nevertheless give ample evidence that the Floss is a symbol of both life and death. The brief reference to Christiana's crossing "the river over which there is no bridge" and its association in context with the Floss (also a river without a bridge) supports part of the meaning which the Floss has in the myth of St. Ogg's. There the woman who is ragged and shivering before crossing the river becomes clothed in the holy light of the Virgin when she reaches the other side. Although the emphasis is clearly on Ogg's kindly act rather than on the woman's transformation into the Virgin, still the trans-

formation which occurs when she steps across on the other
side (Ogg remains in the boat) indicates that the Floss is a
partial equivalent of Bunyan's river of death.

And since there are other references throughout the novel
to *The Pilgrim's Progress*[4] I venture the speculation that
George Eliot's description of the Floss which flows through
a wide plain filled with rich pastures, trees, meadows, and
growing crops is intended to suggest a further comparison between it and Bunyan's river of life "where the fine trees grow
on both sides, " "the meadows are green all the year long, "
and "by this riverside, in the meadows, there were cotes and
folds for sheep . . ." (Bunyan, p. 287). The parallel, if
George Eliot intends it as such, is ironic since the people of
St. Ogg's are out of keeping with the land and Dorl*cote* is a
mill, not a peaceful refuge.

Another indication that the Floss is intended to symbolize
life is that the name itself, undoubtedly chosen with care, suggests the thread of life which the Fates spin and cut off at
death. This meaning is emphasized in a general river image:
"Maggie's destiny, then, is at present hidden, and we must
wait for it to reveal itself like the course of an unmapped river:
we only know that the river is full and rapid, and that for all
rivers there is the same final home" (VI. vi. 203-04). If we can
apply this general image to the Floss, and it would seem quite
accurate to do so, then we arrive at the conclusion that the
Floss is destiny, in particular Maggie's destiny. In the context of the image just presented, George Eliot has made quite
clear that by "destiny" she means both those external circumstances and the internal characteristics which together make
up the course of life. The external circumstances which determine the general course of the river and its final mergence
with the sea also determine the general course of Maggie's
life and her death. Within these limitations Maggie's own nature works out the other part of her destiny. During her trip
down the river with Stephen, Maggie undergoes temptation,
arrives at moral decision, and refuses to drift further. At
the end of the book she is once again in the current of the same
river proceeding in the same direction toward the sea. But
now although the current carries her to death it also carries

her toward that intense spiritual life which is possible only at the moment of vision.

The symbolic connection between the myth of St. Ogg's and the flood scene is that while Maggie is looking at the flood waters and deciding what to do, one of Bob's boats which has broken loose from its mooring appears at the window, crashing its prow through and lodging partially inside. Bob's comment--"It's *wonderful* this fastening isn't broke too, as well as the mooring" (VII. v. 379)--indicates his sense of awe at what has happened. According to the myth, the Virgin blessed Ogg and told him: "And from henceforth whoso steps into thy boat shall be in no peril from the storm; and whenever it puts forth to rescue it shall save the lives of both men and beasts." When Ogg died, the myth continues:

> ". . . behold, in the parting of his soul, the boat *loosed itself from its moorings,* and was floated with the ebbing tide in great swiftness to the ocean, and was seen no more. Yet it was witnessed in the floods of aftertime, that *at the coming on of eventide,* Ogg the son of Beorl was always seen with his boat upon the wide-spreading waters, and the Blessed Virgin sat in its prow, shedding a light around as of the moon in its brightness, so that the rowers in the gathering darkness took heart and pulled anew" [I. xii. 174].

The almost miraculous appearance of the boat which "rescues" Maggie is calculated to recall the myth in an ironic context. The heart's need has been answered by the unseen boatman. When Tom sees Maggie he asks no questions but guesses "a story of almost miraculous divinely protected effort," and once the boat has sunk drowning Maggie and Tom, it reappears once more, "a black speck on the golden water."

The flood scene[5] as a symbolic enactment of Maggie's movement toward vision begins after midnight and ends at sunrise. At first when the boat Maggie is in is driven out upon the flood waters she feels that she is "alone in the darkness with God." What has happened has been "so rapid--so dreamlike" that for a time she has "no distinct conception of her position." Then gradually she is awakened "to fuller consciousness" by the cessation of the rain and her "perception that the darkness was divided by the faintest light. . . ." Gradually she be-

comes aware that this is the flood her father has talked of,
and the memory of him calls up a *"vision* of the old home" and
her family. Aware now that she is lost, she cries out, "Oh,
God, where am I? Which is the way home?"--questions which
in this context take on symbolic meaning. Home is where the
ties are, where one's duty lies. Home, symbolically, is the
harmony which has been the object of Maggie's quest since the
days of her childhood when she sought it in the gypsy camp,
since the days of her adolescence when she had only "a *blind,*
unconscious yearning for something that would link together
the wonderful impressions of this mysterious life, and give
her soul a sense of home in it" (III. v. 353). But home, ironically, is death, since there can be no harmony for Maggie in
life.

Now out on the open flood waters, her mind firmly fixed on
the vision of home and loved ones, "she *strained her eyes*
against the curtain of gloom that she might seize the first
sight of her whereabout. . . ." With "the gradual uplifting of
the cloudy firmament" and "the *slowly defining blackness* of
objects above the glassy dark" she can tell that she is not in
the river. But if she is to get home she must get in its current just long enough to pass the Ripple. *"Looking* behind her,
she *saw* the lines of black trees: *looking* before her, there were
none: then, the river lay before her." Thus as vision increases
she takes her bearing, then begins "to paddle the boat forward
with the energy of wakening hope: the *dawning* seemed to advance more swiftly, now she was in action; and she could soon
see the poor dumb beasts. . . ." Twilight grows and she experiences "a sensation of strength, inspired by a mighty emotion, " a feeling of "strong resurgent love towards her brother." Soon there is a *"dark mass* in the distance" and she is
able to *"discern* the current of the river. The dark mass must
be--yes, it was--St. Ogg's. Ah, now she knew which way to
look for the first glimpse of the well-known trees. . . . But
there was *no colour, no shape yet:* all was *faint* and *dim."*
Nevertheless "with more and more vividness" she creates in
her mind an image of her old home. Then "more and more
clearly in the *lessening distance* and the *growing light* she began to *discern* the objects that she knew must be the well-known
trees and roofs. . . ." The current of the Floss floats her past

the now dangerous Ripple in which there appear undistinguish-
able "floating masses" that are also floated into the Floss.
Aware that she may be crushed by these masses, later identified as part of the mill, she is temporarily horror-struck
but soon concentrates on her struggle to get home. Still her
vision increases: "She *could see* now that the bridge was broken down [the bridge across the Ripple; the Floss has none]:
she *could see* the masts of a stranded vessel. . . ." "Colour
was beginning to awake now, and . . . she *could discern* the
tints of trees--*could see* the old Scotch firs far to the right,
and the home chestnuts. . . ." Finally arriving home she tells
Tom, "God has taken care of me, to bring me to you."

Tom, when he has taken the oars and pushed out on the flood
waters with Maggie, is forced by calamity to attain vision.[6]
Stripped of the artificial concerns of society and "face to face"
with Maggie for the first time in his life, he is capable of
understanding

> the full meaning of what had happened. . . . It came with so over-
> powering a force--it was such a new *revelation* to his spirit, of
> the depths in life, that had lain beyond his *vision* which he had
> fancied so *keen* and *clear*--that he was unable to ask a question.
> They sat mutely gazing at each other: Maggie with eyes of in-
> tense life looking out from a weary, beaten face--Tom pale with
> a certain awe and humiliation. . . . But at last a *mist gathered
> over the blue-grey eyes,* and the lips found a word they could
> utter: the old childish--"Magsie!" [VII. v. 385].

Thus Tom's "very clear, prosaic eyes [which were] not apt
to be dimmed by *mists* of feeling and imagination" have at
last been covered by that "mist" which allows him to imagine
what has happened and to feel the corresponding emotions.
The "vision which he had fancied so keen and clear" is now
supplanted by what George Eliot shows us is genuinely clear
vision "of the depths of life." Whether such a last-minute vision is completely convincing in such a character as Tom is
arguable. But in terms of what has been shown about the novel
as a whole, there is much to be said for it. George Eliot's
own comment surely helps to reveal her intention: ". . . what
quarrel, what harshness, what unbelief in each other can sub-
sist in the presence of a great calamity, when all the *artificial
vesture* of our life is gone, and we are all one with each other

in *primitive mortal* needs ?" The St. Ogg's society has created
such a thick artificial vesture[7] that the awareness of the natural, primitive aspects of human nature has been lost. What
the author seems to be saying through Tom's sudden vision is
that when an individual or a society moves as far away from
clear vision as Tom has moved, nothing less than knowledge
of approaching doom can strip away the barriers and thus make
vision possible. Obviously, this is another way of saying that
such a society or individual is doomed--either to eternal blindness or to vision attained at the cost of life itself. It is further
implied that the Maggies who are capable of attaining vision
through life rather than death must share the doom engendered
by the society of Toms, since the Maggies must either endure
death in life or else be rescued by death.

After the reconciliation between Tom and Maggie, which
could take place only after the enlarging of Tom's vision, the
two of them set out upon the flood waters to rescue Lucy and
the others. To do so, however, they must get back in the current of the Floss. And the Floss--reminding the reader now
of that other river which "once rose, like an angry destroying
god, sweeping down the feeble generations"--the Floss is angry. The river, however, is only the second cause of Maggie
and Tom's death. The first cause is the society itself, as the
symbolism of the following passage will indicate:

> . . . a new danger was being carried towards them by the river.
> Some wooden *machinery* had just given way on one of the wharves,
> and huge fragments were being floated along. The *sun was rising*
> now, and the wide area of watery desolation was spread out in
> dreadful clearness-- in *dreadful clearness* floated onwards the
> hurrying, *threatening masses*. A large company in a boat that
> was working its way along under the Tofton houses, observed
> their danger, and shouted "get out of the current!"
>
> But that could not be done at once. . . . Huge *fragments, cling-
> ing together in fatal fellowship*, made *one wide mass* across the
> stream.
>
> "It is coming, Maggie!" Tom said, in a deep hoarse voice,
> loosing the oars, and clasping her.
>
> The next instant the boat was no longer seen upon the water--
> and *the huge mass* was hurrying on in *hideous triumph*.

It has been made clear earlier that a part of the mill has broken off forming huge "masses" in the river. And it should be

recalled too that Maggie saw "a large dark mass" which she identified as St. Ogg's. These masses are now recalled by the appearance of the fragments of machinery which form "the huge mass" that destroys Maggie and Tom. It is the *machinery* of St. Ogg's, symbolized in general by the mill, which crushes Maggie and Tom. The mill whose function it is to produce the flour for life-giving bread derives its power from the river. But symbolically its function has changed when it becomes life-destroying rather than life-sustaining. It is worth noting that George Eliot personifies the fragments of machinery: "clinging together in fatal fellowship" they constitute a "mass" which performs its destruction and then goes "hurrying on in hideous triumph." The reader could well have been spared such an insistent handling of the symbol; there are, however, some subtleties in meaning. "Fragments" suggests the unwhole and incomplete nature of the St. Ogg's people, and there is a double-play on "fatal fellowship"; it is fatal not only to what lies in its path but also to itself. And the "hideous triumph" therefore becomes ironic. Read in terms of the symbol, it emphasizes the total lack of vision. There are, of course, those in the other boat who see the danger and call to Maggie and Tom to get out of the current. But their attempted help is finally no more effectual than the assistance offered within the community. It is already too late to escape the doom, for "that could not be done at once." The process, George Eliot implies, is long and complex.

In contrast to the lack of vision implied in the ironic symbol above is the "dreadful clearness" with which the rising sun now reveals to Maggie and Tom the watery desolation. Maggie's movement upon the flood waters began in darkness and it now ends in the light of the morning sun. But the watery desolation and approaching death are not to be the final vision for Maggie and Tom. As they are sinking beneath the water, they are "living through again in one supreme moment the days when they had clasped their little hands in love, and roamed the daisied fields together." I have previously indicated why I find this conclusion sentimental and ineffective, but it is more useful to explore what the author has done than to speculate about what she might have done. In this one supreme moment Tom and Maggie create an image of the happy times of their youth, of the time when--to go back to Book I--they "were still very much like young animals, " having still the capacity for spontaneous emotional response so grievously lacking in their rigid society. This, I believe, is not intended to be a sentimentalizing of the past (it is sentimental because it is partially untrue and because it does not include the whole of Maggie's mature vision) but rather the reviving of what was good and unperverted in Maggie and Tom's past, of those moments when their lives together were supposedly harmonious.

The conclusion of *The Mill on the Floss* brings the reader back once more to a view of St. Ogg's that is strongly suggestive of his first view in the opening page. We are told that "Nature repairs her ravages--repairs them with her sunshine, and with human labour. The desolation wrought by that flood had left little visible trace on the face of the earth, five years after. The fifth autumn was rich in golden cornstacks, rising in thick clusters among the distant hedgerows; the wharves and warehouses on the Floss were busy again, with echoes of eager voices, with hopeful lading and unlading. " Thus in a sense we have come full circle; but the circle is a spiral which has widened. What in the first view was the appearance of harmony secured by the exclusion of discordant elements is here known to be an appearance. There is "little *visible* trace" on the earth, but the reader well knows that there are even less easily visible traces in the community itself. And furthermore the preceding paragraph is soon qualified in this symbolic reminder: "Nature repairs her ravages--but not all. The uptorn trees are not rooted again; the parted hills are left scarred: if there is a new growth, the trees are not the same as the old, and the hills *underneath their green vesture* bear the marks of the past rending. To the *eyes* that have dwelt on the past, there is no thorough repair. "

And since symbolically it was man--as in the time of Noah-- who incurred nature's wrath, we are therefore prompted to inquire whether or not man has repaired his ravages even to such an extent as nature has repaired hers. And there is some evidence that he has attempted to do so. Dorlcote Mill has been reconstructed and the tombstone on Mr. Tulliver's grave has been put back in place. We are told that much later Lucy and Stephen are reunited, and we know that they are wiser than before. Philip's vision has been greatly enlarged, and Mrs. Glegg has reaffirmed the best in the Dodson code of morality. What will come of these changes, George Eliot does not choose to prophesy.

The unalterable fact remains: "there is no thorough repair." That *The Mill on the Floss* is a dark and tragic book is, I believe, verified finally by the "rescue" of Maggie and Tom--an ironic reversal of the Noah story--[8] and by the epitaph which appears on their tombstone: "In their death they were not divided." Often read as a sentimental lapse on the part of the author, this epitaph is rather a concluding ironic comment on a society which would not allow that they be united in life. For the people of St. Ogg's are themselves divided, separated by their narrowness and lack of vision from that which is "congruous with the mystery of the human lot."

7. *Middlemarch:* General Patterns of Meaning

I KNOW of no more complex novel than *Middlemarch* and of no complex novel in which there are fewer, if in fact there be any, unassimilated elements. Themes and image patterns are so interrelated here that it is finally an impossible task to explore one theme or image profitably without becoming involved in a discussion of others. I do not attempt the impossible. I hope merely to show some small part of the way various elements are related and of the meaning they thereby create. I shall depend on the reader to remember that vision is always in some way the key to the discussion at hand.

In this chapter my intention is to give some general indication of the complex of elements at work in *Middlemarch*, of the various movements and their subtle interweavings to form the structural movement, of the way that significant image patterns interrelate, reinforcing the central pattern of vision imagery and suggesting the important themes of egoism, expectations, marriage, reform, frustration, and fulfillment. In the following chapter I examine in some detail the individual movements of the major characters, concentrating on one central movement and the way it modifies and is modified by other individual movements toward or away from vision.

In the first chapter of this study, moral vision was defined as the deeply felt perception of what it is to be a human being, a perception so deeply felt that it must profoundly influence what one is in relation to his fellow human beings. When we come to examine *Middlemarch,* there is no need to redefine the term. One of two central facts in *Middlemarch* is that the kind and loving but unheralded private actions which are the result of growing vision do not perfectly fulfill the life which seeks heroic channels but do nevertheless contribute to the moral evolution of mankind. The second is that the petty and selfish private actions which are the result of moral stupidity and lack of vision constitute a friction which retards the forward movement of mankind. In a wide general sense these two antithetical sets of actions create the structural movements toward and away from moral vision and thereby provide the substructural movement of the novel, the forward struggle of humanity. This statement should not be interpreted as implying that George Eliot is setting black against white and showing right and wrong actions to be clear-cut and easily distinguishable but rather that there is no neutral area of indifference, that all human actions--whether trivial or great--have moral consequences. George Eliot is intent on showing her reader how it is that "we insignificant people with our daily words and acts are preparing the lives of many Dorotheas, some of which may present a far sadder sacrifice than that of the Dorothea whose story we know" (Finale), and that we also prepare for the existence of the Bulstrodes, Lydgates, and Rosamonds, as well as the Riggs and Raffles, "those low people by whose interference, however little we may like it, the course of the world is very much determined" (XLI. 208). That is the negative statement. On the other hand, and this is the positive part of the book which has been too often neglected, "the growing good of the world is partly dependent on unhistoric acts" (Finale).

But the term *movement* which at the beginning of this study was chosen as a means of defining the structure of George Eliot's novels has here taken on further extensions. Now the source of an important image pattern, it provides a meaningful part of the metaphoric texture of the novel. Furthermore it is a word which is sometimes used significantly by the author as she indicates the complexity of forces at work in the world she presents. There are several movements in *Middle-*

march. First there is the historical movement of the world, most emphatically called to our attention by Dorothea's scene in Rome, "the city of visible history, where the past of a whole hemisphere seems *moving* in funeral procession with strange ancestral images and trophies gathered from afar," where Dorothea sees "the masquerade of ages . . ." (XX. 278-79). We are reminded that "much the same sort of *movement* and mixture went on in old England as we find in older Herodotus, who also, in telling what had been, thought it well to take a woman's lot for his starting point . . ." (XI. 134). More specifically and in greater detail George Eliot examines the "marital voyage," the movement of medical reform, and the movement of political and social reform as it affects nation, parish, town, and hamlet during the period of the first Reform Bill, from about 1829 to 1832. But, as always, her primary concern is the progression or regression of the human being, of "the human soul [which] *moves* in many channels . . ." (XLII. 220).

Exploration of what I consider to be the governing metaphor of the book may perhaps yield a meaningful point of departure for the examination of structural movement in *Middlemarch*. George Eliot says: "I . . . have so much to do in unraveling certain human lots, and seeing how they were woven and interwoven, that all the light I can command must be concentrated on this particular web, and not dispersed over that tempting range of relevancies called the universe" (XV. 203). Here the author clearly--albeit in general terms--tells us her intention. It is extremely important that she here employs a vision image in relation to her function as novelist. She is intent on "seeing" and making it possible for her reader to see how human lots are related, and all the "light" which she as novelist can command must be focused squarely on the "web" which she invites the reader to explore with her. Thus indirectly she warns her reader that he too must concentrate on seeing that which presumably is not at once discernible. Throughout the whole of *Middlemarch* the vision imagery predominates. We see not only how the web of human lots is constructed but also how the characters themselves come to see it. In this image, then, is the conjunction of two central elements in the novel, for the web metaphor is both idea-giving and form-giving. This study will reveal that it bears a direct relationship to the negative movement away from vision and a less direct relationship to the positive movement. "This particular web" is the fabric constructed by the weaving and interweaving of human lots, and the focus is on the web itself rather than exclusively on one particular human lot, on the way both public and private actions of human beings interrelate. Thus it is that the attention of the reader is constantly being shifted from one episode to another, from one character to another, from one place to another, from private scene to public scene. It is the way in which human actions form the threads of connection that George Eliot would have us examine from various vantage points. "In watching effects, if only of an electric battery, " she says, "it is often necessary to change our place and examine a particular mixture or group at some distance from the point where the *movement* we are interested in was set up" (XL. 187). As we follow the movement of characters from place to place and from group relationship to private relationship we see how their lives become increasingly involved, so enmeshed and interwoven, in fact, that it is impossible to follow one straight narrative line in the life of a character without considering the other lines which intercept and modify it. Hence the effect is a structure made up of many threads rather than a single narrative line. If the term may be used descriptively, we should say that the effect is a *weblike* structure.

Something of both the subtle complexity of this interweaving movement and the author's skillful merging of the particular movement with the general is indicated by the following key passage. George Eliot has been speaking of the first impressions which Lydgate has formed of Dorothea and Rosamond:

> Certainly nothing at present could seem much less important to Lydgate than the turn of Miss Brooke's mind, or to Miss Brooke than the qualities of the woman who had attracted this young surgeon. But any one *watching keenly the stealthy convergence of human lots,* sees a slow preparation of effects from one life on another, which tells like a calculated irony on the indifference or the *frozen stare* with which we *look* at our unintroduced neighbor. Destiny stands by sarcastic with our *dramatis personae* folded in her hand.
>
> Old provincial society had its share of *this subtle movement:* had not only its striking downfalls, its brilliant young professional dandies who ended by living up an entry with a drab and six

children for their establishment, but also those less marked
vicissitudes which are constantly shifting the boundaries of social
intercourse, and begetting new consciousness of interdependence.
Some *slipped* a little downward, some got higher footing: people
denied aspirates, gained wealth, and fastidious gentlemen stood
for boroughs; some *were caught* in political *currents,* some in
ecclesiastical, and perhaps found themselves surprisingly grouped
in consequence; while a few personages or families that stood
with rocky firmness amid all this fluctuation, were slowly presenting new aspects in spite of solidity, and altering with *the
double change of self and beholder.* Municipal town and rural
parish gradually made fresh *threads of connection*--gradually,
as the old stocking gave way to the savings-bank, and the worship of the solar guinea became extinct; while squires and baron-
ets, and even lords who had once lived blamelessly afar from
the civic mind, gathered the faultiness of close acquaintanceship
[XI. 133-34].

Here again George Eliot places emphasis on seeing, on "watching keenly" what is a "stealthy" and "slow" (hence difficult to
observe) process; furthermore she implies a distinction between *seeing* and *staring* or *looking.* Indirectly she asks her
reader to see, to look with sympathetic concern and imagination rather than with "frozen stare" on his unknown neighbor
whose lot is inextricably interwoven with his own. "This subtle movement" which is identified as "the convergence of human lots" is defined in terms of both the individual and the
public. In terms of the individual it is both up and down, in
and out. The up and down movement describes what is primarily the public view of the individual, his degree of success
in the public eye: "some slipped a little downward, some got
higher footing." But in contrast to the "striking downfalls"
are the "less marked vicissitudes" which here seem to assume greater importance because they provide the in and out
movement, the shifting of social boundaries, and the begetting of "new consciousness of social interdependence." Those
who "slipped" or "were caught" in various currents (the phrasing suggests the theme of moral drifting) are in contrast to
those who "stood with rocky firmness, " maintaining their
solidity while "altering with the double change of self and beholder." This double change, I believe, is what George Eliot
means by growth in vision, a change in self which for the bet-

ter alters the way one beholds the world about him but which
does not uproot or dislocate. By this series of general details
the author indicates the nature of the subtle movement she
will present for the reader to see. All of the details have their
counterpart in the story itself: Lydgate's striking downfall,
the less marked vicissitudes of Dorothea and others, the rocky
firmness of the Garths, the political and ecclesiastical currents which catch Mr. Brooke and Mr. Farebrother. Town
and parish do form fresh threads of connection as the railroads
appear and talk of political reform calls attention to conditions
outside the town. And as these "threads" increase--the word
suggests the weblike structure--so does the interdependence.
In such a closely interwoven society there would seem to be
an increasing significance in the personal act which, for good
or ill, must somehow affect the lives of others. In a society
which has no "guiding visions and spiritual directors" (X. 120),
which is helped by "no coherent social faith and order" (Prelude), the frame of reference must be supplied by an individual
sense of morality. Hence the emphasis of this novel lies on
the necessity of seeing "the slow preparation of effects from
one life on another. "

The several movements previously enumerated in brief are
in the above quotation considered by the author to be one subtle movement, the convergence of human lots; and that phenomenon produces what in the governing metaphor the author
has called a web. Throughout the novel there are other significant web images and other important image patterns as well
as isolated images and recurring themes which show themselves to have relevance to this central image. Discussion of
the multiple function of the web image and its complex relationship to other elements in the novel--most especially to
vision--will, I believe, reveal a great deal about theme and
structure in *Middlemarch.*

First of all, the web is the fabric of human life which in
Middlemarch George Eliot partially unravels and examines
in order to discover whatever is discernible about that fabric,
what some of the parts are, and how they relate to the whole.
In the Finale she indicates that the novel proper does not comprehend the entire web. "Every limit is a beginning as well
as an ending. . . . For the fragment of a life, however typi-

cal, is not the sample of an even *web:* promises may not be
kept, and an ardent outset may be followed by declension;
latent powers may find their long-awaited opportunity; a past
error may urge a grand retrieval. " Thus it would seem that
the web is continually extending so that there is finally no even
web, no whole fabric but one that is always in the process of
becoming and will remain so as long as there are human actions to continue the operation of the law of cause and effect
in human affairs. The Finale tells us briefly what happened
to the characters of *Middlemarch,* but such a conclusion does
not give the closed effect which E. M. Forster deplored as
the primary weakness of novels. Rather it opens out, creating the sense of a continuing life pattern. It speaks of marriage, birth, and death, of old age and youth, of reform, in-
heritance, and the daily problems of life. We are not left with
the illusion that our characters live happily ever after, but
with the sure knowledge that while they live out their lives
they are continuing to form fresh threads of connection, some
which will hamper and others which will enrich their lives.

If a web, then, is thought of in the sense indicated above, it
suggests a spread-out, expansive quality. But it also suggests
what is on the surface apparently contradictory, that its intricate structure might impede free and unhampered movement. Both of these qualities are peculiarly suited to George
Eliot's purpose here. This is not to say that the author constantly repeats the image but rather that because it is a rich
image which recurs in significant contexts complementing and
supporting the basic themes and structural movement, it is
therefore useful to the critic as a way of describing the meaning and action of the novel. *Middlemarch* is obviously concerned in large part with the "later-born Theresas" whose
passionate ideal natures can find no adequate channel for heroic action, "no epic life wherein there was a constant unfold-
ing of far-resonant action; perhaps only a life of mistakes, the
offspring of a certain spiritual grandeur ill-matched with the
meanness of opportunity. " Their "loving heart-beats and sobs
after an unattained goodness tremble off and are dispersed
among hindrances, instead of centring in some long-recog-
nizable deed" (Prelude). There are no heroes who will perform
great historic acts, for except in rare instances there is no

longer any channel for such action: "the medium in which their ardent deeds took shape is for ever gone" (Finale). The "hindrances" with which everyday life confronts them cause their energies to be "dispersed" and diffused, resulting in many private actions rather than one grand heroic act. But I believe that it is inaccurate to describe *Middlemarch,* as at least one critic has done, as a study in frustration. [1] Let us say rather that this novel explores the imperfectly fulfilled life, what would be necessary for fulfillment, the elements which prevent fulfillment, the attempts which are made, the nature of the failure, and the known extent of the success. For it is still possible for such lives to fulfill themselves partially if, like Dorothea, they can come to see what their lives should be in relation to those about them--in short, if they can enlarge their vision. George Eliot's last statement about Dorothea (see Finale) implies such a partial fulfillment:

> Her finely-touched spirit had still its fine issues, though they were not widely visible. Her full nature, like that river of which Cyrus broke the strength, spent itself in channels which had no great name on earth. But the effect of her being on those around her was incalculably diffusive: for the growing good of the world is partly dependent on unhistoric acts . . . [pp. 444-45].

Hence the double significance of "this particular web" on which George Eliot chose to focus her light: it is useful as a means of indicating both the meanness of opportunity and the incalculably diffusive effect of human actions performed within such restricting circumstances.

The hindrances which impede the direct movement of the characters toward fulfillment are, as always in George Eliot's scheme of things, the result of causes both inside and outside the character. Therefore one large group of images emphasizes the hampering nature of circumstances, especially of social and financial pressures. Prominent in this group are those thread and string images which are analogous to the central image of the web.

When, for example, Lydgate finds himself involved in the controversy over the appointment of a chaplain for the new hospital, he begins to realize that freedom of action in regard to a public matter can be bought only at the expense of his private plans: "For the first time Lydgate was feeling the hampering *threadlike* pressure of small social conditions, and their frustrating complexity" (XVIII. 260). Much later in a discussion with Dorothea about Farebrother, Lydgate himself verbalizes his own and Farebrother's situation in much the same way:

> "I think him a remarkable fellow; he ought to have done more than he has done."
> "Why has he not done more?" said Dorothea, interested now in all who had slipped below their own intention.
> "That's a hard question," said Lydgate. "I find myself that it's uncommonly difficult to make the right thing work: there are so many *strings* pulling at once" [L. 330].

The question asked here by Dorothea is a crucial one in the book and Lydgate's metaphorical answer indicates the complexity of the problem with which all Middlemarchers are confronted. Even such morally insensitive characters as Mr. Brooke and Mr. Featherstone are partially aware of the web-like circumstances which limit the action of others, although they suppose themselves untouched. Thus Mr. Brooke in a characteristic observation compares himself to Mr. Casaubon who is "a little narrow": "I was always versatile. But a clergy-man is *tied* a little tight. If they would make him a bishop, now! . . . He would have more *movement* then . . ." (XXX. 24). What Mr. Brooke does not realize is that it is not the profession so much as the man himself which ties Casaubon. To Featherstone, less genial than Brooke, it is a source of pleasure rather than sympathy that Bulstrode has a financial hold on Mr. Vincy. Speaking to Fred, he observes: "He's got a pretty strong *string* round your father's leg, by what I hear, eh?" (XIV. 194). The phrase "by what I hear" is significant, since gossip and public opinion in general contribute greatly to the construction of the hampering web. On the obscure backgrounds of both Lydgate and Bulstrode and the nature of the relationship between these two men there is much speculation, some more nearly true and therefore of a more harmful nature than that made by Mrs. Taft: "Many people believed that Lydgate's coming to the town at all was really due to Bulstrode; and Mrs. Taft, who was always counting stitches and gathered her information in misleading fragments caught between rows of her knitting, had got it into her head that Mr. Lydgate was a natural son of Bulstrode's, a fact which seemed to justify her suspicions of evangelical laymen" (XXVI. 382). Simple as this bit of stage business is, it implies that fragments of gossip handled with as little thought as a piece of knitting are just as methodically knit together until they become "fact." And, as the author later questions, "Who can know how much of his most inward life is made up of the thoughts he believes other men to have about him, until that *fabric of opinion* is threatened with ruin?" (LXVIII. 230).

Thus far I have called attention only to those images which suggest the woven web, but exploiting the metaphor further, the author draws on meanings suggested by the spider web. Such meaning seems to be implied in the metaphor contained in the following passage about Lydgate and his arrival in Middlemarch:

> No one in Middlemarch was likely to have such a notion of Lydgate's past as has here been faintly shadowed, and indeed the respectable townfolk there were not more given than mortals generally to any eager attempt at exactness in the representation to themselves of what did not come under their own senses. Not only young virgins of that town, but grey-bearded men also, were often in haste to conjecture how a new acquaintance might be wrought into their purpose, contented with very vague knowledge as to the way in which life had been shaping him for that instrumentality. Middlemarch, in fact, counted on *swallowing* Lydgate and *assimilating* him very comfortably [XV. 221].

Thus at the same time that the people of Middlemarch are likened to "mortals generally" they (and therefore to a certain extent mortals generally) are likened to a smug, complacent spiderlike creature which evinces little or no interest in what its victim really is but is thoroughly assured about what he will become. The relationship between what this image implies about these people and what has been defined as moral vision is clear enough; those who think of their fellow human being merely as one who can be shaped to their own ends are therefore without that profound and moving concern for the lives of others which is vision. Such people, *Middlemarch* shows us, are daily creating the situations and circumstances which will impede the full and natural development of other human beings.

A few chapters earlier George Eliot uses a far more complex image to explore the way one character exerts an influence similar to that which the above image suggests Middlemarch will exert on Lydgate. It provides an example of the way in which other images in the book complement or even parallel images in the web pattern. And it further illustrates the organic relationship between the vision imagery and other patterns. Mrs. Cadwallader, whose mind is as "active as phosphorus, biting everything that came near into the form that suited it . . ." (VI. 83), is the subject which the author asks to observe. But such observation, she tells us, requires more than ordinary eyesight:

> Was there any ingenious plot, any hide-and-seek course of action, which might be detected by a careful telescopic watch? Not at all: a telescope might have swept the parishes of Tipton and Freshitt, the whole area visited by Mrs. Cadwallader in her phaeton, without witnessing any interview that could excite suspicion, or any scene from which she did not return with the same unperturbed *keenness of eye* and the same high natural colour. In fact, if that convenient vehicle had existed in the days of the Seven Sages, one of them would doubtless have remarked that you can know little of women by following them about in their pony-phaetons. Even with a *microscope* directed on a water-drop we find ourselves making interpretations which turn out to be rather coarse; for whereas under *a weak lens* you may *seem to see* a creature exhibiting an active voracity into which other smaller creatures actively play as if they were so many animated tax-pennies, *a stronger lens* reveals to you certain *tiniest hairlets* which make vortices for these victims while *the swallower* waits passively at his receipt of custom. In this way, metaphorically speaking, *a strong lens* applied to Mrs. Cadwallader's matchmaking will show *a play of minute causes* producing what may be called thought and speech *vortices* to bring her the sort of food she needed [VI. 81].

A "careful telescopic watch," then, would reveal nothing significant about Mrs. Cadwallader's actions. For the significant movement here as elsewhere throughout the novel is the subtle play of minute causes, not Mrs. Cadwallader's travels in her pony phaeton. Clearly Mrs. Cadwallader is spiderlike, although the creature to which she is compared is of microscopic size. And that size is an extremely important element in

the successful function of this complex image. It points up the
absurdity of the telescopic watch. But beyond this what is
most important is that it allows for the comparison of three
degrees and two kinds of seeing or observing. The first kind
of observation is the perception with the eye of an animate
object. The greater degree of such perception is achieved
by the use of a microscope with a strong lens, a lesser degree,
by the use of a weak lens. The use of a strong lens enables
the observer to penetrate the illusion which the weaker lens
establishes. By suggestion, there is still another degree of
perception, for the naked eye would allow the observer to
perceive only the drop of water, would in other words create
an illusion that nothing existed in the water drop. The second
kind of observation is the perception of an abstraction, the
play of minute causes of human response. Intricate as this
image is, it readily communicates this comparison to the
reader. In effect, the author is telling her reader that what
she wishes him to see is not easily discernible, that he cannot see merely by looking with a dull eye, and that he must
beware of illusion. This is one of many instances in *Middlemarch* where the author deliberately links a vision image with
another image, calling attention to the way things are, or
should be, looked at. It is such emphasis, as well as the spiderlike characteristic of Mrs. Cadwallader, which connects
this image with that of the author focusing her light on "this
particular web." And further, if we are to appreciate the
complex interrelatedness (were it not confusing, we might
say the interweaving) of thematic and imagistic structure, two
more comparisons should be noted here. First, the "tiniest
hairlets which make vortices" for the victims are, as the
author interprets the metaphor, "thought and speech vortices."
Hence they bear a relationship to the gossip which Mrs. Taft
catches between the rows of her knitting, to the whole idea of
gossip, the "fabric of opinion," as a powerful vehicle which
eventually becomes Bulstrode's nemesis and in part Lydgate's
destruction. Second, in connection with what in previous chapters I have called the imagery of drifting, it is worth pointing
out here that whereas the weak lens shows the small creatures
to be *actively* playing into the vortices, the strong lens shows
them to be the passive victims which are sucked into the vor-

tices. In terms of the plot situation, this is what happens to Sir James when Mrs. Cadwallader's well-placed words about Celia's fondness for him play upon his susceptible nature.

Also to be noted briefly here is another group of images related to the web pattern only in that they too heighten the sense of restless thwarted existence which is the negative half of the book. Although there are several animal images in *Middlemarch,* with one exception they function independently rather than as a pattern of meaning such as is to be found in *The Mill on the Floss*. [2] That exception is a set of metaphors which likens man to a yoked or harnessed animal. Mr. Vincy "felt his neck under Bulstrode's yoke" (XIII. 183), as do most of Bulstrode's associates. Lydgate, when he arrives in Middlemarch, is one of those young hopefuls who think "that Mammon shall never put a *bit* in their mouth and get astride their backs, but rather that Mammon, if they have anything to do with him, shall draw their chariot" (XV. 204). But Farebrother is soon to warn Lydgate: ". . . you must be sure of having the value, and you must keep yourself independent. Very few men can do that. Either you *slip* out of service altogether and become good for nothing, or you wear the *harness* and draw a good deal where your *yoke-fellows* pull you" (XVII. 251). As the financial pressure on Lydgate increases, Farebrother's observation is borne out. Lydgate becomes "galled with his harness" (LVIII. 85); he writhes beneath the "vile yoke" of money worries (LXIV. 170). Then there is also "the yoke of marriage" (XLVIII. 310), an image which is often repeated in one form or another. The chain, for example, which Lydgate picks up on the occasion of his proposal to Rosamond is a symbol of the bondage (a word frequently used to describe marriage) he thereby incurs. Many of the images of restriction are quite naturally connected with the idea of space, movement, and air. On one occasion when he is cheered by Rosamond's increased liveliness, Lydgate thinks of their domestic difficulty as "only a narrow swamp that we shall have to pass in a long journey" (LXIV. 181); soon disabused, however, by knowledge of her latest deception, he feels "as if he had opened a door out of a suffocating place and had found it walled up" (pp. 181-82). An extremely important image suggestive of the web and related to the theme of movement is the labyrinth or maze, which is most often associated with Casaubon or Dorothea. Perhaps nowhere else in the book is there such a piling up of restrictive words as in this description of Dorothea, who when we first see her is "struggling in the *bands* of a *narrow* teaching, *hemmed in* by a social life which seemed nothing but a *labyrinth* of *petty courses,* a *walled in maze* of *small paths* that led no whither . . ." (III.36). But to explore the repeated use of such images as these would be unproductive here since it would necessitate an unnatural separation from patterns of meaning of which they form a lesser part. Therefore I wish merely to indicate their presence and suggest their importance so that they will call attention to themselves when presented in a fuller context.

It will perhaps be fruitful to return to the web imagery in order to see what it further indicates about the interrelatedness of theme, structure, and imagery in *Middlemarch*. The web metaphor is useful not only as a means of describing both the diffuse effect of human actions and the hindrances that prevent man from self-fulfillment but also as a partial way of defining one of the two antithetical movements in the novel, the movement away from moral vision. It is surely of extreme significance that of the four major characters whose downfall the book depicts, all are at some time metaphorically shown to be spinning or weaving a web--all four, but only these four: Lydgate, Rosamond, Casaubon, and Bulstrode. The primary reason that the web image as it is used in relation to these four characters assists in the definition of the movement away from vision is that it either equals an illusion or indicates the means by which an illusion is fixed. Either it represents an insular world or it represents the insulation which makes such a world possible. The distinction here is unimportant--perhaps it does not even have to be made--but what is important is that the web, as used in relation to these characters, is connected with illusion and egoism rather than with reality and fellow-feeling.

Even before she sees Lydgate, Rosamond begins constructing the web of illusion which is eventually to entangle the two of them: "Ever since that important new arrival in Middlemarch she had *woven* a little future, of which something like this scene [her first meeting with Lydgate] was the necessary

beginning" (XII. 166). Rosamond's dream of the future is far
more realistic than the "light web of folly and vain hopes"
which we see Hetty "spinning in young ignorance. "[3] But the
future she constructs with the help of her "remarkably detailed and realistic imagination" rests on a structure of "airy
slightness, " and "there was nothing financial, still less sordid
in her *previsions* . . . " (p. 168). Lydgate, we soon learn, had
not "been *weaving* any future in which their lots were united;
but a man naturally remembers a charming girl with pleasure
. . . " (XIII. 181). After a period of time during which Rosamond "reached her *netting*" (XVI. 234) and Mrs. Bulstrode's
hints about marriage "had managed to get *woven* like slight
clinging *hairs* into the more substantial *web* of his thoughts"
(XXXI. 44), Lydgate becomes so deeply involved that he rationalizes about his firm resolve not to let marriage come
between him and his medical research. Failing to benefit by
the experience of having "once already been drawn headlong
by impetuous folly" (XV. 216), he does not see the real Rosamond beneath the beautiful flowerlike exterior. The fragile
web of courtship is therefore created by Lydgate out of his
illusory expectations of happiness:

> Young love-making--that *gossamer web!* Even the points it clings
> to--the things whence its subtle interlacings are swung--are
> *scarcely perceptible:* momentary touches of finger-tips, meet-
> ings of rays from blue and dark orbs, unfinished phrases, light-
> est changes of cheek and lips, faintest tremors. The *web* itself
> is made of spontaneous beliefs and indefinable joys, yearnings
> of one life toward another, visions of completeness, indefinite
> trust. And *Lydgate fell to spinning that web* from his inward self
> with wonderful rapidity, in spite of experience supposed to be
> finished off with the drama of Laure--in spite too of medicine
> and biology. . . . As for Rosamond, she was in the water-lily's
> expanding wonderment at its own fuller life, and she too was
> *spinning* industriously at the mutual web [XXXVI. 109-10].

Here again the author examines the play of minute causes
which is barely discernible even to the most acute eye, for
this is one of those subtle movements of the soul which *Middlemarch* traces. This image echoes an earlier one the author
uses in pointing up the paucity of genuine knowledge about
each other with which courtship provides two people. "Has
anyone, " she asks, "ever pinched into its pilulous smallness

the *cobweb* of pre-matrimonial acquaintanceship ?" (II. 28).
Seen in full context the image of Lydgate spinning the gossa-
mer web is connected with the gradual lessening of his firm
resolves and most specifically with his resolve not to marry.
Obviously the act of falling in love does not in itself constitute
moral drifting, but in Lydgate it marks the beginning of his
loss of direction. For it is during this period in his life that
Lydgate slowly begins to lose the self-mastery which is necessary to prevent his once more being drawn headlong. But
the signs of his moral drifting are still, like the signs of love,
scarcely perceptible. In fact, it is not so much the entangling
property of the web which is emphasized, although that is implicit in the image, as the unobservable mystery which attends
its creation and its extremely fragile, insubstantial and illu-
sive nature.

Mr. Casaubon also weaves a web of illusion but out of passions which are in themselves ignoble. Fearing that Dorothea
no longer looks on him without criticism, he misinterprets
and builds on certain facts concerning her and Will Ladislaw,
bringing his

> power of suspicious construction into exasperated activity. To
> all the facts which he knew, he added imaginary facts both pres-
> ent and future which became more real to him than those, be-
> cause they called up a stronger dislike, a more predominating
> bitterness. Suspicion and jealousy of Will Ladislaw's intentions,
> suspicion and jealousy of Dorothea's impressions, were con-
> stantly at their *weaving* work.

His vision so blinded that he can see nothing but self, Casaubon
weaves an illusion which further cuts him off from vision;
speaking generally in this passage about Casaubon, the author
asks: "Will not a tiny speck very close to our *vision* blot out
the glory of the world, and leave only a margin by which we
see the blot? I know no speck so troublesome as self" (XLII.
218).

Elsewhere George Eliot explores Casaubon's inner life in
terms which more clearly show the web image in relation to
the themes of egoism and vision. Speaking of his inability to
know the intense joy which can come only when one is at least
partially freed from self, she says: "His experience was of
that pitiable kind which shrinks from pity, and fears most of

all that it should be known: it was that proud, narrow sensitiveness which has not mass enough to spare for transformation into sympathy, and quivers *thread-like* in small currents
of self-preoccupation or at best of an *egoistic* scrupulosity"
(XXIX. 13). These "thread-like currents" form a kind of insular world in which the self is entrapped, cut off from sympathy
and unable to sympathize, cut off finally from the full partici-
pation in life which a wider vision would make possible:

> It is an uneasy lot at the best, to be what we call highly taught
> and yet not to enjoy: to be present at this great spectacle of life
> and never to be liberated from a small, hungry shivering self--
> never to be fully possessed by the glory we behold, never to
> have our consciousness rapturously transformed into the vivid-
> ness of a thought, the ardor of a passion, the energy of an action,
> but always to be scholarly and uninspired, ambitious and timid,
> scrupulous and *dim-sighted*.

Casaubon's "sensibilities [are] thus *fenced* in . . ." (p. 14).
And yet ironically what he wants from marriage is a "soft
fence against the cold, shadowy, unapplausive audience of
his life . . ." (XX. 293). The fence images here emphasize
both the restrictive and insulating qualities suggested by the
threadlike currents of egoism.

Casaubon is not the only character in *Middlemarch* who
feels the need of protective insulation, for Bulstrode badly
needs it if he is to survive in the dual role of hard business-
man and religious fanatic. Hence when he had found himself
engaged in a crooked business entirely incompatible with his
religious position he began a rationalizing process which, con-
tinued over a period of years, gradually creates in him a moral incapacity. In that past life he had acted on the principle
that "his religious activity could not be incompatible with his
business as soon as he had argued himself into not feeling it
incompatible" (LXI. 124). Eventually faced with the problem
of his past in the inescapable fact of Raffles' presence in
Middlemarch, he reiterates his rationale:

> Mentally surrounded with that past again, Bulstrode had the
> same pleas--indeed, the years had been perpetually *spinning*
> them into *intricate thickness, like masses of spider-web, pad-
> ding the moral sensibility;* nay, as age made *egoism* more eager
> but less enjoying, his soul had become more saturated with the

belief that he did everything for God's sake, being indifferent to
it for his own *[ibid.]*.

Thus the weblike padding creates an insular world from which
all of the elements that contradict self-view are excluded in
order that the illusion about self may be perpetuated. Clearly
any action which so pads the moral sensibility and so elevates
the ego constitutes a movement away from moral vision.[4]

A slighter but somewhat similar image is used to describe
Rosamond, whose egoism, if second to that of any character
in *Middlemarch,* is second only to Bulstrode's. On one of the
numberless occasions when Rosamond employs her cleverness
to secure her own way in opposition to Lydgate, he gradually
comes to understand the egoistic nature of this cleverness
which had so attracted him to her: "He had regarded Rosamond's cleverness as precisely of that receptive kind which
became a woman. He was now beginning to find out what that
cleverness was--what was the shape into which it had run as
into *a close network* aloof and independent" (LVIII. 76). This
passage partially indicates the illusion about Rosamond out
of which Lydgate spun his share of the "mutual web, " the illusion that her cleverness is receptive and womanly. The
"close network" of Rosamond's cleverness is indeed neither
fragile nor dependent on any other creature. Rather the image
effectively suggests the strong impenetrable nature of Rosamond's egoism. "What she liked to do was to her the right
thing, and all of her cleverness was directed to getting the
means of doing it" (p. 75). When, however, what is needed
is not something she likes, the cleverness remains neutral
and apart:

> "What can *I* do, Tertius?" said Rosamond. . . .
> That little speech of four words, like so many others in all
> languages, is capable by varied inflexions of expressing all
> states of mind from helpless dimness to exhaustive argumen-
> tative perception, from the completest self-devoting fellowship
> to the most neutral aloofness. Rosamond's thin utterance threw
> into the words "What can *I* do?" as much neutrality as they could
> hold [p. 89; author's italics].

It is, of course, Lydgate's inability to penetrate Rosamond's
aloof neutrality that finally makes impossible any reasonable
solution to their domestic difficulty. Rosamond does not, like

Casaubon and Bulstrode, create a padding against a world which she fears will find her culpable--"In fact there was but one person in Rosamond's world whom she did not regard as blameworthy . . ." (LXV.195)--but the aloof and independent network of her cleverness is just as sure a means of preserving her egoism and cutting her off from fellow feeling.

It is, however, not only the Bulstrodes, Casaubons, and Rosamonds whose moral sensibility is padded but those of every human being, George Eliot reminds us: "If we had a *keen vision* and feeling of all ordinary human life, it would be like hearing the grass grow and the squirrel's heart beat, and we should die of that roar which lies on the other side of silence. As it is, the quickest of us walk about well *wadded* with stupidity" (XX.281). Obviously we do not need to supply further protection, since truly keen vision and feeling of all ordinary human life can never be achieved. *Middlemarch* is therefore dedicated to showing another kind of death, that which occurs as the result of too much padding.

≪-≪-≪-≪-≪-≪-≪

That the web image has relevance to the theme of egoism, especially in such explicit terms as are used above to describe Bulstrode's rationalizing, is one more indication of its power to function in relation to the important elements of the book. For the theme of egoism is central throughout *Middlemarch*. It bears a direct relationship not only to the movements toward and away from moral vision but also to the themes of reform and expectations. That relationship can perhaps be most succinctly indicated by exploration of a small group of images.

One of these figures further illustrates the author's habit of showing the reader how to observe, once again, how an illusion is created. The image presents, perhaps unintentionally but not incidentally, an interesting recurrence of web-like configuration:

> Your pier-glass or extensive surface of polished steel made to be rubbed by a housemaid, will be minutely and multitudinously scratched in all directions; but place now against it a lighted candle as a centre of illumination, and lo! the scratches will

seem to arrange themselves in a fine series of concentric cir-
cles round that little sun. It is demonstrable that the scratches
are going everywhere impartially, and it is only your candle
which produces the *flattering illusion* of a concentric arrangement, its light falling with an exclusive optical selection. These
things are a parable. The scratches are events, and the candle
is the *egoism* of any person now absent--of Miss Vincy, for example [XXVII. 383].

It is, of course, common in George Eliot's works to find that
such subdued light creates illusion; that idea is a part of the
whole pattern of light imagery. But nowhere is it more precisely demonstrated than in this image which the author expli-
cates. Here again is an insular world very much akin to that
created by Bulstrode's masses of spider web. The egoistic
belief that events arrange themselves around one person for
the special benefit of that person creates in him a cheerful
confidence in luck or fate, a naïve expectation that the world
will provide him with whatever is necessary to make him
happy. Carried to its fullest extensions this belief would encourage a passive state of moral irresponsibility, of moral
drifting. One of the things which moral vision naturally en-
tails is the arranging of one's expectations in accordance with
the complex reality of a world that does not revolve about the
candle of egoism.

In fact, *Middlemarch* clearly seems to be saying that the
maturity of one's moral vision is in part defined by the nature
of his expectations, since what he expects of the world about
him is inseparable from the way he regards the world. Thus
in the following image the author shows the egoistic view with
which we all begin life as constituting the state of moral infancy: "We are all of us born in moral stupidity, *taking the
world as an udder* to feed our supreme selves" (XXI. 306).
Mr. Farebrother, in a passage which we can assume is presenting the author's own comment, uses a similar image to
characterize Bulstrode and his religious group: ". . . they
are a narrow ignorant set, and do more to make their neighbours uncomfortable than to make them better. Their system
is a sort of worldly-spiritual cliqueism: they really *look* on
the rest of mankind as a *doomed carcass* which is to nourish
them for heaven" (XVII. 254). This egoistic view that the many

exist in a contemptible state divested of human properties and
suitable only for the nourishment of the few is one which clearly cuts off expectations of a mature nature. It indicates what
is only a slightly more sophisticated state of moral infancy
than that noted above. Initiated by such a viewpoint as this,
reform would necessarily become, as it does in Bulstrode's
hands, a kind of spiritual barter. The emphasis is on what
one expects or needs, the assumption of such a viewpoint being that the world is already doomed and therefore needs nothing.

Elsewhere in indicating that although Bulstrode rationalizes,
he is not characterized by hypocrisy, the author speaks of him
generally in an image strikingly similar to those above:

> If this be hypocrisy, it is a process which shows itself occasion-
> ally in us all, to whatever confession we belong, and whether we
> believe in the future perfection of our race or in the nearest date
> fixed for the end of the world; whether we regard the earth as a
> *putrefying nidus* for a saved remnant, including ourselves, or
> have a passionate belief in the solidarity of mankind [LXI. 128].

The image of the earth as a "putrefying nidus" is somewhat
incidental in this context where the primary purpose is to
point up similarity in spite of the difference in points of view,
but it is calculated to recall Farebrother's figurative statement concerning Bulstrode's view of mankind as "doomed
carcass." Both images suggest that the world, as seen from
a certain viewpoint, is doomed and decaying and that its only
function is to serve the saved remnant by providing nourishment or breeding place. And in the repetition of the theme of
egoistic expectations both images may well recall the parable
of the scratched surface and the image of "the world as an
udder to feed our supreme selves. "

George Eliot points up still another general egoistic attitude
in an image which works negatively to indicate the nature of
Lydgate's egoism:

> Some gentlemen have made an amazing figure in literature by
> general discontent with the universe as a *trap of dulness* into
> which their great souls have fallen by mistake; but the sense of
> a stupendous self and an insignificant world may have its conso-
> lations. Lydgate's discontent was much harder to bear: it was
> the sense that there was a grand existence in thought and effective
> action lying around him, while his self was being narrowed into

the miserable isolation of *egoistic fears,* and vulgar anxieties
for events that might allay such fears [LXIV. 169].

The image of the universe as a "trap of dulness" into which
the great soul has fallen by mistake is related to the image of
the spider web. But furthermore it implies both contrast and
likeness to the attitude defined in the images of the udder, the
doomed carcass, the putrefying nidus, and the candle. All of
these images place the self as the superior center of a decidedly inferior world; but whereas the first viewpoint begets the
falsely confident and egoistic expectation that such a world
will provide the means of salvation for the self, the image of
the trap implies a cynical pessimism, a lack of any such expectation. Conversely, Lydgate has a sense of a grand existence and a trapped, narrowed self, an incongruity which becomes so frustrating that it induces a set of egoistic desires,
a state not so much of confident expectancy that events will
arrange themselves advantageously as of desperate hopeful-
ness that they somehow might do so. There is, however, a
crucial difference between Lydgate's egoism at this point (the
passage occurs in Book VII) and that of the moral infant described by previous images: Lydgate is aware of the narrowing,
isolating effect of his egoistic fears and anxieties. Even at an
earlier stage in his life when his egoistic expectations have
about them an air of haughty ease, when he is one of those
young men who are confident "that Mammon shall never put a
bit in their mouths, " he is fully cognizant of a grand existence
outside himself.

The theme of expectations is of course present in the earlier
novels, but in *Felix Holt* it gains emphasis and becomes increasingly important in *Middlemarch* and *Daniel Deronda.*
Aside from its inclusion in the above pattern of images, this
theme, as it is presented in *Middlemarch,* receives its most
cogent metaphorical statement in the description of the nearest of kin in Featherstone's funeral procession; they are the
"Christian Carnivora" who are "naturally impressed with the
unreasonableness of expectations in cousins" (XXXV. 87). The
most pointed rhetorical emphasis is the author's humorous
comment during the reading of the will: "O possibilities! O
expectations founded on the favor of 'close' old gentlemen! O
endless vocatives . . . " (p. 95). And in terms of character

relationship the most decided contrast is between Mary Garth, who has had "strong reason to believe that things were not likely to be arranged for her peculiar satisfaction" (XXXIII. 65) and Fred Vincy, who thinks, "what can the fitness of things mean, if not their fitness to a man's expectations?" (XIV. 193).

⁂⁂⁂⁂⁂

I wish now to call attention to a group of images which in large part derive their meaning from the archetypal symbol of life as a journey or pilgramage. In *Adam Bede* and *The Mill on the Floss* the journey symbol figures prominently, and in fact it underlies the central concept of this entire study: that George Eliot's novels are a study in movement toward and away from moral vision. But in *Middlemarch* it provides-- as I am not aware that it has done in preceding novels--a complex pattern of images which help to define most of the characters in terms of attitudes, intentions, and purpose. The cumulative effect of these images is a sense of movement in the novel (or of attempted movement as the case may be), a sense that all of the Middlemarchers although they usually are not marching steadily forward are nevertheless struggling to move along some path or perhaps along more than one path. The nature of movement is in some cases so generally characterizing that it will be valuable to use the images as points of departure leading into a discussion of the characters in larger terms.

The stages in Dorothea's life can be sketchily traced through this imagery: her early dissatisfaction with her narrow life and her hopes for a better life, her disillusionment, and some indication of her more realistic knowledge about what life holds for her. To the youthful Dorothea, as we have noted earlier, her life seemed "nothing but a *labyrinth* of petty *courses*, a walled-in *maze* of small *paths* that led no whither." Discontented with all of her attempts to do good because, as she phrases it, "everything seems like *going on a mission* to a people whose language I don't know," she believes that her union with Casaubon will "give her the freedom of voluntary submission to a guide who would take her along *the grandest path*" (III. 36-37). In marrying him she feels that she is "get-

ting away from Tipton and Freshitt, and her own sad liability
to *tread* in the wrong places *on her way* to the New Jerusalem"
(IV.49). The movement image which describes her state of
disillusionment is quite naturally connected with a vision image: "Like one who has lost his way and is weary, she sat and
saw as in one glance all the *paths* of her young hope which she
should never find again. And just as clearly in the *miserable
lights* she *saw* her own and her husband's solitude--how they
walked apart . . . " (XLII.229). Also related to vision is this
image which indicates something of Dorothea's growth since
the time when she sought for a guide to take her along the
"grandest paths": ". . . in the long valley of her life which
looked so flat and empty of way-marks, guidance would come
to her as she *walked along the road,* and *saw* her fellow passengers by the way" (LXXVII.354). Now, the passage seems
to imply, she will find her guidance through her sympathetic
contact with fellow passengers along a common road.

   Similarly this image group brings into focus a pattern of
observations about Lydgate's life. Lydgate, who on arrival
in Middlemarch intends not to marry "until he had *trodden
out a good clear path* for himself away from the *broad road*
which was quite ready-made" (XI.132), unequivocally states
his determination not to allow any interference. "'I hope I
shall have nothing to do with clerical disputes, ' said Lydgate
[in a conversation with Bulstrode]. 'The *path* I have chosen
is to work well in my own profession'" (XIII.180). And since
"medical practice was still *strutting* or *shambling* along the
old paths" (XV.213), there is room for exploration of a new
path, one which is not "ready-made. " "Perhaps, " George
Eliot says, "that was a more cheerful time for observers
and theorizers than the present; we are apt to think it the finest
era of the world when America was beginning to be discovered,
when a bold *sailor,* even if he were wrecked, might alight on
a new kingdom; and about 1829 the dark territories of Pathology
were a fine America for a *spirited young adventurer"* (pp.
211-12). The explorer image is, I believe, the most important in the pattern because its repetition in terms of other
characters points up significant contrasts and because in this
specific instance it indicates that for Lydgate there is still
a channel for historic action, a grand path which does not

exist for Dorothea or for other Middlemarchers. Something more about the new path Lydgate intends to travel and his proposed mode of exploration is revealed in a widely relevant passage containing a less explicit but more significant explorer metaphor. What is most striking about this passage, aside from the beauty and power of the image, is that here as elsewhere (see conclusion of the next chapter) in defining Lydgate's intention as a scientific explorer, George Eliot also defines her own intention as novelist; and in defining imagination as a mode of exploration she also defines poetic imagination as contrasted with poetic fancy:

> Many men have been praised as vividly imaginative on the strength of their profuseness in indifferent drawing or cheap narration:--reports of very poor talk going on in distant orbs; or portraits of Lucifer coming down on his bad errands as a large ugly man with bat's wings and spurts of phosphorescence; or exaggerations of wantonness that seem to reflect life in a diseased dream. But these kinds of inspiration Lydgate regarded as rather vulgar and vinous compared with the *imagination that reveals subtle actions inaccessible by any sort of lens,* but *tracked in that outer darkness through long pathways of necessary sequence by the inward light* which is the last refinement of Energy, capable of bathing even the ethereal atoms in its *ideally illuminated* space. He for his part had tossed away all cheap inventions where ignorance finds itself able and at ease: he was enamored of that arduous invention which is *the very eye of research,* provisionally framing its object and correcting it to more and more exactness of relation; he wanted to *pierce the obscurity* of those minute processes which prepare human misery and joy, those *invisible thoroughfares* which are the first lurking places of anguish, mania, and crime, that delicate poise and transition which determine the growth of happy or unhappy consciousness [XVI. 236-37].

The light which the author focuses on the web of human lots can safely be equated with "the inward light which is the last refinement of energy": it is "the imagination that reveals subtle actions inaccessible by any sort of lens." In contrast to the telescopic watch and microscopic scrutiny which have been referred to from time to time is this third way of seeing. Although Lydgate's concern is to track in "that outer darkness," the object which George Eliot provisionally frames and then explores has also, as the whole book demonstrates,

its "long pathways of necessary sequence." *Middlemarch,*
like Lydgate, is dedicated to piercing "the obscurity of those
minute processes which prepare human misery and joy." How
it is that Lydgate and George Eliot differ in their conception
of the minute processes which have such important effects
must be considered in a fuller discussion of Lydgate's vision.
At the moment what is important is that Lydgate among all
of the characters in the novel is the one who has found a grand
path and the most adequate means of exploring it.

That the acute Mr. Farebrother recognizes in Lydgate the
qualities of "the spirited young adventurer" and that George
Eliot wishes to emphasize it is confirmed by the rector's
metaphoric comment: "You are a sort of *circumnavigator*
come to settle among us, and will keep up my belief in the
antipodes" (XVII. 254). Farebrother's acuteness, however,
extends further; this observation occurs at the end of a conversation during which he has warned Lydgate about the necessity of keeping himself independent. But Lydgate, the author points out, is adventuresome only in one area of life:

> We may handle even extreme opinions with impunity while our
> furniture, our dinner-giving, and preference for armorial bear-
> ings in our own case, link us indissolubly with the established
> order. And Lydgate's tendency was not toward extreme opinions:
> he would have liked no barefooted doctrines, being particular
> about his boots: he was no radical in relation to anything but
> medical reform and the prosecution of discovery. In the rest of
> practical life he *walked* by hereditary habit . . . [XXXVI. 113].

It is Lydgate's tragic dilemma that he cannot walk both the
ready-made road of hereditary custom and the new path of
discovery. By the time he is ready to eschew the hereditary
habit of fine furniture and dinner-giving, his lot is inextricably interwoven with Rosamond's. He "accepted his narrowed
lot with sad resignation. He had chosen this fragile creature,
and had taken the burthen of her life upon his arms. He must
walk as he could, carrying that burthen pitifully" (LXXXI.
392).

In fine contrast to Lydgate, whose ambition it is to discover "the primitive tissue" which is the source of life (see
XV. 213), is Casaubon, who calls himself a "scrupulous explorer" (XX. 291), but who with a "small taper of learned

theory [is] *exploring* the tossed ruins of the world" (X. 116),
the realm of the dead past. [5] Speaking to Mr. Brooke, he defines his own movement more accurately than he himself
elsewhere seems to realize: "I feed too much on the inward
sources; I live too much with the dead. My mind is something
like the *ghost* of an ancient, *wandering about the world* and
trying mentally to construct it as it used to be, in spite of
ruin and confusing changes" (II. 20-21). Ladislaw, a severer
critic of Casaubon than George Eliot approves of, does put
his finger on what the book gives us every reason to believe
is true when he compares Casaubon with German historical
scholars: ". . . the Germans have taken the lead in historical
inquiries, and they laugh at results which are got by *groping
about* in the woods with a pocket-compass while they have
made *good roads"* (XXI. 301). In effect, then, Casaubon uses
an outmoded and inadequate means to explore an area which
is already being settled, or, to quote Ladislaw again, he goes
"crawling a little way after men of the last century . . ."
(XXII. 322). The result is that even the "small monumental
records of his *march"* (XXIX. 13), the pamphlets which he
publishes, remain relatively unnoticed by his colleagues. And
at the end of his life as he prepares instructions for Dorothea
regarding his unfinished work, he is "oppressed in the plan of
transmitting his work, as he had been in executing it, by the
sense of *moving heavily* in a dim and clogging medium . . ."
(L. 328).

And in contrast to both Lydgate and Casaubon, who have a
definite direction and purpose even though their purposes remain unfulfilled and in the one instance unworthy of fulfillment,
is Mr. Brooke, whose way it was "to go about everywhere and
take in everything" (IV. 51) up to his "certain point. " But as
Mrs. Cadwallader emphasizes, no one knows where that certain point is: "I should like to be told how a man can have any
certain point when he belongs to no party--leading *a roving
life,* and never letting his friends know his address" (VI. 73).
Mr. Brooke's most uncertain point is his own ineffectual safe-
guard against going too far in any one of his several hobbies,
the thing in life which he most fears: "Hobbies are apt to run
away with us, you know; it doesn't do to be run away with. We
must keep the reins. I have never let myself be run away with;

I always pulled up. That is what I tell Ladislaw. He and I are alike, you know: he likes to go in everything" (XXXIX. 172). But ironically it is this very fear of committing himself to any one course which causes him to be run away with, as Mr. Cadwallader observes in a very apt image: "Brooke is a very good fellow, but pulpy; he will run into any mold, but he won't keep shape" (VIII. 97).

Mr. Brooke carries his idea of roaming far and wide into his political position, if it can be said to be a position. Speaking as a "close neighbor" of those assembled for the political rally, he exhorts:

". . . everything must go on--trade, manufactures, commerce, interchange of staples--that sort of thing--since Adam Smith, that must go on. We must *look* all over the globe: *'Observation with extensive view,'* must *look everywhere*, 'from China to Peru,' as somebody says--Johnson, I think, *The Rambler*, you know. That is what I have done up to a certain point--not as far as Peru; but I've not always stayed at home--I saw it wouldn't do. I've been in the Levant, where some of your Middlemarch goods go--and then, again in the Baltic. The Baltic, now" [LI. 344-45].

Thus in a rambling rhetoric decidedly suited to a rambling view, Mr. Brooke expounds his theory of reform which goes too far afield ever to reach his "neighbors" who listen. It is regrettable that we cannot adequately explore the comic effects that George Eliot achieves in her presentation of this superbly comic character. [6] But it is a far more relevant and necessary side-step to consider the implications of Mr. Brooke's particular kind of movement in relation to the themes of reform and vision.

First it should be noted that Mr. Brooke says we "must *look* all over the globe, " "must *look* everywhere, " but that he gives no indication about what we should look for or at. Again there is the implied contrast between "observation with extensive view" and careful scrutiny of minute causes which the book posits as prerequisite to the extensive view, between the telescopic watch and the microscopic examination which George Eliot has discussed in relation to Mrs. Cadwallader's matchmaking. Mr. Brooke speaks in wide generalities and abstractions--"everything must go on--trade, manufacture . . .

that kind of thing"--but he does not once consider the concrete
problems of his neighbors whom he proposes to represent.
His criterion for progress seems to be movement for its own
sake regardless of direction, as this bit of vague conversation indicates: "Well, what do you think of things?--going on
a little fast! It was true enough, what Lafitte said--'Since
yesterday, a century has passed away':--they're in the next
century, you know, on the other side of the water. Going on
faster than we are" (XXXVIII. 163). Once more we note that
his interest is in an undefined movement in a distant place,
and although he remarks that "things" are "going on a little
fast" he is nevertheless impressed by that phenomenon.

It is in this scene that Mr. Cadwallader reads from the
Pioneer a passage of criticism attacking Mr. Brooke, one
which is obviously intended to be read as the author's most
direct comment not only on this kind of man but also on reform:

> *If we had to describe a man who is retrogressive in the most*
> *evil sense of the word--we should say he is one who would dub*
> *himself a reformer of our constitution, while every interest for*
> *which he is immediately responsible is going to decay: a philan-*
> *thropist who cannot bear one rogue to be hanged, but does not*
> *mind five honest tenants being half-starved: a man who shrieks*
> *at corruption, and keeps his farm at rack rent: . . . a man very*
> *open-hearted to Leeds and Manchester, no doubt. . . . But we*
> *all know the wag's definition of a philanthropist: a man whose*
> *charity increases directly as the square of the distance* [pp. 164-
> 65; author's italics].

Finally, then, the significance of Mr. Brooke's rambling
movement and his theory that we must go about and look everywhere is cogently expressed in the wag's definition of a philan-
thropist. True reform, George Eliot is saying, begins at home
in small but charitable actions, not at a distance in abstractions and generalities. It is begun by men of vision who, seeing what the lives of their neighbors are like and responding
to their needs, can then extend the area of their reforming
actions.[7] This is, in fact, the crux of George Eliot's political
position as it has been stated one novel earlier by Felix Holt.
In his attack against a Radical electioneer, Felix deprecates
any plan which will give the vote to ignorant men who will
thereby be able to exert an irresponsible power. The idea of

the vote as a panacea, Felix asserts, is built on a false expectation: "Now, all the schemes about voting, and districts, and annual Parliaments, and the rest, are engines, and the water or steam--the force that is to work them--must come out of human nature--out of men's passions, feelings, and desires. Whether the engines will do good work or bad depends on these feelings; and if we have *false expectations* about men's characters, we are very much like the idiot who thinks he'll carry milk in a can without a bottom. In my opinion, the notions about what mere voting will do are very much of that sort. " The greatest power, he further asserts, is "public opinion--the ruling belief in society about what is right and what is wrong, what is honorable and what is shameful" (XXX. 84-85). Implicit in this position is the idea of moral vision as a greater power than the vote and as a prerequisite to the vote. The novel *Felix Holt* provides several rewarding comparisons with *Middlemarch*. Mr. Lignon's election speech on behalf of Harold Transome (see chapter xix) points Lignon up as a lesser Mr. Brooke, both of whom contrast with Felix, who says: "one must begin somewhere. I'll begin at what is under my nose" (XI. 189).

What Mr. Brooke has been quoted above as saying about Will Ladislaw is one of the important clues to Ladislaw as a character: "He and I are alike, you know. He likes to go in everything. " In fact these two characters are in decided contrast to Lydgate and Casaubon, the explorers. Ladislaw, frequently compared to a gypsy, is a wanderer who, as Mr. Casaubon describes him, is preparing "to go abroad again, without any special object, save the vague purpose of what he calls culture, preparation for he knows not what" (IX. 112). But for reasons which Casaubon with only superficial accuracy explains to Mr. Brooke, Ladislaw is no explorer:

"He has a *thirst for travelling;* perhaps he may turn out a Bruce or a Mungo Park, " said Mr. Brooke. "I had a notion of that myself at one time. "

"No, he has *no bent toward exploration,* or the enlargement of our geognosis: that would be a special purpose which I could recognize with some approbation. . . . But so far is he from having any desire for a more accurate knowledge of the earth's surface that he said he should prefer not to know the sources of the Nile, and that there should be some unknown regions preserved as *hunting-grounds for the poetic imagination*"[pp. 112-13].

To Casaubon this attitude of Ladislaw's is nothing more than part of a "general inaccuracy and indisposition to thoroughness of all kinds, " an indication of his noticeable lack of direction. And, in fact, so it is. But whereas Casaubon would grant no validity to the poetic imagination as a means of exploring unknown regions, George Eliot would accredit it as a primary mode of exploration. That Casaubon does not himself have imagination is clearly the cause of his pitiful failure as an explorer. That Lydgate has both the imagination and an adequate channel for it to work in is the tragic element in his failure. And that Ladislaw--unlike Lydgate, who "was enamoured of that arduous invention which is the very eye of research, provisionally framing its object and correcting it to more and more exactness of relation"--is given to easy and fanciful invention rather than imaginative exploration is the clue to his formless, imperfectly fulfilled life. In a passage which shows something of his attitude toward Dorothea--obviously in the best chivalric tradition--George Eliot clearly associates wit and fancy with his imagination and indicates that it functions primarily to delight and charm its possessor. Once more a movement image is employed:

> . . . Will was not one of those whose *wit* "keeps the roadways": he had his *bypaths* where there were little joys of his own choosing, such as gentlemen cantering on the *high-road* might have thought rather idiotic. The way in which he made a sort of happiness for himself out of his feeling for Dorothea was an example of this. . . . What others might have called the futility of his passion, made an additional *delight* for his *imagination:* he was conscious of a generous movement, and of verifying in his own experience that higher love-poetry that had *charmed* his *fancy.* Dorothea, he said to himself, was forever enshrined in his soul: no other woman could sit higher than her footstool. . . . She had once said that she would like him to stay; and stay he would, whatever *fire-breathing dragons* might hiss around her [XLVII. 292-93].

Ladislaw, like Lydgate, does not choose the "high-road" which is ready-made. Nor does he, until the end of the novel, choose any one road, although he allows himself to drift into one.

In fact, in Ladislaw's scheme of things it is of central importance that he be allowed complete freedom of movement:

> Indeed, Will had declined to fix on any more precise destination
> than the entire area of Europe. Genius, he held, is necessarily
> intolerant of fetters: on the one hand it must have utmost play
> for its spontaneity; on the other, it may confidently await those
> messages from the universe which summon it to its peculiar
> work, only placing itself in an attitude of receptivity toward all
> sublime chances [X.115].

Like Lydgate, Ladislaw is "intolerant of fetters," a phrase
which recalls the images of the web and the trap. But in his
passivity and lack of direction unlike Lydgate, Ladislaw insists on the freedom not to choose any given path but to make
himself completely receptive to whatever might choose him.
This attitude expressed in terms of movement imagery is so
basic in Ladislaw's make-up that it is reflected in his personality and appearance, in his thinking and feeling. As external
stimuli play upon him he undergoes a "metamorphosis": "The
first impression on seeing Will was one of sunny brightness,
which added to the uncertainty of his changing expression.
Surely, his very features changed their form. . . ." And
what first impresses Dorothea about him is his "openness to
conviction," the fact that he is "quick and pliable, so likely
to understand everything" (XXI.303-4). He is not, however,
so likely to maintain a consistent attitude toward what he
understands: he "was made of very impressible stuff. The
bow of a violin drawn near him cleverly would at one stroke
change the aspect of the world for him, and his *point of view
shifted* as easily as his mood" (XXXIX.171). Finally, then,
his only consistency at this point in his life is his hedonism;
pointing out the fallacy in Dorothea's fanatical sympathy, he
proposes his method of reforming the world:

> "If you carried it out you ought to be miserable in your own good-
> ness, and turn evil that you might have no advantage over others.
> The best piety is to enjoy--when you can. You are doing the most
> then to save the earth's character as an agreeable planet. And
> enjoyment radiates. It is of no use to try and take care of the
> world; that is being taken care of when you feel delight . . ."
> [XXII.318].

But much later Ladislaw has come to know that he must
choose some consistent and direct course if he is to make

himself worthy of Dorothea. The change is pointed up in terms
of movement: despairing of ever winning her, ". . . he felt
himself *plodding along* as a poor devil seeking a position in a
world which in his present temper offered him little that he
coveted . . ." (LXII. 152). By now there has been a decided
change in his expectations in relation to the universe. And
still later, having discovered Rosamond's dependence on
him, he feels "no more foretaste of enjoyment in the life before him than if his limbs had been lopped off and he was *making his fresh start on crutches*" (LXXXII. 396). His world is
considerably narrowed by acceptance of this responsibility:
"The Rubicon, we know, was a very insignificant stream to
look at; its significance lay entirely in certain invisible conditions. Will felt as if he were forced *to cross* his small
boundary ditch, and what he *saw* beyond it was not empire,
but discontented subjection" *(ibid.)*. And finally during his
last appearance in the book, Ladislaw makes an observation
which even more completely indicates the change in his expectations from the time when he had confidently waited for
the universe to beckon him to great endeavor. ". . . I shall
most likely always be very poor: on a sober calculation, one
can count on nothing but *a creeping lot*" (LXXXIII. 407). Although the immediate context seems to indicate that Ladislaw
is speaking only of financial circumstances, the statement
nevertheless has about it the air of a more generally applicable pronouncement which reveals the fundamental change
in Ladislaw.

A fruitful comparison could be made between Ladislaw and
Daniel Deronda. Daniel's problem, much simplified of course,
is that his sympathy is so all-embracing that he remains unformed, somewhat as Ladislaw is, until his Jewishness imposes form. I would suggest--merely suggest--that Ladislaw's
wandering and the fact that he is part Jewish together hint at
the theme of the wandering Jew and that George Eliot works
from Ladislaw to Deronda. Deronda moves from an undirected
and too diffuse vision to a heroship which justifies partiality
of vision; Ladislaw, however, must learn to give up the idea
of heroship.

A few more images which point up the general movements
of the characters in *Middlemarch* may be noted briefly in or-

der to indicate the scope of the pattern. The significant occurrence in Rosamond's life is outlined by two contrasting
images. During the happy days of courtship "she seemed to
be sailing with a fair wind just whither she would go . . ."
(XXVII. 387).[8] But during the crucial period of her life when
for a brief time her dream world collapses, she is shattered
with "a sense that she had been *walking* in an unknown world
which had just broken in upon her" (LXXXI. 386-87). Fred,
who begins life with confident expectations that the world will
make things easy for him, gradually comes "to *see* that this
was a world in which even a spirited young man must sometimes *walk* for want of a horse to carry him . . ." (LVII.
55). According to his own view of himself, Bulstrode is trying "to thread a path for principles in the intricacies of the
world . . ." (XIII. 186); but the author herself in one telling
metaphor illuminates the entire movement of his life:

> Strange, piteous conflict in the soul of this unhappy man, who
> had longed for years to be better than he was--who had taken his
> selfish passions into discipline and clad them in severe robes,
> so that he had *walked with them as a devout choir,* till now that
> a terror had risen among them, and they could chant no longer,
> but threw out their common cries for safety [LXX. 254-55].

This image of Bulstrode walking with his passions as a devout
choir is one of the finest in the book. It emphasizes his asceticism, his attempt to order his life, and at the same time it
points up the falsity of the appearance he wishes to present
to the world and to himself. It suggests his isolation, how
he walks through life surrounded only by himself. But most
of all in the poignantly rendered breakdown of that appearance,
it reveals the internal struggle and secures the reader's sympathy for this man who has so deluded himself. And so it is
that in almost every instance the movement images used to
define a character either directly or indirectly indicate something about that character's vision.

Obviously the imagery of drifting is itself largely a pattern
of movement imagery. Here it differs from the drifting pattern
in George Eliot's other novels only in detail and emphasis. The

state of will-lessness, for example, is often more emphatically related to the theme of expectations, as the following passage indicates: ". . . *indefinite visions* of ambition are weak against the ease of doing what is habitual or *beguilingly* agreeable; and we all know the difficulty of carrying out a resolve when we secretly long that it may turn out to be unnecessary. In such states of mind the most incredulous person has a private leaning toward a miracle . . ." (LX. 103). The state of moral drifting is sometimes presented in physiological images: Bulstrode's misdeeds are frequently "like the *subtle muscular movements* which are not taken account of in the consciousness, though they bring about the end that we fix our mind on and desire" (LXVIII. 227); and Lydgate's lack of resolve is referred to both by himself and by the author as "creeping paralysis." But much of the drifting imagery is derived from the idea of movement on water, as in the other novels. Lydgate wants no hobby besides his profession because he has "the sea to swim in there" (XVII. 248), but unfortunately he loses "the niceties of inward balance, by which a man *swims* and makes his point or else *is carried headlong*" (XV. 214). Eventually he and Rosamond find themselves shipwrecked: ". . . it was as if they were both *adrift* on one piece of wreck and *looked away from each other*" (LXXV. 330). The recurrent shipwreck image is connected with the theme of expectation in the author's description of Bulstrode: ". . . in the midst of his fears, like many a man who is in danger of *shipwreck* or of being dashed from his carriage by runaway horses, he had the clinging impression that *something would happen* to hinder the worst . . ." (LXVIII. 231-32). Ladislaw, in a state of crisis, is like "the man who has escaped from *wreck* by night and stands on unknown ground in *darkness*" (LXXXII. 398). Lydgate is sometimes associated with a swamp, as in the following passage: ". . . he was every day getting deeper into that *swamp*, which *tempts* men toward it with such a pretty covering of flowers and verdure. It is wonderful how soon a man gets up to his chin there . . ." (LVIII. 79).

In general the elements in the pattern of vision imagery are also basically the same here as in the first novels. But central now in the pattern and to some extent counterbalancing the governing metaphor of the web is the symbol of the window. George Eliot employs the usual symbolic implications of a window as an opening through which one may see the world outside or through which light is admitted to reveal what is inside--hence a means of increasing vision. Thus, for example, Casaubon, whose extremely weak and "blinking" eyes and "burrowing" tendency are generally symbolic of his poor vision, is associated with the heavily shuttered library and the small-windowed side of the house, with candlelight rather than sunlight: "With his taper stuck before him he forgot the absence of windows . . . had become indifferent to the sunlight" (XX. 286). In extreme contrast, of course, is Dorothea who is associated with the bow-window. But, as in the case of the web, George Eliot further exploits the symbol by drawing on its antithetical implications. Thus, for example, Bulstrode's window does not open out but rather thrusts back upon him his past life:

> Night and day, without interruption save of brief sleep, which only *wove* retrospect and fear into a fantastic present, he felt the scenes of his earlier life coming between him and everything else, as obstinately as, when we look through the *window* from a lighted room, the objects we turn our backs on are still before us, instead of the grass and the trees [LXI. 122].

Even more important, however, is the negative implication in relation to Dorothea; for whereas a window is an opening through which one may see, it is also a transparent covering which removes one from immediate contact with what is seen. In one sense like the web, then, it may help provide an insular world, one in which the detached role of spectator may be assumed.

8. *Middlemarch:* The Window and the Web

IN THE preceding chapter I attempted to give some general indication of the complex elements at work in *Middlemarch*. I wish now to consider in some detail the individual movements in *Middlemarch*, concentrating on one movement and the way others merge with it and are affected by it. The two characters whose influence is most profoundly felt throughout *Middlemarch* are Bulstrode and Dorothea. Either by marriage or money, Bulstrode is in some way connected with all of the major characters except Dorothea. Always carefully scrutinizing the circumstances surrounding his numerous loans, he thus increases his power: "In this way a man gathers a domain in his neighbours' hope and fear as well as gratitude; and power, when once it has got into that subtle region, propagates itself, spreading out of all proportion to its external means. It was a principle with Mr. Bulstrode to gain as much power as possible, that he might use it for the glory of God" (XVI. 223). Therefore it is ironic that Bulstrode's tyrannical influence hovers over the whole of *Middlemarch* like an evil spirit; even some of his supporters disagree with his policies but rationalize that it is sometimes necessary "to hold a candle to the Devil" (p. 222). But obviously more important in terms of the entire novel is the counterinfluence of Dorothea, whose individual movement joins and modifies the movement of four other lives. I therefore intend to trace the stages in Dorothea's advance toward moral vision, to explore the way she affects the vision of those whose lives become interwoven with hers, and, finally, in the light of this examination to show further where true reform really lies--to discover the book's answer to Dorothea's constantly reiterated question: how close can the individual come to leading "a grand life here--now--in England" (III. 37). Much of this, I believe, can be accomplished through calling attention to the vision imagery as it reinforces the dramatic line of the individual movement, but it will also be necessary to draw on other elements.

In view of the response some readers apparently have to Dorothea, one of the most crucial questions which need to be asked about *Middlemarch* is whether Dorothea actually does move toward a wider vision or whether George Eliot considers her to be so good and noble that very much change in her way of looking at things would be superfluous. The question appears to be loaded, and yet it states an important issue. It is a question, however, which would have far more valid grounds for argument in relation to Dinah than Dorothea, for here I believe the answer is unequivocal. Dorothea does have a fine and noble nature; but the reader who objects to references which associate her with the Virgin Mary or to her queenly and naïvely idealistic attitude would do well to consider the full context and the author's intention, an intention which, I believe, is carefully executed in terms of expository, dramatic, and imagistic emphasis.

We learn in chapter one that according to rural opinion, ". . . Miss Brooke's large eyes seemed, like her religion, too unusual and striking" (p. 9), but the first significant indication about the peculiar quality of her sight comes in the quotation which prefaces chapter ii: "'Seest thou not yon cavalier who cometh toward us on a dapple-grey steed, and weareth a golden helmet?' 'What I see,' answered Sancho, 'is nothing but a man on a gray ass like my own, who carries something shiny on his head.' 'Just so,' answered Don Quixote: and that resplendent object is the helmet of Mambrino.'" This quotation is obviously intended not only as a comment on Dorothea's quixotic view of Casaubon, with which the chapter is primarily concerned, but also as a partial definition of her habitual way of looking at things in general. The role of Sancho is filled by Celia, who later finds it necessary to

tell Dorothea what "everyone can see, " that Sir James is in
love with her: "I thought it right to tell you, because you went
on as you always do, *never looking* just where you are, and
treading in the wrong place. You always *see what nobody else
sees;* it is impossible to satisfy you; yet you *never see what
is quite plain.* That's your way, Dodo" (IV. 47). Speaking of a
small terrier Celia once had, Dorothea partially confirms
Celia's observation: "It made me unhappy, because I was
afraid of treading on it. I am rather short-sighted" (III. 39).

In many instances throughout the novel Celia serves as a
humorous but sympathetic foil to Dorothea, frequently a reminder of Dorothea's habit of treading in the wrong places
and looking at the world with an unrealistic eye. It is no accident that Celia's pet name for Dorothea is Dodo. The incongruity between the sound of the childish nickname and
Dorothea's high seriousness often punctures her excessively
idealistic attitude, calls attention to her childishness, and
thereby sets her in proper perspective for the reader. Furthermore the name may very well be intended to suggest the
dodo, a now extinct, clumsy, flightless bird whose name is
derived from a Portuguese word meaning *silly*. A superb
illustration of the use of this name and Celia's general function in relation to Dorothea is the conversation between the
two sisters immediately after Dorothea has discovered Rosamond and Ladislaw in what she thinks is a love scene:

> "Dodo, how very bright your eyes are'. " said Celia. . . . "And
> you don't see anything you look at, Arthur or anything. You are
> going to do something uncomfortable, I know. Is it all about Mr.
> Lydgate, or has something else happened?" Celia had been used
> to watch her sister with expectation.
> "Yes, dear, a great many things have happened, " said Dodo,
> in her full tones.
> "I wonder what, " said Celia, folding her arms cozily and lean-
> ing forward upon them.
> 'Oh, all the troubles of all the people on the face of the earth'. "
> said Dorothea, lifting her arms to the back of her head.
> "Dear me, Dodo, are you going to have a scheme for them?"
> said Celia, a little uneasy at this Hamlet-like raving [LXXVII.
> 358-59].

This verbal exchange, occurring as it does at the end of
one of the most important dramatic scenes in the book, clear-

ly indicates the author's intention to reveal the absurdities of her character as well as the virtues; her own repetition of the nickname--"said Dodo, in her full tones"--and her descriptive phrase--"this Hamlet-like raving"--should leave no doubt about that. Furthermore, Celia's remark about Dorothea's having a scheme for the troubles of the world is ironic in view of the fact that none of Dorothea's relatively less grandiose schemes have been carried out. Celia's placid serenity, indicated by her response of "folding her arms cozily" and merely wondering what has happened, contrasts sharply with Dorothea's excessive emotionalism here. One might question whether or not George Eliot is showing her characteristic sympathy in so presenting Dorothea at a time when she has just undergone a tremendous shock. But Dorothea is not really suffering, for she is still too much engrossed in the experience of new emotion: "She had never felt anything like this triumphant power of indignation in the struggle of her married life, in which there had always been a quickly subduing pang; and she took it as a sign of new strength" (p. 358). Her extravagant speech is therefore accurately labeled as histrionic. The passage, merely one of many such, is, I believe, a fair example of the objectivity with which the author presents Dorothea. It should be added, however, that because Celia remains static she also serves as a measuring stick by which we can observe Dorothea's change. Thus there is sometimes, especially at the end of the book, a reverse twist when Celia's conversation ironically turns upon the position she represents and thus emphasizes the rightness of Dorothea's position.

It is absolutely necessary to distinguish between the idealization which Dorothea receives at the hands of other characters and the actual Dorothea as the author wishes the reader to regard her. It is true that on the first page George Eliot suggests that Dorothea has the kind of beauty with which the Italian painters visualized the Blessed Virgin and that her plain garments give her "the impressiveness of a fine quotation from the Bible." The German painter Naumann observes that she is "the most perfect young Madonna" (XIX. 274) he has ever seen and insists on painting her as Santa Clara. But these are indications of appearance, and in George Eliot's

novels appearance is never to be used as an indiscriminate
basis for conclusions. In this case, however, the appearance
is not deceptive, for Dorothea is described with some accuracy by Lydgate, who--after Dorothea has taken her stand in
his behalf--has stronger basis than appearance for his conclusion: "This young creature has a heart large enough for
the Virgin Mary. She evidently thinks nothing of her own future, and would pledge away half her income at once, as if
she wanted nothing for herself but a chair to sit in from which
she can look down with those clear eyes at the poor mortals
who pray to her" (LXXVI. 347). The extent of Lydgate's accuracy here and most especially the extent to which the author
considers such a characteristic praiseworthy must be considered later, but there is indeed something queenly and noble
about Dorothea which causes her to be enthroned by others.
"'It is a pity she was not a queen,' said the devout Sir James"
(LIV. 4), whose "chivalrous nature" makes him her most determined protector; for, as the author questions in a paren-
thesis, "was not the disinterested service of woman among
the ideal glories of old chivalry?" Something of Ladislaw's
chivalrous attitude toward Dorothea has already been noted;
the following passage makes that attitude quite clear: "The
remote worship of a woman throned out of their reach plays
a great part in men's lives, but in most cases the worshipper
longs for some queenly recognition, some approving sign by
which his soul's sovereign may cheer him without descending
from her high place. That was precisely what Will wanted"
(XXII. 316). Although she finds it frustrating to have her movements checked, Dorothea cannot be said to be wholly averse
to the homage paid her. As early as chapter i we are told
that "Miss Brooke presided in her uncle's household, and
did not at all dislike her new authority, with the homage that
belonged to it" (p. 10). Much later the author observes that
"Dorothea had little vanity, but she had the ardent woman's
need to rule beneficently by making the joy of another soul"
(XXXVII. 132).

But whether or not George Eliot considers the beneficent
rule from the height of a throne to be the best way of making
the joy of another soul is a question which needs some attention. To trace the progress of Dorothea's growth in vision is

also to trace her movement from the throne into the world. Before that movement is examined, however, one more point in modification of the preceding statements concerning the author's handling of Dorothea needs to be made.

And this point, I believe, is finally the one which most complicates the problem of accurately interpreting Dorothea as a character. Here is the crucial spot for determining whether or not Dorothea is sentimentalized. The point is that Dorothea's idealistic way of looking at people is not always to be condemned as poor vision, that, in fact, it is one of her most positive characteristics:

> There are natures in which, if they love us, we are conscious of having a sort of baptism and consecration; they bind us over to rectitude and purity by their pure belief about us; and our sins become that worst kind of sacrilege which tears down the invisible altar of trust. . . .
>
> Dorothea's nature was of that kind: her own passionate faults lay along the easily-counted open channels of her ardent character; and while she was full of pity for the visible mistakes of others, she had not yet any material within her experience for subtle constructions and suspicions of hidden wrong. But that simplicity of hers, holding up an ideal for others in her believing conception of them, was one of the great powers of her womanhood [LXXVII. 351-52].

That the use of certain words here--*baptism, consecration, sins, sacrilege,* and *altar*--gives a decidedly religious overtone to this description of character should not be interpreted as the apotheosizing of Dorothea, whose childlike faith and simplicity are the characteristics being stressed. Rather it implies that human beings, in their very capacity as human beings, can affect each other in such a way as to create what is essentially a religious experience, as for example the upper room scene in *Adam Bede.* But it seems to me that an important and rather difficult distinction needs to be made here, since there are times when Dorothea's idealizing is decidedly an example of poor vision. The distinction is this: that it is one thing to fail to see aright what already exists as an accomplished fact of a person's life, and it is another to see and act in terms of a potential--even a slightly potential --good which for a complex of reasons does not become an accomplished fact of a person's life. The first we must call lack of vision; the second we must call vision of the ideal. The first, if it consists in seeing a weakness as less weak or even as a strength, is the idealizing, seeing an illusion rather than a reality. The second, by setting up for another person an ideal of himself, may cause him to raise himself up toward it. The distinction is important because Dorothea does both.

꙰꙰꙰꙰꙰

The point, then, at which Dorothea begins her slow and painful movement is one which allows much room for growth. Quixotic, childishly naïve--"compared with her the innocent-looking Celia was knowing and worldly-wise" (I. 9)--Dorothea usually sees people in the narrow world about her through rose-colored glasses, although "across all her imaginative adornment of those whom she loved, there darted now and then a keen discernment, which was not without a scorching quality" (pp. 15-16). She has "very childlike ideas about marriage," one of them being that "the really delightful marriage must be that where your husband was a sort of father, and could teach you even Hebrew, if you wished it" (p. 10), "Enamoured of intensity and greatness" and yearning for "some lofty conception of the world which might frankly include the parish of Tipton and her own rule of conduct there" (p. 6), she believes that the "provinces of masculine knowledge" would be "a standing-ground from which all truth could be *seen* more truly" (VII. 88). Dorothea, then, wishes to see more truly, to have vision. In view of these facts it is therefore to be expected that the first in a long series of visions which together create her movement toward wider vision should be an unrealistic view of a future with "a man who [she believes] could understand the higher inward life, and with whom there could be some spiritual communion; nay, who could *illuminate* principle with the widest knowledge . . ." (II. 27).

This initial vision, occurring even before Casaubon's proposal, is a dream filled with youthful expectancy. As Dorothea is walking in the park on a beautiful autumn afternoon,

> there had risen before her the *girl's vision* of a possible future
> for herself to which she looked forward with trembling hope, and

she wanted to wander on in that *visionary* future without interrup-
tion . . . there was nothing of an ascetic's expression in her
bright full eyes, as she *looked* before her, *not consciously seeing,* but absorbing into the intensity of her mood, the solemn
glory of the afternoon with its long swathes of light between the
far-off rows of the limes, whose shadows· touched each other
[III. 34].

If we are to be aware of the rhythmic variations of elements
appearing in Dorothea's visions it is necessary to remember
that this is an *inward* vision. Dorothea *looks* before her but
she does not consciously *see* what is there, for she is intent
on seeing with her mind's eye what she has imaginatively constructed. On some subsequent occasions the author uses the
terms "inward vision" and "outward vision" in relation to
Dorothea's experience, and it is important to observe the way
Dorothea comes to connect the inward with the outward. The
reader who has been aware of the vision imagery in George
Eliot's earlier novels will recognize the reappearance here
of characteristic components. It is afternoon, the time of
illusion rather than clear vision of reality, and the light falls
in long narrow strips creating shadows among the far-off
trees. There is in this detail the symbolic suggestion of interrelatedness, but it is shadow rather than substance that
forms the relationship. The intensity of mood is also characteristic of the time of vision. It is significant and fitting that
the "girl's vision" which rises before Dorothea is only partially described for the reader by means of an image but rather more in terms of Dorothea's thought about the future life
she would have; she desires abstractions rather than material
objects, and these abstractions are extremely vague. If Casaubon were to ask her to become his wife, Dorothea muses,
". . . it would be almost as if a winged messenger had suddenly stood beside her path and held out his hand towards
her!" (p. 35). The choice of image here is a reference to an
earlier passage:

Dorothea by this time had looked deep into the ungauged res-
ervoir of Mr. Casaubon's mind, *seeing reflected there in vague
labyrinthine extension every quality she herself brought;* had
opened much of her own experience to him, and had understood
from him the scope of his great work, also of attractively laby-

rinthine extent. For he had been as instructive as Milton's *"af-
fable archangel"*; and with something of the archangelic manner
he told her how he had undertaken to show (what indeed had been
attempted before, but not with that thoroughness, justice of comparison, and effectiveness of arrangement at which Mr. Casaubon
aimed) that all the mythical systems or erratic mythical fragments in the world were corruptions of a tradition originally revealed. Having once mastered the true position and taken a firm
footing there, the vast field of mythical constructions became
intelligible, nay, *luminous* with the *reflected light* of corres-
pondences [pp. 29-30].

Small wonder then that the credulous Dorothea wishes to be
a "lampholder" for this "winged messenger" about whom her
girlish vision is constructed; he seems to offer the promise
of a way toward the vision she seeks, a way out of the oppres-
siveness which has made vision impossible: "For a long while
she had been oppressed by the indefiniteness which hung in
her mind, like a thick summer haze, over all her desire to
make her life greatly effective. What could she do, what ought
she to do? . . ." (p. 35). In her visionary dreams of the future she thinks of her winged messenger as one who will help
her to "learn everything. . . . It would be like marrying
Pascal. I should learn to *see* the truth by the same *light* as
great men have seen it by" (pp. 36-37). The primary illusion
in Dorothea's first vision is that Casaubon is a hero, "a modern Augustine" who "would take her along the grandest path"
(III. 30. 36). This vision, then, is made up of dreams, "the
dreams of a girl whose notions about marriage took their
colour entirely from an exalted enthusiasm about the ends of
life, an enthusiasm which was *lit* chiefly by its own fire . . ."
(p. 35).

When Dorothea receives Casaubon's proposal she has no
distinct vision of the future, but 'her whole soul was possessed
by the fact that a fuller life was opening before her; she was
a neophyte about to enter on a higher grade of initiation. She
was going to have room for the energies which stirred uneasily
under the dimness and pressure of her own ignorance and the
petty peremptoriness of the world's habits" (V. 58). Neophyte
that she is--and the choice of the word suggests her nunlike
attitude--Dorothea is nevertheless beginning a life which will
eventually take her into the world. For as the author observes

in a context which relates to Dorothea, "starting a long way off the true point, and proceeding by loops and zigzags, we now and then arrive just where we ought to be" (III. 31). Her first step, then, is an attempt to put herself in contact with a life nobler than those she now finds about her. "How can one ever do anything nobly Christian, living among people with such petty thoughts?" she asks in response to Celia's comment about Dodo's "favorite *fad*" (author's italics) of drawing plans. This is a question to which she is eventually to find an answer, but for the moment it is rhetorical. "No more was said: Dorothea was too much jarred to recover her temper and behave so as to show that she admitted any error in her self. She was disposed rather to accuse the intolerable narrowness and the *purblind* conscience of society around her . . ." (IV. 48). But at other times, however, Dorothea is "visited with con-scientious questionings whether she were not exalting these poor doings above measure and contemplating them with that self-satisfaction which was the last doom of ignorance and folly" (III. 44).

The house in which Dorothea is to take up her secluded nunlike existence as wife of Casaubon is "small-windowed and melancholy looking." But it has its "happy side" where "from the drawing-room windows the glance swept uninterrupt-edly along a slope of greensward till the limes ended in a level of corn and pastures, which often seemed to melt into a lake under the setting sun" (IX. 100-1). This is the view which Dorothea's bow-windowed room upstairs affords. And this view and this room are to recur significantly in nearly all of Dorothea's subsequent visions. The first description of the room defines a highly romantic world in which every-thing appears artificial:

> The bow-window looked down the avenue of limes: the furniture was all of a faded blue, and there were miniatures of ladies and gentlemen with powdered hair hanging in a group. A piece of tapestry over a door also showed a blue-green world with a pale stag in it. The chairs and tables were thin-legged and easy to upset. It was a room where one might fancy the ghost of a tight-laced lady revisiting the scene of her embroidery. A light book-case contained duodecimo volumes of polite literature in calf, completing the furniture [p. 103].

Here are represented the two worlds with which the young
and unformed Dorothea must come to terms. The window
rounds out to give a view of the real world which contrasts
with the romantic world of the pale stag. In short, the room
represents the polite world of the gentlewoman whose characteristic activity is embroidering. When Mr. Brooke suggests
that the room be refurnished for Dorothea, she replies, "Pray
do not speak of altering anything. There are so many other
things in the world that want altering--I like to take these
things as they are" (p. 104). What she here seems not to recognize is that she cannot go about effecting meaningful reform
until she has put her own inner world in order. It is significant that what she sees outside the window is described briefly and in such terms as to recall the time of her first vision
when the lime trees formed shadows: ". . . she turned to
the window to admire the view. The sun had lately pierced
the grey, and the avenue of limes cast shadows" (p. 105).
Here the lack of definition of the outside world is, I believe,
intended to suggest that Dorothea's own concept of it is shadowy and unformed.

The second of Dorothea's series of visions occurs during
her honeymoon in Rome when she is discovered by Ladislaw
and Naumann in a state of intense abstraction. "She was not
looking at the sculpture, probably not thinking of it: her large
eyes were fixed dreamily on a streak of sunlight which fell
across the floor" (XIX. 273). The content of this vision is not
revealed until several pages later, during which time her nunlike appearance is the subject of much conversation between
Ladislaw and his friend and her internal life is explored by
the author. This is a crucial time in Dorothea's life, and the
vision she has as she looks at the streak of sunlight is a culmination of her experience in Rome. Two elements here com-
bine to bring Dorothea to a state of somewhat wider vision:
her "real" rather than "imaginary" marriage and the impact
of Rome. The "stupendous fragmentariness" of Rome "heightened the dreamlike strangeness of her bridal life" (XX. 279).
To Dorothea, even the art objects in her uncle's home had
been "painfully inexplicable, staring into the midst of her
Puritanic conceptions: she had never been taught how she
could bring them into any sort of relevance with her life"

(IX. 102). Now she is confronted by Rome, an experience so important that it is hereafter associated with certain times of vision in her life:

> . . . all this vast wreck of ambitious ideals, sensuous and spiritual, mixed confusedly with the signs of breathing forgetfulness and degradation, at first jarred her as with an electric shock, and then urged themselves on her with that ache belonging to a glut of confused ideas which check the flow of emotion. *Forms* both pale and glowing took possession of her young sense, and *fixed themselves* in her memory even when she was not thinking of them, preparing strange associations which remained through her after-years. Our moods are apt to bring with them *images* which succeed each other like the magic-lantern pictures of a doze; and in certain states of dull forlornness Dorothea all her life *continued to see* the vastness of St. Peter's, the huge bronze canopy, the excited intention in the attitudes and garments of the prophets and evangelists in the mosaics above, and the red drapery which was being hung for Christmas spreading itself everywhere *like a disease of the retina* [XX. 280-81].

The red drapery, here presumably a symbol of the worldly beauty and richness which Dorothea's "fanaticism of sympathy" will not allow her to appreciate, is compared to a disease of the retina because it colors the whole image which Dorothea retains just as a disease of the retina might affect the entire image which the retina of the eye receives from the lens. This vision image is most effective simply as a suggestion that there is something faulty about Dorothea's vision. Here she sees forms and faces of those who like herself have been enamored of intensity and greatness, but she also sees signs of human failure and degradation. She is not yet ready to order these contradictory elements into a whole.

Just as Dorothea does not in the least comprehend what Rome means to her, so too she does not know what is happening to her marriage. To have tried to verbalize the cause of her unhappiness

> would have been like trying to give a history of the lights and shadows; for that new *real* future which was replacing the *imaginary* drew its material from the endless minutiæ by which *her view* of Mr. Casaubon and her wifely relation, now that she was married to him, was gradually changing with the secret motion of a watch-hand from what it had been in her maiden *dream* [pp. 281-82].

The illusion is being slowly dispelled but reality has not yet become defined. Perception is now more a matter of feeling than of seeing: "How was it that, in the weeks since her marriage, Dorothea had not distinctly observed, but felt with a stifling depression, that the *large vistas* and *wide fresh air* which she had dreamed of finding in her husband's mind were replaced by *anterooms* and *winding passages* which seemed to lead nowhither?" George Eliot's answer to this question brings together not only the images of movement and restriction which the question itself contains but also points up the theme of expectation and its effect on vision; it contains as well a significant recurrence of the explorer image. These two passages will perhaps illustrate the difficulty of discussing separate patterns of meaning in the novel as well as the difficulty of showing how they relate. The author answers:

> I suppose it was that in courtship everything is regarded as provisional and preliminary, and the smallest sample of virtue or accomplishment is taken to guarantee delightful stores which the broad leisure of marriage will reveal. But the door-sill of marriage once crossed, *expectation* is concentrated on the present. Having once embarked on your *marital voyage,* it is impossible not to be aware that you make no way and that the sea is *not within sight*--that, in fact, you are *exploring* an *enclosed basin* [pp. 283-84].

Clearly Dorothea must now come to rearrange her expectations in accordance with the limitations imposed on her by the nature of her marriage. No longer can she expect to be taken along the grandest path; and, in fact, we soon learn that she "was gradually ceasing to *expect* with her former delightful confidence that she should *see* any *wide opening* where she followed him" (p. 286). But she has as yet no conception of his inner life: "She was as *blind* to his inward troubles as he to hers: she had not learned those hidden conflicts in her husband which claim our pity" (p. 290). She only feels that so far their wedded life has "seemed like a catastrophe, changing all prospects . . ." (p. 293). In the light of this whole situation, then, it is to be expected that Dorothea's second vision, in which she is interrupted by Ladislaw and the painter Naumann, should be of a less idealized but still not adequately envisioned future:

She did not really see the streak of sunlight on the floor more
than she saw the statues: she was *inwardly seeing* the light of
years to come in her own home and over the English fields and
elms and hedge-bordered highroads; and feeling that the way in
which they might be filled with joyful devotedness was *not so
clear* to her as it had been. But in Dorothea's mind there was
a current into which all thought and feeling were apt sooner or
later to flow--the reaching forward of the whole consciousness
toward the fullest truth, the least partial good. There was clearly
something better than anger and despondency [p. 294].

During the remainder of her time in Rome, Dorothea comes
to a relatively deeper understanding of herself and her husband. She recognizes that her own ignorance is the cause of
her blindness to the beauty of art: "It must be my own dulness, " she tells Ladislaw. "I am seeing so much all at once,
and not understanding half of it. That always makes one feel
stupid. It is painful to be told that anything is very fine and
not be able to feel it is fine--something like being *blind,* while
people talk of the sky" (XXI. 298-99). But what is more decidedly an advance in her progress toward moral vision is
her growing awareness of her husband as a real rather than
ideal human being. Now she feels "that new alarm on his behalf which was the first stirring of a pitying tenderness fed
by the realities of his lot and not by her own dreams" (p. 303).
Their first argument marks a decided change in Dorothea's
vision:

. . . Dorothea remembered it to the last with the vividness with
which we all remember epochs in our experience when some dear
expectation dies, or some new motive is born. To-day she *had
begun to see* that she had been under a *wild illusion in expecting*
a response to her feeling from Mr. Casaubon, and she had felt
the *waking* of a presentiment that there might be a sad consciousness in his life which made as great a need on his side as on
her own [pp. 305-6].

She has begun to be aware of an inner life other than her own,
and she has furthermore begun to see that her expectations
about marriage and life in general have been based on girlish
dreams. This is the first stage in the total disillusionment
which--according to George Eliot's well-established pattern

in movement toward vision--must take place before a wider
and more complete vision may be achieved.

Her next vision is therefore of a wholly "disenchanted"
world. [1] Occasioned by her return from Rome, this scene is
a rhythmic variation on the first scene which describes Dorothea's boudoir at Lowick. One of the elements in the scene
which emphasizes its prominence in the series of visions com-
posing Dorothea's movement is the complex repetition. It re-
flects, causing the reader to remember details in the previous
scene which are here repeated though with considerable variation; it contains within itself much repetition of words and
descriptive detail which not only creates a mood but also emphasizes the nature of Dorothea's vision at this moment; and
finally because of these two kinds of repetition this scene
causes the reader to anticipate its recurrence with meaningful
variation in a subsequent scene which will reveal a difference
in Dorothea's vision. The contrast between the present picture
and the picture presented by a similar set of details in the
earlier scene is readily apparent. Both the blue-green boudoir
and the view from the bow-window have shrunken and changed
in aspect, although slightly more detail is used to describe
the outside world:

> . . . she saw the long avenue of limes lifting their trunks from
> a white earth, and spreading white branches against the dun and
> motionless sky. The distant flat shrank in uniform whiteness and
> low-hanging uniformity of cloud. The very furniture in the room
> seemed to have shrunk since she saw it before: the stag in the
> tapestry looked more like a ghost in his ghostly blue-green world;
> the volumes of polite literature in the bookcase looked more like
> immovable imitations of books [XXVIII.3].

Dorothea becomes "absorbed in looking out on the still, white
enclosure which made her visible world"; but the very description of the world, "the still, white enclosure," indicates the
absence of space, color, and human activity. She feels the
duties of her married life to be "shrinking with the furniture
and the white *vapour-walled landscape*. The clear heights
where she expected to walk in full communion had become *difficult to see even in her imagination . . .* "(p. 4). Most of
all she feels "the stifling oppression of that gentlewoman's
world, where everything was done for her and none asked for

aid--where the *sense of connection* with a manifold pregnant
existence had to be kept up painfully as an *inward vision,* instead of coming from without in claims that would have shaped
her energies" (p. 5). Here the author clearly indicates that
the outward vision which connects the individual with "a manifold pregnant existence" outside himself is finally preferable
to an "inward vision" (although the latter is prerequisite to
the former) because the former imposes claims which would
direct action, whereas the latter can do no more than preserve
the idea of connection. Such outward vision is not yet possible
for Dorothea, and there is as yet nothing but "the low arch of
dun vapor" outside the window. Therefore outside and inside
merge as she stands "in a moral imprisonment which made
itself one with the chill, colourless, narrowed landscape, with
the shrunken furniture, the never-read books, and the ghostly
stag in a pale fantastic world that seemed to be vanishing from
the *daylight"* (p. 5). The unreality of this world is revealed to
Dorothea by the daylight or, to be more exact, by the early
morning daylight. Everything in the room is "withering and
shrinking away from her"; everything in the room is "disenchanted, " everything but the miniature of Ladislaw's grand-
mother. Now Dorothea feels a "new companionship" with it,
for now she is able to comprehend at least something of what
that woman had suffered and borne in marriage. Slight as it
may seem, this last detail is a symbolic indication of Dorothea's growing sympathetic perception into the lives of real
people about her as contrasted with the still somewhat abstract idea of having sympathy for the lowly underprivileged,
who in Dorothea's experience are represented by the cottager.

Further indication of this growth in Dorothea comes in a
group scene where her attention is beginning to be directed
not merely toward the cottagers for whom she makes plans
that are never executed but rather toward people of all classes,
people for whom the act of living among them with sympathy
may constitute the most valuable reform. At the instigation
of Mrs. Cadwallader, who enjoys seeing "collections of strange
animals, " the gentry have gathered to watch the Featherstone funeral procession from a window in Casaubon's upstairs sitting room, the bow window in Dorothea's room obviously being reserved for Dorothea's private vision. Doro-

thea's response to this visual scene is so intense that it subsequently becomes a part of her inward vision:

> . . . aloof as it seemed to be from the tenor of her life, [this scene] always afterwards came back to her at the touch of certain sensitive points in memory, just as the *vision* of St. Peter's at Rome was inwoven with moods of despondency. Scenes which make vital changes in our neighbour's lots are but the background of our own, yet, like a particular aspect of the fields and trees, they become associated for us with the epochs of our own history, and make a part of that unity which lies in the selection of our keenest consciousness [XXXIV. 79].

This association is explained in the extremely significant passage which follows:

> The dreamlike association of something alien and ill-understood with the deepest secrets of her experience seemed to *mirror* that sense of loneliness which was due to the very ardour of Dorothea's nature. The country gentry of old time lived in a rarefied social air: dotted apart on their stations up the mountain *they looked down with imperfect discrimination* on the belts of thicker life below. And Dorothea was not at ease in the *perspective and chilliness of that height.*

Thus the author makes an acute observation about the vision of the gentry at the same time that she indicates the general direction in which Dorothea's desire for vision must take her; she must move downward from the height and outward among people in order that she may be better able to see and feel what their lives are like. [2] It is because she associates the atmosphere of the occasion, an emotional blank in both the people who observe from the heights and those who form the procession, with an emotional blank in her own life that she can enter into the situation this far: "This funeral seems to me the most dismal thing I ever saw. It is a blot on the morning. I cannot bear to think that anyone should die and leave no love behind" (p. 82). The scene establishes a subtly complex perspective from which the reader views the wealthy farming and manufacturing class through the eyes of the gentry and thereby views the gentry: Mrs. Cadwallader, to whom this class beneath her is "as curious as any buffaloes or bison"; Mr. Brooke, who comments that a funeral is a solemn thing, "if you take it in that light, you know"; Celia, who says, "I

shall not look any more" but supposes that "Dodo likes it; she
is fond of melancholy things and ugly people"; and Dorothea,
who answers this charge: "I am fond of knowing something
about the people I live among. . . . It seems to me we know
nothing of our neighbours unless they are cottagers." This is
one of several group scenes whose primary purpose it is to
point up essential differences in the way certain characters
look, or fail to look, at a given situation.

The next time of vision in Dorothea's life is marked by the
repetition of the complex of details associated with the blue-
green boudoir and the bow window. In the interim between the
disenchantment and the reinvestment of meaning, Dorothea
has "looked steadily at her husband's failure" (XXXVII. 138)
and has faced the seriousness of his physical condition. She
has lived a more intense inner life, and that life has gradually
come more and more to be identified with the world of the bow-
windowed room:

> Any private hours in her day were usually spent in her blue-
> green boudoir, and she had come to be very fond of its pallid
> quaintness. Nothing had been outwardly altered there; but while
> the summer had gradually advanced over the western fields be-
> yond the avenue of elms, the bare room had gathered within it
> those memories of an inward life which fill the air as with a
> cloud of good or bad angels, the invisible yet active forms of
> our spiritual triumphs or our spiritual falls. She had been so
> used to struggle for and to find resolve in looking along the ave-
> nue toward the arch of western light that *the vision itself had
> gained a communicating power* [pp. 146-47].

The rhythmic recurrence of this particular element in the
novel is one of the primary means by which the author secures
the unity of the Dorothea story. The fact that much has tran-
spired between the times when we see Dorothea in the blue-
green room only makes its changing aspect more emotionally
convincing as an objectification of Dorothea's inner change.
One of the objects in the room whose meaning has greatly increased for Dorothea is the miniature of Ladislaw's grand-
mother; for as Dorothea has learned more about Ladislaw's
life and the circumstances which have linked it with her husband's life, she has become increasingly concerned about the
disinheritance of that lady and its subsequent effect on Ladis-

law. It comes to her now as a revelation that her husband
must alter his will in such a way as to discharge his responsibility to Ladislaw:

> The *vision* of all this as what ought to be done seemed to Dorothea
> like a sudden *letting-in of daylight,* waking her from her previous
> stupidity and incurious self-absorbed ignorance about her hus-
> band's relations to others . . . Mr. Casaubon had never him-
> self *seen fully* what was the claim upon him. "But he will!" said
> Dorothea. "The great strength of his character lies here" [p.
> 149].

What here indicates Dorothea's growth in vision is her new
awareness of her husband as a human being who has a relationship to others than herself, but what also shows her to be naïvely blind is her miscalculation of the "great strength" of
Casaubon's character. Her very blindness, however, provides
her protection: "She was *blind,* you see, to many things obvious to others--likely to tread in the wrong places, as Celia
had warned her; yet her *blindness* to whatever did not lie in
her own pure purpose carried her safely by the side of preci-
pices where *vision* would have been perilous with fear." The
tone of the author's comment here indicates that the blindness
of the innocent is sometimes preferable to the vision of the
experienced, since it allows the blind to act generously in accordance with a generous spirit. George Eliot apparently intends to suggest that this blindness is actually moral vision
because man is seen in terms of his potential goodness. But
the fact remains that Casaubon does not have this potential,
that he has not seen any moral necessity to include Ladislaw
in his will. Dorothea's appraisal of him is therefore an idealization; and the author's appraisal of Dorothea at this point
seems too partial. In terms of the dramatic structure this
moment of partial vision and partial blindness is very important, since it occasions Dorothea's plea that Casaubon change
his will, a plea ironically resulting in the codicil which finally
necessitates Dorothea's abdication.

Of less importance to the plot but nevertheless also of dramatic significance is the next scene which marks a further
step in Dorothea's movement toward vision. Ending in a superbly rendered moment which climaxes the dramatic interchange of two characters, it marks as well Casaubon's finest

achievement. It explores the imperfectly fulfilled life, indicating what constitutes a partial fulfillment and what may hinder fulfillment. For, George Eliot insists, it is not merely the general circumstances of Middlemarch life which constitute the meanness of opportunity but the particular commonplace acts of human beings. Just such an act was Casaubon's rejection of Dorothea's attempt to support him during the moment of his greatest suffering following his crucial interview with Lydgate:

> Mr. Casaubon kept his hands behind him and allowed her pliant arm to cling with difficulty against his rigid arm.
> There was something horrible to Dorothea in the sensation which this unresponsive hardness inflicted on her. That is a strong word, but not too strong: it is in *these acts called trivialities* that the seeds of joy are forever wasted, until men and women look round with haggard faces at the devastation their own waste has made, and say, the earth bears no harvest of sweetness--calling their denial knowledge [XLII. 227].

Casaubon having shut himself in the library, Dorothea retires to her boudoir. "The open bow-window let in the serene glory of the afternoon lying in the avenue, where the lime-trees cast long shadows. But Dorothea knew nothing of the scene." Rather, she "saw as in one glance" both "her own and her husband's solitude . . ." (pp. 228-29). Sitting thus through the afternoon and into the night, Dorothea undergoes a severe struggle, fighting the anger which she feels at first and finally, through a series of visions, arriving at the point of submission:

> That thought with which Dorothea had gone out to meet her husband--her conviction that he had been asking about the possible arrest of all his work, and that the answer must have wrung his heart, could not be long without rising beside the *image* of him, like a shadowy monitor looking at her anger with sad remonstrance. It cost her a *litany of pictured* sorrows and of silent cries that she might be the mercy for those sorrows--but the resolved submission did come . . . [p. 230].

The "litany of pictured sorrows" is an extremely complex metaphor whose religious overtones are emphasized by the use of the word *mercy.* What it implies is that Dorothea imagines so vividly what sorrows her husband must have that she constructs them into a series of images which appear before

her as the supplications in a litany to which her own cry forms
the response. In effect, she not only imaginatively probes
Casaubon's life so that she may be able to feel compassion
for him, but she sees him as suppliant, the very opposite of
the proud unresponsive man who has angered her; in order
that she may be able to respond to him she imagines that he
wishes a response. And in her "silent cries that she might
be the mercy for those sorrows," she herself enters the ritual as suppliant. As a result of this communion Dorothea
reaches the state of submission but does not retain the illusory expectation that her husband will actually be suppliant.
She has made herself ready to "risk incurring another pang.
She would never again *expect* anything else." What happens,
however, when he comes upstairs and finds her waiting quietly for him in the darkness outside her room is in effect a partial actualization of the communion she has imagined:

> When her husband stood opposite to her she saw that his face was
> more haggard. He started slightly on seeing her, and she looked
> up at him beseechingly, without speaking.
>   "Dorothea!" he said, with gentle surprise in his tone. "Were
> you waiting for me?"
>   "Yes. I did not like to disturb you."
>   "Come, my dear, come. You are young, and need not to ex-
> tend your life by watching."
>   . . . She put her hand into her husband's, and they went along
> the broad corridor together [XLII. 231].

This far, then, has Casaubon's life been fulfilled: for one
brief moment he has reached the point of being able to give
and receive human sympathy. This far, too, has Dorothea's
life been fulfilled: she has, to that extent at least, enlarged
the moral sensibility of a fellow human being.

In the interim between this and the next stage in Dorothea's
movement toward vision, her world undergoes "a state of
convulsive change" (L. 324). Her attitude toward both her husband and Ladislaw is affected by the situation which Casaubon's
will places her in after his death, and as her world changes
she feels that she herself is undergoing a "metamorphosis."
She is, however, still faced with the same problem now made
more pressing by her greatly increased wealth: how to fulfill
her moral responsibility in the world. Mrs. Cadwallader,

aware of Dorothea's queenly attitude, warns of a danger that
may befall her when she returns as sole mistress of Lowick:

> "I dare say you are a little bored here by our good dowager; but
> think what a bore you might become yourself to your fellow-crea-
> tures if you were always playing tragedy queen and taking things
> sublimely. Sitting alone in that library at Lowick you may fancy
> yourself ruling the weather; you must get a few people around
> you who wouldn't believe you if you told them. That is a good
> lowering medicine" [LIV. 6].

To her husband, Mrs. Cadwallader confides that Dorothea
must marry again and that "Lord Triton is precisely the man:
full of plans for making people happy in a soft-headed sort of
way" (p. 7). And Dorothea, sitting once more in her blue-green
boudoir, "looking out along the avenue of limes to the distant
fields," sees a coming danger: "every leaf was at rest in the
sunshine, the familiar scene was changeless, and seemed to
represent the prospect of her life, full of motiveless ease--
motiveless, if her own energy could not seek out reason for
ardent action" (p. 11).

During this period she has no clear conception of what
Ladislaw is coming to mean to her. At first she has only the
"hurrying, crowding *vision* of unfitting conditions" (L. 324).
Later she stands beside him in the drawing room whose bow
window beneath that of the blue-green boudoir is thereby associated in the reader's mind with Dorothea's private vision,
giving an emotional undertone to the scene. Knowing that he
is leaving, she looks out "on the rose-bushes, which seemed
to have in them the summers of all the years when Will would
be away" (LIV. 14). But even then she did not know that "it
was Love who had come to her briefly, *as in a dream before
awaking* . . . " (LV. 21). And once she is almost certain that
Ladislaw does love her, "so heavily did the world weigh on
her in spite of her independent energy that with this idea of
Will as in need of such help and at a disadvantage with the
world, there came always the *vision of that unfittingness* of
any closer relation between them which lay in the *opinion* of
every one connected with her" (LXII. 152). Clearly Dorothea
is in a transitional stage when such visions as she has are
negative. Some deeper, more profound experience is wanting

to bring her to a clearer vision of what is genuinely fitting for a rich and useful life.

Such an experience is being prepared for her in the Raffles-Bulstrode-Lydgate affair. This complex incident may seem indeed to be remote from the life of this wealthy Lowick widow, but it is far more than a plot contrivance intended to fuse the two major story elements. For it emphasizes the primary point of the novel, the interweaving of human lots, "the slow preparation of effects from one life on another, which tells like a calculated irony on the indifference or the frozen stare with which we look at our unintroduced neighbour."

Dorothea's involvement in this situation begins with the stand she takes when Lydgate's alleged guilt is being discussed among a group. A recurrent variation of the Featherstone funeral scene, this conversation emphasizes differences in points of view (chapter lxxii). Dorothea proposes that Lydgate's friends attempt to vindicate him. Sir James makes a direct answer: "He must act for himself." Mr. Farebrother, well-meaning but cautious, says: "I think his friends must wait till they find an opportunity." Mr. Brooke awakens from his nap, "not quite knowing at what point the discussion had arrived, but . . . with a conversation generally appropriate. 'It is easy to go too far, you know.'" Celia, whose wifely attitude the younger Lydgate would have found so admirable, says: "Now, Dodo, do listen to what James says. . . . He lets you have your plans, only he hinders you from being taken in." This time, however, Celia mistakenly assumes that Dorothea's current plan is of no more consequence than all of her previous plans. Dorothea's own position is clearly the only right one: "I should not be afraid of asking Mr. Lydgate to tell me the truth, that I might help him. . . . Then we would all stand by him and bring him out of his trouble. People glorify all sorts of bravery except the bravery they might show on behalf of their nearest neighbours." In an earlier conversation with Mr. Farebrother, Dorothea says: "I feel convinced that his conduct has not been guilty: I believe that people are almost always better than their neighbours think they are." And the author explains: "Some of her intensest experience in the last two years had set her mind strongly in opposition to any unfavorable construction of others." Thus we are reminded that this attitude is not merely the result of Dorothea's ardent and idealizing nature but that it has been validated by the firsthand knowledge Dorothea has had, Casaubon having mistakenly judged both Ladislaw and Dorothea.

⬗⬗⬗⬗⬗⬗

Now, "another's need having once come to her as a *distinct image*" (LXXVI. 335), Dorothea moves out of the period of motiveless ease into a situation which is to be the crisis in four lives, finally culminating in the moment of greatest vision for Lydgate, Ladislaw, Rosamond, and Dorothea. It is here that the four major private movements of *Middlemarch* meet, mutually reinforcing one another and thus fulfilling the dramatic, thematic, and structural necessity previously established in this novel.

Dorothea's approach to Lydgate's problem is simple and direct:"'I beseech you to tell me how everything was,' said Dorothea, fearlessly. 'I am sure that the truth would clear you'" (LXXVI. 337). Her own moral responsibility is quite clear to her: "It is wicked to let people think evil of any one falsely, when it can be hindered." The effect of such a generous action, the author points out, is to change one's vision, and Lydgate begins to respond accordingly:

> The presence of a noble nature, generous in its wishes, ardent in its charity, *changes the light for us:* we *begin to see* things again in their larger, quieter masses, and to believe that we too can be seen and judged in the wholeness of our character. That influence was beginning to act on Lydgate, who had for many days been *seeing* all life as one who is dragged and struggling amid the throng. He sat down again, and felt that he was recovering his old self in the consciousness that he was with one who believed in it [pp. 337-38].

And although Lydgate is not long to retain his old self--so much more hopelessly entangled is he in circumstances than the childlike Dorothea can anticipate--he is nevertheless permanently affected by her somewhat quixotic action:

> Dorothea's voice, as she made this childlike picture of what she would do, might have been almost taken as a proof that she could do it effectively. The searching tenderness of her woman's tones

seemed made for a defense against ready accusers. Lydgate did
not stay to think that she was Quixotic: he gave himself up, for
the first time in his life, to the exquisite sense of leaning entirely on a generous sympathy, without any check of proud reserve.
And he told her everything . . . [pp. 338-39].

Thus the effect of Dorothea's life on this self-contained and
often arrogant man who had once observed of Dorothea that
she "did not look at things from the proper feminine angle"
(XI. 133) is that his life now opens out to receive gratefully
the human sympathy he has heretofore disdained. And he, on
the other hand, thus partially enables her to fulfill her own
moral purpose.

But he is not, however, to be the means through which she
will finally be able to realize one of her "plans." Although
she has come to know that she cannot do anything on such a
grandiose scale as to found the village which she has planned,
she is still naively idealistic about what use her money may
be put to:

"So you see that what I should most rejoice at would be to have
something good to do with my money: I should like it to make
other people's lives better to them. It makes me very uneasy--
coming all to me who don't want it."
    A smile broke through the gloom of Lydgate's face. The child-
like grave-eyed earnestness with which Dorothea said all this
was irresistible--blent into an adorable whole with her ready
understanding of high experience. (Of lower experience such as
plays a great part in the world, poor Mrs. Casaubon had a very
blurred, shortsighted knowledge, little helped by her imagination.) [LXXVI. 341-42].

Here we may assume that the significant comment in the pa-
rentheses is the author's own addition to Lydgate's amused
but tender observation. That indeed Dorothea does have a
"blurred, shortsighted knowledge" of "lower experience" has
been emphasized in every possible way. And it is to receive
further demonstration here. Dorothea simply assumes that
moral support and relief of all financial burdens will make
Lydgate's life "quite whole and well again." And when Lydgate
explains that he owes it to his wife to leave town as she desires, Dorothea replies: "But when she *saw* the good that might
come of staying--," thus indicating her inability to conceive
of any other outcome. But Lydgate's curt reply, "She would

not *see* it, " and his explanation that he cannot even discuss the problem with Rosamond leave Dorothea still undaunted and eager to visit Rosamond: "I would tell her that you shall be cleared in every fair mind. I would cheer her heart. " So firmly convinced of the powerful persuasiveness of the truth is Dorothea that she must be credited here with more than naïve zeal; for she actually does manage to clear Lydgate in some fair minds and she has a decidedly positive effect on Rosamond.

But what Dorothea's blurred, shortsighted knowledge of lower experience does not allow her to know is that the effects of moral drifting cannot so easily be righted. Dorothea's proposal that she clear Lydgate with friends and subsidize him in his hospital work brings him finally face to face with himself, with the necessity to decide whether or not he is worthy of such trust. And facing himself, he is left with the fact that he has lost his self-mastery and can no longer trust himself. The only moral act he is capable of at this point therefore is to decline any new responsibility that he might not be capable of fulfilling. Consequently when Dorothea urges him to take more time to consider her proposal, he replies:

> 'No; I prefer that there should be no interval left for wavering. I am no longer sure enough of myself--I mean of what it would be possible for me to do under the changed circumstances of my life. It would be dishonourable to let others engage themselves to anything serious in dependence on me. . . . I cannot consent to be the cause of your goodness being wasted" [p. 345].

When Dorothea reasserts her faith in his "power to do great things" and her own desire to share her fortune, he is even more convinced of the necessity to appraise himself truly:

> "It is good that you should have such feelings. But I am not the man who ought to allow himself to benefit by them. I have not given guarantees enough. I must not at least sink into the degradation of being pensioned for work that I never achieved. It is very *clear* to me that I must not count on anything else than getting away from Middlemarch as soon as I can manage it. . . . I must do as other men do, and think what will please the world and bring money; look for a little opening in the London crowd, and push myself; set up in a watering-place, or go to some southern town where there are plenty of idle English, and get myself

puffed, --that is the sort of shell I shall *creep* into and try to keep
my soul alive in. "

"Now that is not brave, " said Dorothea, "to give up the fight. "

"No, it is not brave, " said Lydgate; "but if a man is afraid of
creeping paralysis ?" [pp. 345-46].

What has become "very clear" to Lydgate, then, is that he
can no longer expect anything of himself nor can he allow himself to create expectations in anyone else. But such vision as
he has of himself and his relationship to other people has come
too late to save him from the "creeping paralysis" which he
fears is setting in. The metaphor which he as a medical man
chooses to describe his moral condition is peculiarly fitting
as a way of indicating the results of moral drifting: the gradually increasing loss of the power of *voluntary* motion. Now it
seems that the only right action is "to give up the fight. " This
Lydgate forms a tragic contrast to the young doctor who came
to Middlemarch with "a fearless *expectation* of success, a
confidence in his own powers and integrity much fortified by
contempt for petty obstacles or seductions of which he had had
no experience" (XIII. 177).

Dorothea's plan for rehabilitating Lydgate has failed because,
like all of her other plans, it is unrealistic. Lydgate at first
"did not stop to think that she was Quixotic" but he comes to
know it and so does the reader, as George Eliot intends him to.
But however quixotic Dorothea may be in supposing that Lydgate's life can again be put to right, she is decidedly clear-
sighted in perceiving that he is innocent of complicity in the
death of Raffles and in further perceiving that it is her own
moral responsibility to indicate her faith in his innocence
and attempt to establish it before the community. And the effects of that action are finally positive; for although it is too
late for the whole direction of Lydgate's life to be changed, it
is not too late for him to benefit by the trust and sympathy
Dorothea gives him. ". . . You have made a great difference
in my courage by believing in me, " he tells her. "Everything
seems more bearable since I have talked to you . . . " (LXXVI.
346). It is because of Dorothea's goodness that Lydgate finds
it necessary to determine the truth about himself. But the effects of this action are to have far-reaching extensions, for

Dorothea has merely begun one of those minute processes whose consequences are finally incalculable.

I wish now to put in context a passage previously cited in part:

> As Lydgate rode away, he thought: "This young creature has a heart large enough for the Virgin Mary. She evidently thinks nothing of her own future, and would pledge away half her income at once, as if she wanted nothing for herself but a chair to sit in from which she can look down with those clear eyes at the poor mortals who pray to her. She seems to have what I never saw in any woman before--a fountain of friendship towards men--a man can make a friend of her. Casaubon must have raised some heroic hallucination in her. I wonder if she could have any other sort of passion for a man? . . . Well--her love might help a man more than her money" [p. 347].

There are several reasons why Lydgate's comparison of Dorothea to the Virgin Mary is fitting here. Her action has clearly indicated largeness of heart; and so purely gratuitous is it and in such sharp contrast to the condemnatory actions of neighbors with whom Lydgate has been far more closely associated than with Dorothea that it would quite naturally assume for him extraordinary proportions to be expressed in extraordinary terms. On a religious level the comparison works accurately, for Dorothea has heard his case, has granted him mercy, and has assumed the role of intercessor. But there is still another very important reason why Lydgate's description of Dorothea is fitting: it indicates that he has arrived at a fuller conception of womanhood than he had before his marriage. During his engagement, Lydgate

> thought that . . . he had found perfect womanhood . . . an accomplished creature who venerated his high musings and momentous labours and would never interfere with them; who would create order in the home and accounts with still magic, yet keep her fingers ready to touch the lute and transform life into romance at any moment; who was instructed to the true womanly limit and not a hair's breadth beyond--docile, therefore, and ready to carry out behests which came from beyond that limit [XXXVI. 119].

Marriage has disenchanted him and has taught him the negative
aspects of woman's peculiar influence, her capacity for destruction. But he has not until now been able to perceive the
positive aspects of womanly influence. This is a point which
has received much emphasis throughout the novel, one of
Lydgate's first observations about Dorothea having been that
"it is troublesome to talk to such women. They are always
wanting reasons, yet they are too ignorant to understand the
merits of any question, and usually fall back on their moral
sense to settle things after their own taste." But the author
points out that Lydgate "might possibly have experience before him which would modify his opinion as to the most excellent things in woman" (X. 130-31). The central irony of the
book is that it is precisely because she does fall back on her
moral sense that Dorothea is his sole support during this crisis. Lydgate's inadequate view of woman and her role has
played a decidedly important part in his downfall; it is therefore natural that during his moment of clearest vision he
should come to see in Dorothea what he "never saw in any
woman before." What he sees is one indication of his increased vision.

But there might still remain the problem of determining to
what extent George Eliot countenances such a description of
Dorothea. For Dorothea has created the impression that "she
wanted nothing for herself but a chair to sit in from which she
can look down with those clear eyes at the mortals who pray
to her." It should be recalled, however, that "Dorothea was
not at ease in the perspective and chilliness of that height"
from which the gentry "looked down with imperfect discrimi-
nation on the belts of thicker life below" (see p. 188 above);
and further, we who have seen something of Dorothea's inner
life know that she desires an active life. But even if it were
true that at this time in her life Dorothea prefers the role
Lydgate ascribes to her, her final vision--one which follows
as a result of her support of Lydgate--shows her to have
changed her attitude. Lydgate himself, in observing that
"her love might help a man more than her money," indicates
awareness of the more positive and realistic role to which
George Eliot finally assigns Dorothea. Furthermore, the

two stanzas of Blake's poem with which the chapter (lxxvi) is prefaced should be noted:

> "To mercy, pity, peace, and love
>   All pray in their distress
> And to these virtues of delight,
>   Return their thankfulness.
>
> . . . .
>
> "For Mercy has a *human* heart,
>   Pity a *human* face;
> And Love the *human* form divine;
>   And Peace the *human* dress."

Here is George Eliot's comment on Dorothea as she appears in this scene.

Up to this point in her life Dorothea "had not yet any material within her experience for subtle constructions and suspicions of hidden wrong" (LXXVII. 352). It is partly for that reason that she can so forthrightly believe in Lydgate's innocence and that in spite of gossip she can furthermore believe that Ladislaw is innocent of anything dishonorable in his relationship with Rosamond. Since, therefore, she consistently believes the best of people and has noted with disappointment that even such a fine man as Mr. Farebrother has not done so, it becomes a nice irony that because of her attempt to free Lydgate from the appearance of guilt she likewise becomes one who judges guilt by appearance. Now she is to be in a situation which causes her to suspect a hidden wrong against herself. That experience is the extreme crisis in her own life through which her blurred, shortsighted knowledge of lower experience is to become greatly enlarged.

On the occasion of Dorothea's first visit to Rosamond in the role of intercessor for Lydgate, the author notes that "Dorothea had *less* of *outward vision* than usual this morning, being filled with *images* of things as they had been and were going to be" (LXXVII. 356). Absorbed in the past and future but divorced from the present, she is suddenly brought into a shocking present revealed "in the terrible *illumination* of a certainty which filled up all outlines. . . ." For what merely appears to be a love scene between Rosamond and Ladislaw assumes a dreadful certainty for Dorothea.

Having spent the day in feverish activity Dorothea retires to her boudoir, where she undergoes the suffering that initiates her into a new state of being (LXXX. 373-78). At first two intensely vivid images appear before her as "living forms," one an image of Ladislaw as she had thought him to be and the second as she believes she has discovered him to be:

> Here, with the nearness of an answering smile, here within the vibrating bond of mutual speech, was the bright creature whom she had trusted--who had come to her like the spirit of morning visiting the dim vault where she sat as the bride of a worn-out life; and now, with a full consciousness which had never awakened before, she stretched out her arms toward him and cried with bitter cries that their nearness was *a parting vision:* she discovered her passion to herself in the unshrinking utterance of despair.
> And there, aloof, yet persistently with her, moving wherever she moved, was the Will Ladislaw who was a changed belief exhausted of hope, a detected illusion--no, a living man toward whom there could not yet struggle any wail of regretful pity, from the midst of scorn and indignation and jealous offended pride. . . . Why had he brought his cheap regard and his lip-born words to her who had nothing paltry to give in exchange? . . . Why had he not stayed among the crowd of whom she asked nothing--but only prayed that they might be less contemptible" [p. 374].

Through the first image Dorothea discovers and acknowledges the depths of a passionate love which she has never before experienced. Through the second she experiences passions of a different order: pride, anger, indignation, self-esteem, self-righteousness, contempt, and scorn. Here indeed is no Virgin Mary but a woman who feels herself betrayed and who reacts accordingly. Dorothea's last question reveals the other side of an ambivalence about mankind which has heretofore received only partial expression in her remarks about the pettiness of the world. It points up her sense of superiority which has perhaps in part been both cause and effect of her queenly role.

Having sobbed herself to sleep on the floor, Dorothea passes the night and wakes in the early morning: "In the chill hours of the *morning twilight,* when all was *dim* around her, she awoke--not with any amazed wondering where she was or what had happened, but with the *clearest consciousness* that

she was *looking into the eyes of sorrow.* She rose . . . and
seated herself in a great chair where she had often *watched*
before. " The waking at dawn is, of course, a symbolic act
which will readily suggest parallels in George Eliot's other
novels. We note that all about her is "dim" but that she has
a clear consciousness of her internal condition. And having
placed herself in the position from which she has "watched
before, " she is now ready for the culminating vision. She
has reached the point of resignation after the struggle:

> . . . she had *waked to a new condition:* she felt as if her soul
> had been liberated from its terrible conflict; she was no longer
> wrestling with her grief, but could sit down with it as a lasting
> companion. . . . It was not in Dorothea's nature, for longer
> than the duration of paroxysm, to sit in the *narrow cell* of her
> calamity, in the besotted misery of a consciousness that only
> *sees* another's lot as an accident of its own [p. 375].

Here the image of restriction, "the narrow cell, " is linked
with the egoistic vision of one who "sees another's lot as an
accident of its own, " thereby recalling not only the other images of restriction but also the egoistic images of the world
as an udder, as a putrefying nidus, and as a doomed carcass.
Moved by "the dominant spirit of justice within her, " Dorothea
has been shown "the truer measure of things. " Now she relates her own marriage troubles to these "hidden as well as
evident troubles" in Lydgate's marriage, and ". . . all this
vivid, sympathetic experience returned to her now as a power; it asserted itself as acquired knowledge asserts itself, and
will not let us see as we saw in the day of our ignorance. "
Thus her own painful experience has brought about a change
in vision. Now she considers the possibility of a crisis in
the lives of Lydgate, Rosamond, and Ladislaw and concludes
that the contact of their lives with hers has laid an obligation
on her. Accepting this obligation, she asks herself the crucial
question: "What should I do--how should I act now, this very
day, if I could clutch my own pain, and compel it to silence,
and think of those three ?" This question is somewhat comparable to Maggie's anguished "Oh, God, if my life is to be
long, let me live to bless and comfort--": each represents
the crisis in the movement toward vision.

What follows now has been anticipated by all of Dorothea's visions in the bow-windowed room:

> It had taken long for her to come to that question, and there was *light* piercing into the room. She *opened her curtains,* and *looked out* towards the bit of road that lay in view, with fields *beyond outside* the entrance-gates. On the road there was a man with a bundle on his back and a woman carrying her baby; in the field she could *see* figures moving--perhaps the shepherd with his dog. *Far off* in the bending sky was the *pearly light;* and she felt the largeness of the world and the manifold wakings of men to labour and endurance. She was a part of that involuntary, palpitating life, and *could neither look out on it from her luxurious shelter as a mere spectator, nor hide her eyes in selfish complaining* [pp. 376-77].

Here we recognize the repetition of elements present not only in Dorothea's preceding visions but in crucial moments of vision everywhere in George Eliot's novels.[3] Here again there is a sense of light, the change from dawn twilight to daylight having paralleled Dorothea's internal change. Here, too, is a sense of space and above all a sense of connection between this one life and the world which lies outside. This time it is not the details of the blue-green room that are seen but what lies outside the bow-window; this time Dorothea looks *out, beyond, outside, far off.* What was once merely an "avenue of limes" or a "low arch of dun vapor" has now become a road, the fields beyond, and a far-distant sky. But what is more important is that the field contains "figures moving-- perhaps the shepherd with his dog" and the road contains "a man with a bundle on his back and a woman carrying her baby." The scene becomes a miniature allegory of life, with man, woman, child, bundle, road, and shepherd as symbols. In fact, the pattern of movement imagery culminates here in the progression of man, woman, and child along this road. Dorothea recognizes that she is a part of that life--of all life. How she shall assume her position within the real world is implied in terms of the negation of her past position: she can neither "look out on it" as a "spectator" who has her own luxurious life behind the bow window, nor can she "hide her eyes" and see it not at all. Once she has seen it she must descend and take up her place as part of it. Thus the passage serves as a comment both on Dorothea's past life and on her future. Now with "the tradition that fresh garments belonged to all *initiation* haunting her mind, " Dorothea performs the symbolic act of putting off her mourning garments and putting on a new dress and bonnet. And so it is that she ritualizes her acceptance of "that involuntary, palpitating life" which her bow window now rounds out to disclose.

Balancing the irony of Dorothea's judgment of Ladislaw is the poetic justice which is the result of her next action. For it is singularly fitting that Dorothea's selfless desire to attend to the needs of others whose lives have touched hers during their crises should be the incidental means by which she recovers her own chance for a more richly fulfilled life. Her decision to see Rosamond again in order to carry out her original plan of interceding for Lydgate is to have far-reaching effects on her own life and the lives of Rosamond, Lydgate, and Ladislaw.

Dorothea is aware that "this might be a turning-point in three lives--not in her own; no, there the irrevocable had happened, but--in those three lives which were touching her own with the solemn neighbourhood of danger and distress" (LXXXI. 386). But she is completely unaware that her action penetrates untouched depths in Rosamond:

> It was a newer crisis in Rosamond's experience than even Dorothea could imagine: she was under the first great shock that had shattered her dream-world in which she had been easily confident of herself and critical of others; and this strange, unexpected manifestation of feeling in a woman whom she had approached with a shrinking aversion and dread, as one who must necessarily have a jealous hatred toward her, made her soul totter all the more with the sense that she had been walking in an unknown world which had just broken in upon her [pp. 386-87].

Dorothea's impassioned plea for understanding and trust between Lydgate and Rosamond becomes so keenly connected with her own new sorrow that Dorothea herself is overcome, ending her plea with the confession: "I am weak. " Rosamond has never before been placed in contact with such a life as this. Incapable as she is of having a clear vision of her own responsibility--no clear-cut vision images are used here--the

habitually unbending and neutrally aloof Rosamond is for one
critical moment in her life brought to the point of acting as
if she does have moral vision. What happens at this moment
is the kind of result that Lydgate has been incapable of effecting
in his relationship with Rosamond. George Eliot defines it on
the occasion of Rosamond and Lydgate's single conversation
about his plight:

> Perhaps if he had been strong enough to persist in his deter-
> mination to be the more because she was less, that evening
> might have had a better issue. If his energy could have borne
> down that check, he might still have wrought on Rosamond's
> *vision and will*. We cannot be sure that any natures, however in-
> flexible or peculiar, will resist this effect from a more massive
> being than their own. They may be taken by storm and for the
> moment converted, becoming part of the soul which enwraps
> them in the ardour of its *movement* [LXXV. 333].

This passage is obviously intended to indicate Lydgate's loss
of strength and by contrast to point up what occurs between
Dorothea and Rosamond:

> Rosamond, *taken hold of* by an emotion stronger than her own--
> *hurried along in a new movement* which gave all things some new,
> awful, undefined aspect--could find no words, but *involuntarily*
> she put her lips to Dorothea's forehead which was very near her,
> and then for a minute the two women clasped each other as if
> they had been in a shipwreck [LXXXI. 389].

Caught in the movement of Dorothea's soul, Rosamond tells
the truth about Ladislaw. She has "delivered her soul under
influences which she had not known before." Having "begun
her confession under the subduing influence of Dorothea's
emotion," she has concluded it with the sense that she has
freed herself of Ladislaw's reproaches--not, however, with
the sense that she has restored his chance for happiness, for
she has not that much vision. Dorothea's response to Rosamond
is one of unchecked sympathy, and although she now has a
more profound vision of the lives of others, nevertheless she
imperfectly understands what has happened in Rosamond:
"With her usual tendency to overestimate the good in others,
she felt a great outgoing of her heart toward Rosamond, for
the generous effort which had redeemed her from suffering,
not counting that the effort was a *reflex of her own energy*"

(p. 390). Thus George Eliot indicates that one never reaches perfect vision (the term is always relative) but that even those who together have undergone such a deep experience as this still see each other's lives imperfectly. And she further demonstrates that the effects of our actions--for good or ill--are never completely known even to ourselves. Judging before the fact, we should have called Dorothea childishly naïve and lacking in vision to have assumed that Rosamond could be brought to perform such an action; judging after the fact, we can but say that George Eliot has demonstrated the nearly miraculous power of a genuinely moral vision which, because it is human, frequently errs but errs on the side of right.

Once more, therefore, we have an example of the extent to which a private action can bring self-fulfillment by enlarging the lives of others. Dorothea has been the means of bringing Rosamond and Lydgate to a more bearable relationship. Lydgate's question about whether Dorothea has made Rosamond feel "less discontented" with him receives the following response:

> "I think she has," said Rosamond, looking up into his face. "How heavy your eyes are, Tertius--and do push your hair back." He lifted up his large white hand to obey her, and felt thankful for this little mark of interest in him. Poor Rosamond's vagrant fancy had come back terribly scourged--meek enough to nestle under the old despised shelter. And the shelter was still there: Lydgate had accepted his narrowed lot with sad resignation. He had chosen this fragile creature, and had taken the burthen of her life upon his arms. He must walk as he could, carrying that burthen pitifully [p. 392].

Considered in the full context of Rosamond's selfish life, her one minute sign of sympathy for someone other than herself is rendered poignant. Like Casaubon's "Come, my dear, come. You are young and need not to extend your life by watching," Rosamond's "How heavy your eyes are, Tertius" becomes one of the nondramatic high points in the book. Dorothea's effect on Rosamond has carried over far enough that Rosamond is herself able to make this gesture.

In order to see the double effect which Dorothea's action in behalf of Lydgate has on Will Ladislaw, it is necessary to consider the situation he has unwittingly allowed himself to

slip into. In the early days of the Lydgate marriage when
Ladislaw is a frequent visitor, Rosamond discovers that a
married woman may still "make conquests and enslave men."
"How delightful, " she thinks, "to make captives from the
throne of marriage with a husband as a crown prince by your
side--himself in fact a subject--while the captives look up
forever helpless, losing their rest probably, and if their ap-
petite too, so much the better!" (XLIII. 243). [4] But Ladislaw
is not himself aware of any such intentions on Rosamond's
part nor does he become aware that he is in danger of en-
slavement until the occasion of Dorothea's discovering him
with Rosamond: ". . . what seemed a foreboding was pressing
upon him as with slow pincers:--that his life might come to
be enslaved by this helpless woman who had thrown herself
upon him in the dreary sadness of her heart" (LXXVIII. 364).
In the light of this awareness, then, Lydgate's comment when
the two men talk about living in London becomes ironic: "We
shall have you again, old fellow, " says Lydgate. Ladislaw
does not answer but he has a vivid vision of himself in a state
of moral drifting, a state which the author points up as far
more common than the Faustian dilemma:

> . . . it seemed to him as if he were beholding in a magic pano-
> rama a future where he himself was *sliding* into that pleasure-
> less *yielding* to the small solicitations of circumstance, which
> is a commoner history of perdition than any single momentous
> bargain.
>   We are on a perilous margin when we begin to *look* passively
> at our future selves, and *see* our own figures *led* with dull con-
> sent into insipid misdoing and shabby achievement. Poor Lydgate
> was inwardly groaning on that margin, and Will was arriving
> at it [LXXIX. 368-69].

Yet it is to Ladislaw's credit, as the same fact is credit to
Lydgate, that he is temperamentally incapable of rejecting
one who is dependent on him because of expectations he has
aroused. He is caught therefore in the conflicting claim of
Lydgate's friendship and Rosamond's dependency, and ". . .
the revelation that Rosamond had made her happiness in any
way dependent on him was a difficulty which his outburst of
rage toward her had immeasurably increased for him" (LXXXII.
395). His way out of this impossible situation is secured for

him by Dorothea's action which causes Rosamond to release him from bondage.

The second effect of Dorothea's action on Ladislaw is of course the change in his relationship with Dorothea. It is a subtle change which involves their movement from the romantic idealistic world into the actual world in which they are to share the problems of their married life. When Ladislaw learns of the conversation between Rosamond and Dorothea, it seems to him as if what he has shared with Dorothea has been permanently lost: "until that wretched yesterday . . . all their *vision,* all their thought of each other, had been as in a world apart, where the sunshine fell on tall white lilies, where no evil lurked, and no other soul entered. But now-- would Dorothea meet him in that world again?" (p. 398).

This romantic world of white lilies and sunshine has, in fact, been lost; what Dorothea and Ladislaw now see as they move toward the window together in their final scene is a stormy, tumultuous world: "they stood silent, not looking at each other, but looking at the evergreens which were being tossed, and were showing the pale underside of their leaves against the blackening sky. . . . Leaves and little branches were hurled about, and the thunder was getting nearer. The light was more and more sombre, but there came a flash of lightning which made them start and look at each other and then smile" (LXXXIII. 405-6). Standing thus in the somber light Dorothea asserts the truth she has discovered: "if we had lost our own chief good, other people's would remain, and that is worth trying for. Some can be happy. I seemed to *see* that more *clearly* than ever, when I was the most wretched." But there is still another truth to discover, that renunciation for the sake of appearances is false renunciation.

The storm in this scene is more than a dramatic background for a correspondingly dramatic situation, and more than a mere symbol of the real world in contrast to the unreal world of lilies and sunshine. It is in itself such a brilliantly shocking revelation of the overwhelming forces at work in the real world that it arouses a sense of awe and mystery, thus cutting through to another level of reality where the fittingness of union between man and woman is to be measured against something more than appearances. In contrast to George Eliot's habit-

ual use of dawn light and a waking scene to indicate the natural awakening of consciousness and growth in vision is the
vivid flash of lightning which is necessary for such a revelation:

> . . . there came a vivid flash of lightning which *lit* each of them
> up for the other--and the light seemed to be the terror of a hope-
> less love. Dorothea darted instantaneously from the window;
> Will followed her, seizing her hand with a spasmodic move-
> ment; and so they stood, with their hands clasped, like two chil-
> dren, looking out on the storm, while the thunder gave a tremen-
> dous crack and roll above them, and the rain began to pour down.

The sense of awe is made even more explicit: "The rain was
dashing against the window-panes as if an angry spirit were
within it, and behind it was the great swoop of the wind; it
was one of those moments in which both the busy and the idle
pause with a certain awe" (pp. 406-7).

Dorothea's insistence that their lives need not be maimed
by separation becomes unrealistic to Ladislaw, for whom the
chivalrous attitude no longer holds any charm: "You may *see*
beyond the misery of it, but I don't. " When Dorothea suggests
that they might be married sometime, Ladislaw realistically
appraises his expectations: "What is the use of counting on
any success of mine ? It is a mere toss-up whether I shall
ever do more than keep myself decently, unless I choose to
sell myself as a mere pen and mouthpiece. I can *see* that
clearly enough" (p. 408). Having once drifted into selling himself as a pen to the ineffectual Mr. Brooke, Ladislaw clearly
does not entertain such a future. Now he stands before Dorothea, "rayless" at last, no longer a bright and sunny romantic
hero whose credo is delight, but a man who having made a
"sober calculation" knows that he "can count on nothing but
a creeping lot. "[5] Perhaps Ladislaw has been reduced to something less than he was in his formlessness when everyone
speculated about how he would "turn out. " Life has imposed
its limitations on him and forced him down a certain path. But
as a child in becoming a man becomes both something less
and something more, so Ladislaw has become something more
in the very process of taking on form. Dorothea has been for
him a shaping influence. And she accepts him now, not as one
who can take her "along the grandest path, " but simply as the

man she loves. For him she renounces the wealth which she has never known how to use and the position of beneficent spectator from a gentlewoman's world which has now become incompatible with the degree of moral vision she has attained.

The basis for community disapproval of Dorothea's marriage to Casaubon had been primarily the disparity between Dorothea's youthful vigor and the aging Casaubon's lifelessness. But that marriage represented no change--unless for the better--in social position. Dorothea's marriage to Ladislaw, however, represents a radical change in Dorothea's whole way of life. The case of the opposition is, as usual, stated by Celia, who has always felt that she can influence her sister "by a word judiciously placed--by opening a little *window* for the *daylight* of her own understanding to enter among the *strange coloured lamps by which Dodo habitually saw*" (LXXXIV. 420). At this point, however, Dorothea has already seen the world by a more realistic daylight than Celia has:

". . . You never can go and live in that way. And then there are all of your plans! You can never have thought of that. James would have taken any trouble for you, and you might have gone on all your life doing what you liked."

"On the contrary, dear," said Dorothea, "I never could do anything that I liked. I have never carried out any plan yet" [p. 421].

Celia's primary concern for Dorothea is that she will no longer be what she has been in the past, that she "will go away among queer people" in London and live "in a street" rather than in a gentlewoman's world. If Dorothea were to remain unmarried, Celia tells her:

". . . there would be nothing uncomfortable. And you would not do what nobody thought you could do. James always said you ought to be a queen; *but this is not at all like being a queen.* You know what mistakes you have always been making, Dodo, and this is another. . . . "

"It is quite true that I might be a wiser person, Celia," said Dorothea, "and that I might have done something better, if I had been better. But this is what I am going to do" [pp. 422-23].

Having accepted a position which is "not at all like being a queen," Dorothea "had no dreams of being praised above other women, feeling that there was always something better which she might have done, if she had only been better and known better" (Finale). She is no longer disposed "to accuse the intolerable narrowness and the purblind conscience of the society around her" for her failure to be everything that she has dreamed of being. In the role of wife and mother, however, she does have a life of "beneficent activity." It is, I believe, to be assumed that George Eliot thus supplies her answer to the problem she has proposed for Dorothea: to "see how it was possible to lead a grand life here--now--in England." Certainly the telescopic watch would not reveal that Dorothea's life was grand, nor in fact that there were any grand lives in England then. But to the reader, who has been enabled to see not only by means of microscopic scrutiny but also through "the imagination that reveals subtle actions inaccessible by any sort of lens," Dorothea's life does reveal itself to be of grand, though necessarily limited, proportions.

♣♣♣♣♣♣♣♣♣♣♣♣♣

Dorothea has learned that the channels for doing good are narrow and indirect, that Utopian plans are ineffective, that human life is limited, and that waste of potential good is in the scheme of things. The tragic element in Dorothea's life remains; but *Middlemarch* is finally affirmative in implying that the waste of potential good can be lessened by people who live in the world with charity and love. The action of this novel covers roughly 1829-32, and private actions are frequently established in time by reference to the progress or regress of the Reform Bill. But George Eliot does not use this historic undercurrent merely as background; rather she uses it and all other attempts at public reform as a counterrhythm playing against that of the commonplace, unhistoric act. It is significant that, although the Reform Bill actually passed in 1832, *Middlemarch* ends just after it was rejected by the House of Lords: the most effective reform, the book implies, is that which enlarges moral vision.

And the focal point from which such reform radiates to touch the neighbor, the community, and the world is the hearth, the marriage, and the family. Marriage is a bondage, a lim-

itation, but "every limit is a beginning as well as an ending."
And marriage "is still a great beginning. . . . It is still the
beginning of the home epic--the gradual conquest or irremediable loss of that complete union which makes the advancing
years a climax, and age the harvest of sweet memories in
common" (Finale). Whether it results in gradual conquest or
irremediable loss is greatly dependent on what is expected of
it. Middlemarchers take many views of marriage. Mr. Brooke
explains his bachelorhood: "The fact is, I never loved any one
well enough to put myself into a noose for them. It *is* a noose,
you know" (IV. 54; author's italics). Mr. Trumbull presents
another bachelor's view: "A man whose life is of any value
should think of his wife as a nurse; that is what I should do, if
I married. . . . Some men must marry to elevate themselves
. . ." (XXXII. 63). Casaubon looked upon marriage as an "outward requirement" (XXIX. 15) and as "a soft fence against
the cold, shadowy, unapplausive audience of his life . . ."
(XX. 293). To Rosamond it represented the "prospect of rising
in rank" (XVI. 239) and the opportunity to enslave an admirer.
The youthful Ladislaw preferred to remain the knight-errant,
and the youthful Dorothea saw in marriage the prospect of being taken along the grandest path; but she also considered it
a "spiritual communion." And George Eliot's view of the ideal
marriage seems to be presented in the stories of Mary Garth
and Fred Vincy and the Caleb Garths. Mary and Fred's courtship is not a "cobweb" of "pilulous smallness" but rather a
time of testing and growth, at least for Fred. Mary remains
a static character who serves as a kind of model indicating
the shaping influence of a woman who is enthroned only in
the sense that she is loved. And Fred, in his response to her
influence, also represents an ideal. The Garth and the Mary-
Fred stories function primarily to comment on and point up
other elements in the book. That is not to say that they are
unassimilated elements: I repeat that I know of no complex
novel which has so few, if any, unassimilated elements.

Lydgate's view of marriage is in itself perhaps no more destructive than others presented in the book, but it is finally
so for him because in him the life potential is greater than
in anyone else save Dorothea. That this adventuresome young
explorer who had intended to track in that outer darkness

should find it necessary to creep into a shell is not to be explained by any formula: "It always remains true that if we had been greater, circumstances would have been less strong against us. Lydgate was aware that his concessions to Rosamond were often little more than the lapse of slackening resolution, the *creeping paralysis* apt to seize an enthusiasm which is out of adjustment to a constant portion of our lives" (LVIII. 78). But the ironic fact remains that although he had once dedicated himself to "piercing the obscurity of those minute processes which prepare human misery and joy" (see pp. 159-61 above), he did not fully consider what those processes might be. For he brought

> a much more *testing vision* of details and relations into this pathological study than he had ever thought it necessary to apply to the complexities of love and marriage, these being subjects on which he felt himself amply informed by literature, and that traditional wisdom which is handed down in the genial conversation of men. Whereas Fever had *obscure* conditions . . . [XVI. 236].

As Lydgate had pursued the study of certain diseases, George Eliot tells us, he had come to feel the need for "that fundamental knowledge of structure." And because no one "can understand and estimate the entire structure or its parts--what are its frailties and what its repairs--without knowing the nature of the materials," he had questioned further: What were the "primary *webs* or tissues" out of which the organs of the body were composed? ". . . Have not these structures some common basis from which they have all started, as your sarsnet, gauze, net, satin, and velvet from the raw cocoon?" What Lydgate most desired, then, was "to demonstrate the more intricate relations of living structure . . ." (XV. 212-13). But, ironically, what prevents him is his failure to bring that same "testing vision" to the consideration of a different structure: that which results from the interweaving of human lots. The careful and obedient reader of *Middlemarch* has seen such a structure.

A Final Word

THE CAREFUL and obedient reader has, in fact, seen "the more intricate relations of living structure" in all three of the novels examined here. But to say, as I do, that all these novels have the same basic structural movements and the same primary image patterns is obviously not to say that George Eliot has written the same novel three times over. For, as the preceding chapters have indicated, the structure of movement toward and away from moral vision and the complex of vision imagery--both capable of intricate and expansive variation--provide an artistic means whereby the human condition may be endlessly explored.

In *Adam Bede* the two countermovements form a shifting tension which is finally resolved in the positive movement. In *The Mill on the Floss* the single movement is achieved in a milieu of constant tension as Maggie struggles against the negative forces within her society. And in *Middlemarch* the several individual movements conjoin, interweave, and interact among themselves and with the general historical movement in such a way as to create the most highly complex structure in George Eliot's works. In all three of these novels and-- if I may presume to go beyond my demonstration here--in the other novels of George Eliot, there is finally more emphasis on the positive movement than on the negative. For with one exception (see *Romola*, where Tito's movement ends in his total destruction) the negative movements are ultimately reversed by one means or another and dissolved into the posi-

tive movement toward vision. If the negative movement has
been such as to lead inevitably toward catastrophe, then the
reversal may initiate a penitential movement, as in the case
of Hetty, Arthur, Tom, Bulstrode, and--a most notable example not examined here--Gwendolen Harleth in *Daniel Deronda*.

The reason for this emphasis on the positive movement is,
I believe, that George Eliot is always concerned with asserting and exploring the moral evolution of mankind. In fact, if
we were to adopt her own use of the motto, we might select
one from among those with which she so meticulously prefaced
her books and chapters of books and allow it to stand as a general thematic statement for all of her novels. Since it implies
not only theme but image and structure as well, no motto would
be more apt than the last part of the verse which she herself
apparently wrote for chapter xli of *Felix Holt:*

> . . . the soul can grow
> As embryos, that live and move but blindly,
> Burst from the dark, emerge regenerate,
> And lead a life of vision and of choice.

The use of the motto now strikes the twentieth-century reader
as a quaint Victorian habit which, because it is too suggestive
of the text prefacing a sermon, could better have been omitted.
And, happily, it can be omitted. For obviously no mere motto
could ever begin to suggest what image, theme, and structure
have artistically created in the novels of George Eliot.

That George Eliot is a highly conscious artist should at
this point be so obvious as to need no further comment. Also
superfluous is the observation that she is as much concerned
with making her reader see and feel as with making him think,
in short, that she wishes to aid her reader in his struggling
movement toward vision. A final word which does, however,
remain to be said, even though it has been said before, is that
Adam Bede is a great novel and that *Middlemarch* is one of
the greatest novels ever written. All three of the novels considered here are capable of increasing the reader's awareness of that most uncommon of all commonplace things, "that
roar which lies on the other side of silence."

Notes

Chapter I

1. *Confessions of Saint Augustine* (Everyman ed.; 1950), pp. 300-1.

2. George Eliot, *Adam Bede,* chapter xv, in *The Writings of George Eliot, Together with the Life by J. W. Cross* (Warwickshire ed.; 25 vols.; New York: Houghton Mifflin, 1907), III, 216. The Warwickshire edition has been used throughout this study. To avoid confusion between the editor's volume numbers and the author's book numbers and to make the reference more readily transferable to other editions, I shall hereafter give the chapter number in Roman numerals followed by page reference to the edition used. An exception must be made in dealing with *The Mill on the Floss,* where chapters are numbered separately within each of the seven books. Except for foreign words, all italics throughout this study are mine unless otherwise noted. Subsequent references will be made within the text.

Chapter II

1. An illustration of how one of the minor elements contributes to the poetic texture of the book may be noted here. Thias, who has been a "thorn" in the side of his loved ones, is buried, at Lisbeth's insistence, under the white thorn. There are several references to it throughout. For example, Lisbeth in a

characteristically complaining mood says: "The sooner I'm laid under the thorn the better. I'm no good to nobody now." She later refers to her remaining life as the time "afore I go to bed to my old man under the white thorn." If we consider also the part that Arthur plays in Adam's life, the name Donnithorne is suggestive.

2. It should be fruitful here to compare the decidedly similar but far more complex process which Gwendolen Harleth goes through. In the section of *Daniel Deronda* which introduces Mordecai, George Eliot describes the visionary in general terms--terms which are so startlingly applicable to Gwendolen that the connection could hardly be accidental: ". . . there are persons whose yearnings, conceptions--nay, travelled conclusions--continually take the form of images which have a foreshadowing power: the deed they would do starts up before them *in complete shape,* making a coercive type; the event they hunger for or dread rises into a *vision* with a seed-like growth, feeding itself fast on unnumbered impressions" (XXXVIII. 426). Such a phenomenon occurs when Gwendolen hopes for Grandcourt's death: "Fantasies moved within her like ghosts, making no break in her more acknowledged consciousness and finding no obstruction in it: dark rays doing their work invisibly in the broad light" (XLVIII. 91). These vague "fantasies" take on more form as Gwendolen's "vision of deliverance" comes to be an "image" of "some possible accident" (LIV. 186). This image is actualized in the drowning scene, of which Gwendolen subsequently observes: "I only know that I *saw* my wish outside me."

Chapter III

1. If the details here seem too incidental to support such an interpretation, we need only compare the scene in chapter xxv between old Mr. Donnithorne and Mrs. Irwine, both of whom give ample indication of being out of contact with the common ordinary life around them:

> "What excellent *sight* you have!" said old Mr. Donnithorne, who was holding a *double glass* up to his *eyes*, "to *see* the expression of that young man's face so far off. His face is nothing but a pale blurred spot to me. But I fancy I have the advantage

of you when we come to look close. I can read small print without *spectacles*."

"Ah, my dear sir, you began with being very *near-sighted*,
and those *near-sighted* eyes always wear the best. I want very
strong spectacles to read with, but then I think my *eyes* get better and better for things at a distance. I suppose if I could live
another fifty years, I should be *blind* to everything that wasn't
out of other people's *sight*, like a man who stands in a well, and
sees nothing but the stars" [pp. 394-95].

One of the primary characterizing devices in all of George
Eliot's novels is eyesight. Romola's godfather Bernardo, who
like Bartle Massey shifts his spectacles, observes that "old
men's eyes are like old men's memories; they are strongest
for things a long way off" (*Romola*, XXXI. 411). The Floren-
tines in *Romola* are generally said to be "blind, " a people
who "put on their eyes when they went abroad, and took them
off when they got home again" (V. 75); and the blindness of
Romola's father is symbolic. The first specific point made
about any character in *Silas Marner* is that "those large brown
protuberant eyes in Silas Marner's pale face really saw nothing very distinctly that was not close to them" (I. 5). Silas,
whose "unexampled eyes" are "short-sighted, " is in fact one
of many shortsighted characters who people George Eliot's
novels. Another is Mr. Lyon, whose "large eyes looked dis-
cerningly through the spectacles" which "he was in the habit
of using when he wanted to observe his interlocutor more
closely than usual" (*Felix Holt*, V. 84). And so on throughout
the novels.

2. Only one other chapter in the book begins in a similar
style (see the opening of chapter iv: "A green valley with a
brook running through it, full almost to overflowing with the
late rains; overhung by low stooping willows"), and it too sets
the stage for a crisis in Adam's life.

3. Mr. George H. Creeger is to my knowledge the only critic
who has noted the symbolic import of this scene. I completed
my study of *Adam Bede* in December, 1954, almost two years
before his excellent article appeared in print. There is a
large area of agreement between Mr. Creeger's reading of
this novel and mine, but I have in no way drawn on his work.
See "An Interpretation of *Adam Bede*, " *English Literary History*, XXIII (September, 1956), 218-27.

Chapter IV

1. John S. Diekhoff, for example, maintains ("The Happy
Ending of *Adam Bede,*" *English Literary History,* III [1936],
221-27) that "the absence of a consistently developed moral
purpose in *Adam Bede* is . . . its weakness." The wedding,
Adam's forgiveness of Arthur, and Hetty's pardon are all
necessary elements in the happy ending which compromises
the book, Mr. Diekhoff argues. In real life the marriage
might possibly have happened, but in the book it is inartistic
and untrue to the characters, thus defeating the "transcendent
purpose of the novel." Mr. Diekhoff asks: "what now of the
wrongs that can never be righted?" I believe that what Mr.
Diekhoff sees as the "transcendent purpose" is only one part
of a much larger purpose, which has on the whole been accomplished. The wrongs and sufferings in *Adam Bede* remain
for me as uncanceled as they are, for example, in *Troilus
and Criseyde.*

Chapter V

1. Since chapters are numbered separately within each of
the seven books of *The Mill on the Floss,* it will here be necessary to indicate both book and chapter. The page reference
will still be to that particular book and chapter in the Warwickshire edition. This reference is to II.ii.228.
2. This pattern of imagery was only germinal in *Adam Bede*
where its most concentrated use was the characterization of
Hetty. She is, for example, frequently compared to a lamb,
bird, or butterfly.
3. Luke, the hired man, makes this significant observation
about the death of the rabbits: "they're nash things, them lop-
eared rabbits--they'd happen ha' died, if they'd been fed.
Things out o' natur niver thrive: God A'mighty doesn't like
'em. He made the rabbits' ears to lie back, an' it's nothin'
but contrariness to make 'em hing down like a mastiff dog's.
Master Tom 'ull know better nor buy such things another time"
(I.iv.42).
4. The image of the Hamadryad provides a definite clue to

the meaning of the chapter entitled "The Cloven Tree." In the preceding chapter while Philip tries to persuade Maggie to reject her asceticism and think only of their love, he observes that she turns away from him to look at a tree. He pleads with her: "Look at me, Maggie; tell me again, it is possible for you to love me. Don't look away from me to *that cloven tree;* it is a bad omen" (V.iv.102). In the next chapter Tom discovers Maggie's secret meetings with Philip through a chance remark dropped by Aunt Pullet: "the channel of fatality--the pathway of the lightning--was no other than Aunt Pullet" (V.v.105). But Tom is the lightning itself which cleaves the tree when he makes it impossible for Maggie to continue her secret relationship with Philip. What Philip does not realize and what Maggie herself is not consciously aware of is that her love for Philip is a part of the self-denial she has been practicing. After an intense scene with Tom, Maggie realizes that she can no longer "stand on serene heights above the worldly temptations and conflict" and that she is once more "in the thick of a hot strife with her own and others' passions" (p. 121). Still she is "now and then conscious of a certain dim background of relief in the forced separation from Philip." Although she believes that the relief is occasioned by "the sense of a deliverance from concealment," the reader knows that the state of captivity from which she has "just issued" has been partially instituted by Philip.

5. That George Eliot wished to emphasize this tendency in Tom is indicated by the following passage which occurs two pages later:

> Tom, as I said, had never been so much like a girl in his life before, and at that epoch of irregular verbs his spirit was further depressed by a new means of mental development which had been thought of for him out of school hours. Mrs. Stelling had lately had her second baby, and as nothing could be more salutary for a boy than to feel himself useful, Mrs. Stelling considered she was doing Tom a service by setting him to watch the little cherub Laura while the nurse was occupied with the sickly baby. It was quite a *pretty* employment for Tom. . . .

6. Note the similarity between Hetty's wandering and Maggie's when she searches for the gypsy camp. See the second

paragraph of chapter ix, Book I. Maggie also leaves the "high-road" and walks through the fields. She too becomes frightened and isolated. She too desires to return to the community from which she has sought escape. The situation is, of course, essentially different: Hetty seeks to escape from a good community because she has violated its moral code; Maggie seeks to escape from a destructive community whose rigidity has violated her nature.

7. This, I believe, is an excellent example of the poetic use George Eliot sometimes makes of a word or of language in general when the context is suitable. The imaginative use of the word *truant* is startling; it brings the image of the sun driving home the *heavenly* blue into sharp focus. The effect is a delightful whimsey.

Chapter VI

1. Cf. the two chapters in *Romola* entitled "Drifting Away" and "Romola's Waking." In a letter to Sara Hennell dated August 23, 1863, George Eliot explains that although she was forced into a "more ideal treatment of Romola" than she had anticipated, the "Drifting Away" was a part of her "earliest vision" of the novel and was "by deliberate forecast adopted as [one of the] romantical and symbolical elements" (*The George Eliot Letters*, ed. Gordon S. Haight [7 vols; New Haven: Yale University Press, 1954-55], IV, 103-4).

2. Compare the literalness with which Mrs. Tulliver interprets her husband's metaphorical language (I. ii. 9). Mr. Tulliver tells his wife: "That's the fault I have to find wi' you, Bessy; if you see a stick i' the road, you're allays thinkin' you can't step over it. You'd want me not to hire a good wag-goner, 'cause he'd got a mole on his face." Mrs. Tulliver's response is one of surprise: "Dear heart! . . . when did I iver make objections to a man because he'd got a mole on his face? I'm sure I'm rether fond o' the moles; for my broth-er, as is dead an' gone, had a mole on his brow." Mr. Tulliver explains that he "meant it to stand for summat else" and con-cluded that "it's puzzling work, talking is."

3. Not, however, too sudden. There has been ample prep-

aration throughout the entire novel, and the last chapter begins with a description of the heavy rains and talk of flood. The reader has already been so carefully prepared both on a literal and dramatic level that the symbolic coincidence of Maggie's renunciation and the appearance of the flood waters is not only expected but demanded.

4. The most direct of these is George Eliot's title of Book IV, "The Valley of Humiliation." Maggie makes reference to the devil "in his true shape, as he fought with Christian" (I.iii.22), to Apollyon (I.xi.158), and to Mr. Greatheart (p. 166). The enchanted world which holds Maggie under a spell is suggestive of "the Enchanted Ground, where the air naturally tended to make one drowsy" (John Bunyan, *The Pilgrim's Progress* [New York: Thomas Nelson and Sons, 1905], p. 303). At the risk of going too far I suggest that Mudport is so named because it is Maggie's Slough of Despond.

5. Unless otherwise indicated, further references are to VII.v.379-86.

6. Some characters in George Eliot's novels (Hetty and Arthur, for example) are incapable of reaching vision any other way. Daniel Deronda recognizes that Gwendolen Harleth may be such a person. Instructing her in the art of vision, he says: "Lives are enlarged in different ways. I dare say some would never *get their eyes opened* if it were not for a *violent shock* from the consequences of their own actions" (*Daniel Deronda*, XXXVI.239). Felix Holt, who assumes a similar role in relation to Esther Lyon, tells her: "I want you to have such a *vision* of the future that you may never lose your best self. Some charm or other may be flung about you . . . and nothing but a good strong *terrible vision* will save you" (*Felix Holt*, XXVII.39). Many characters throughout the seven novels are helped by an image of good in another's life (as Esther is through Felix), but Esther is the only character who is saved from becoming her worst self by a "terrible vision" of another's (Mrs. Transome's) life. Gwendolen is saved by an even more terrible vision of her own potential self. Her saving vision is far more compelling and far more complex in the making than Esther Lyon's.

7. Several minor elements in the book emphasize the theme

of the artificial. Note, for example, that Mrs. Pullet's door mats are not what they seem, for they "were by no means intended to wipe shoes on: the very scraper had a deputy to do its dirty work" (I.ix.129). Consider also the mock ritual of the visit to Mrs. Pullet's wardrobe, the unlocking of doors, the "procession," the "funereal solmenity of the scene," and the "process" of producing the bonnet (pp. 131-33). Mrs. Tulliver's "household gods" (see IV.ii), the dispute over the relative merit of stripes or spots in table linen, all of these details and many more provide a comic element at the same time that they indicate the artificiality of St. Ogg's life.

8. This parallel seems justified by echoes in the book of the Biblical story. When Bob and Tom discuss "the big flood" of long ago, Tom tells Bob that when he is a man he will build a boat "like Noah's ark" (I.vi.71). The flood is referred to as "that awful visitation of God" (VII.v.380), and George Eliot's phrase, "the feeble generations whose breath is in their nostrils" (IV.i.3), is a deliberate echo of Genesis 7: 22: "All in whose nostrils was the breath of life. . . ."

Chapter VII

1. Edward Wagenknecht, *Cavalcade of the English Novel: From Elizabeth to George VI* (New York, 1943), p. 326. But see also Joan Bennett, *George Eliot: Her Mind and Her Art* (Cambridge, 1948) and Gerald Bullett, *George Eliot: Her Life and Books* (New Haven, 1948). Both authors point to the positive aspects of *Middlemarch*.

2. A few examples will illustrate the difference. The rhetoric of Mr. Casaubon is "as sincere as the bark of a dog, or the cawing of an amorous rook" (V.67). Lydgate compares himself to a bear and Rosamond to "an exquisite bird" (XVI. 230). During the period of courtship, Rosamond, who knows "the notes of many birds" (p. 228), wishes that Lydgate "had known his notes so that his enchantment under her music had been less like an emotional elephant's . . ." (XXVII.388). The bird, bear, and elephant images are all repeated. Mr. Featherstone is "like an aged hyena" (XXXIII.71); Mr. Brooke is "like a stray tortoise" (XXXVII.127); Miss Noble is like "a tiny timid quadruped" (XVII.243) which makes "small com-

passionate mewings" (LIX. 96). More such images appear, but these are representative. In themselves they all function to establish the various characters, but they do not seem to me to function as a unit which reveals a pattern of meaning such as the animal imagery of *The Mill* or the web imagery of *Middlemarch*.

3. Such images do appear in the other novels, but except in *Silas Marner* George Eliot does not exploit their thematic and structural implications. During the first period of his isolation in Raveloe, Silas "seemed to weave, like the spider, from pure impulse, without reflection." His life is reduced to "the unquestioning activity of a spinning insect" and he is intent only on "looking toward the end of his pattern, or toward the end of his web" (II. 21-22). Thus the web imagery is used to point up the deficiency in Silas' vision. The insular world he creates can be entered only by the child, and she alone can lead him out of it.

4. Mr. Vincy's fleshly theory provides a comic contrast here: "It's an uncommonly dangerous thing to be left without any *padding* against the shafts of disease . . ." (X. 130). Elsewhere in reprimanding Bulstrode for his dietary habits, he says: "I've no opinion of that system. Life wants *padding* . . ." (XIII. 182).

5. In Romola's father, the old scholar who is both literally and figuratively blind, we recognize the fictional prototype of Casaubon. Bardo, who lives in a small-windowed house and is cut off from the world about him by "the prison of his blindness," accurately characterizes himself:

". . . for what is that grosser narrower light by which men behold merely the petty scene around them, compared with that far-stretching, lasting light which spreads over centuries of thought, and over the life of nations, and makes clear to us the minds of the immortals who have reaped the great harvest and left us to glean in their furrows. For me, Romola, *even when I could see, it was with the great dead that I lived:* while the living often seemed to me mere spectres . . ." [*Romola*, V. 74].

No reader of George Eliot could possibly conclude that she, like Bardo, abjures the "petty scene" and looks upon the living as "mere spectres."

6. Much of this effect is achieved by skillful repetition not only of phrases like "you know" and "up to a certain point" but also of quotations from conversations with people he has known and from authors whom he sometimes forgets he could not have known. He is an empty echo of himself as well as everyone he has read. Therefore it is a brilliant stroke on George Eliot's part when she breaks up his political speech by the appearance of his effigy and the "parrot-like, Punch-voiced echo of his words." This echo "had a wicked choice of the words it overtook"; that is, it repeats his phrases in the precise way that he echoes himself and others (see chapter li).

7. The most extensive exploration of reform is the debate between Ladislaw and Lydgate, chapter xlvi.

8. The same image is used in reference to Tito, who is in some basic ways similar to Rosamond. As he makes his way upward in the political and social life of Florence he is said to be "sailing under the fairest breeze" (*Romola*, IX.14).

Chapter VIII

1. Cf. Barbara Hardy, "The Moment of Disenchantment in George Eliot's Novels," *Review of English Studies*, N.S., V (July, 1954), 256-64. I have not in any way depended on Miss Hardy's observations, since my initial work on *Middlemarch* was completed several months before her article appeared in print.

2. In this sense Dorothea is very much like Romola. In his most piercing condemnation of Romola, Savonarola tells her: "Your life has been spent in *blindness*, my daughter. You have lived with those who *sit on a hill aloof*, and look down on the life of their fellow men" (*Romola*, XL.104). Compare also Romola's relationship with her father, the aged scholar, and Dorothea's relationship with Casaubon.

3. Compare, for example, the crisis in Esther Lyon's life. Faced with the decision of her response to Harold Transome's proposal and "desiring to see with undisturbed clearness," she goes to her bedroom window: "she drew up the blinds, liking to see the grey sky, where there were some veiled glimmerings of moonlight, and the lines of the forever running river,

and the bending movement of the black trees. She wanted the largeness of the world to help her thought" (*Felix Holt,* XLIX. 325).

4. The difference between Rosamond's rule from the throne and Dorothea's needs no comment. This is merely one example of the way in which countless elements play upon each other in *Middlemarch.* Compare also Bulstrode's use of power. He is a "ruler" who is "ready to confer obligations, and severe in watching the result" (XVI. 222). Vincy, who among others has "felt his neck under Bulstrode's yoke" speaks of Bulstrode's "tyrannical spirit, wanting to play bishop and banker everywhere . . ." (XIII. 183, 187).

5. This phrase is especially meaningful in terms of frequent references to Ladislaw as a winged creature.

Bibliography

The items in this bibliography have been primarily selected as representative of the relatively recent Eliot criticism. From among the early critical works I have included only the indispensable essays by Henry James and the standard work by Leslie Stephen. I have attempted to avoid needless repetition of material familiar to any student of George Eliot. Rather I have tried to bring together those works which, either by comparison or contrast, have relevance to this study.

Books and Theses

Beaty, Jerome. "Middlemarch" from Notebook to Novel: A Study of George Eliot's Creative Process. Unpublished Ph. D. thesis, University of Illinois, 1956.
Bennett, Joan. *George Eliot: Her Mind and Her Art*. Cambridge: Cambridge University Press, 1948.
Bullett, Gerald. *George Eliot: Her Life and Books*. New Haven: Yale University Press, 1948.
Diamond, Naomi J. Vision and the Role of the Past in George Eliot's Novels. Ph. D. thesis in progress, University of Washington.
Eliot, George. *The Writings of George Eliot, Together with the Life by J. W. Cross*. Warwickshire Edition, 25 vols. Boston: Houghton Mifflin Co. , 1907.
Haight, Gordon S. , ed. *The George Eliot Letters*. 7 vols. New Haven: Yale University Press, 1954-55.

Hanson, Lawrence and Elisabeth. *Marian Evans and George Eliot: A Biography*. London: Oxford University Press, 1952.

Speaight, Robert. *George Eliot*. New York: Roy Publishers, n. d.

Stephen, Leslie. *George Eliot*. London: Macmillan & Co., 1919.

Essays

Arthos, John. "George Eliot: 'The Art of Vision,'" *Rivista di Letterature Moderne*, III (1952), 260-70.

Beaty, Jerome. "Visions and Revisions: Chapter LXXXI of *Middlemarch*," *Publications of the Modern Language Association of America*, LXXII (September, 1957), 662-79.

Beebe, Maurice. "'Visions Are Creators': The Unity of *Daniel Deronda*," *Boston University Studies in English*, I (Autumn, 1955).

Bethell, S. L. "The Novels of George Eliot," *Criterion*, XVIII (1938), 39-57.

Bissell, Claude T. "Social Analysis in the Novels of George Eliot," *English Literary History*, XVIII (September, 1951), 221-39.

Creeger, George H. "An Interpretation of *Adam Bede*," *English Literary History*, XXIII (September, 1956), 218-38.

Diekhoff, John S. "The Happy Ending of *Adam Bede*," *English Literary History*, III (September, 1936), 221-27.

Eliot, George. "Quarry for Middlemarch," ed. with introduction and notes by Anna Theresa Kitchel, 1950. Accompanying *Nineteenth-Century Fiction*, Vol. IV (1949-50).

Fyfe, Albert J. "The Interpretation of 'Adam Bede,'" *Nineteenth-Century Fiction*, IX (September, 1954), 134-39.

Haight, Gordon S. "Introduction," in *Middlemarch* by George Eliot. Boston: Houghton Mifflin Co., 1956, pp. v-xx.

Hardy, Barbara. "Imagery in George Eliot's Last Novels," *Modern Language Review*, L (January, 1955), 6-14.

-------. "The Moment of Disenchantment in George Eliot's Novels," *Review of English Studies*, N.S., V (July, 1954), 256-64.

Heilman, Robert B. "The Return to Raveloe: Thirty-five Years After," *The English Journal*, XLVI (January, 1957), 1-10.

Holloway, John. "George Eliot," in *The Victorian Sage: Studies in Argument*. London: Macmillan & Co., 1953, pp. 111-58.

Hussey, Maurice. "Structure and Imagery in 'Adam Bede,'" *Nineteenth-Century Fiction*, X (September, 1955), 115-29.

James, Henry. "George Eliot's 'Middlemarch,'" *Nineteenth-Century Fiction*, VIII (December, 1953), 161-70.

-------. "The Life of George Eliot" and "Daniel Deronda: A Conversation," in *Partial Portraits*. New York: Macmillan & Co., 1905, pp. 37-93.

Kettle, Arnold. "George Eliot," in *An Introduction to the English Novel*. 2 vols. New York: Hutchinson House, 1951. I, 171-90.

Leavis, F. R. "George Eliot," in *The Great Tradition*. London: Chatto & Windus, 1948, pp. 28-125.

Naumann, Walter. "The Architecture of George Eliot's Novels," *Modern Language Quarterly*, IX (March, 1948), 37-50.

Praz, Mario. "The Decline of the Hero: George Eliot," in *The Hero in Eclipse in Victorian Fiction*, tr. Angus Davidson. London: Oxford University Press, 1956, pp. 319-83.

Rubin, Larry. "River Imagery as a Means of Foreshadowing in *The Mill on the Floss*," *Modern Language Notes*, LXXI (January, 1956), 18-22.

Schorer, Mark. "Fiction and the 'Analogical Matrix,'" in *Critiques and Essays on Modern Fiction 1920-1951*, ed. John W. Aldridge. New York: Ronald Press, 1952, pp. 83-98.

Steiner, F. George. "A Preface to 'Middlemarch,'" *Nineteenth-Century Fiction*, IX (March, 1955), 262-79.

Steinhoff, William R. "Intent and Fulfillment in the Ending of *The Mill on the Floss*," *University of California Publications, English Studies*, XI (1955), 231-51.

Thale, Jerome. "River Imagery in 'Daniel Deronda,'" *Nineteenth-Century Fiction*, VIII (March, 1954), 300-7.

Van Ghent, Dorothy. "On *Adam Bede*," in *The English Novel, Form and Function*. New York: Rinehart & Co., 1953, pp. 171-81.

Wagenknecht, Edward. "The 'New' Novel: George Eliot," in *Cavalcade of the English Novel: From Elizabeth to George VI*. New York: Henry Holt and Co., 1943, pp. 319-35.

Woolf, Virginia. "George Eliot, " in *The Common Reader:*
First and Second Series Combined in One Volume. New York:
Harcourt, Brace & Co. , 1948, pp. 229-42.

J